planet chicken

D1586085

992025932 4

Also by Hattie Ellis

Sweetness & Light:
The Mysterious History of the Honey Bee

planet chicken

the shameful story of
the bird on your plate

hattie ellis

SCEPTRE

Gloucestershire County Council	
GL	
992625932 4	
Askews	07-Feb-2008
338.176	£7.99

First published in Great Britain in 2007 by Sceptre
An imprint of Hodder & Stoughton
An Hachette Livre UK company

First published in paperback in 2008

The right of Hattie Ellis to be identified as the Author of the Work has been
asserted by her in accordance with the Copyright, Designs and Patents Act 1988.

1

All rights reserved. No part of this publication may be reproduced, stored in
a retrieval system, or transmitted, in any form or by any means without the
prior written permission of the publisher, nor be otherwise circulated in
any form of binding or cover other than that in which it is published and
without a similar condition being imposed on the subsequent purchaser.

A CIP catalogue record for this title is available from the British Library

ISBN 978 0 340 921883

Typeset in Sabon by Hewer Text UK Ltd, Edinburgh
Printed and bound by Clays Ltd, St Ives plc

Hodder Headline's policy is to use papers that are natural, renewable
and recyclable products and made from wood grown in sustainable
forests. The logging and manufacturing processes are expected to
conform to the environmental regulations of the country of origin.

Hodder & Stoughton Ltd
A division of Hodder Headline
338 Euston Road
London NW1 3BH

www.hodder.co.uk

To Sophie Orloff and Julia Ellis

Contents

Foreword by Hugh Fearnley-Whittingstall   ix

Part One   What We Are Doing

1 Chicken Pieces   3
2 From Jungle to Farm   12
3 From Farm to Factory   21
4 Meat and Eggs   32
5 Drugs, Bugs and Poo   46
6 Killing   64
7 Frozen, Fast, Processed   81
8 International Chicken   100

Part Two   What We Can Do

9 The Whole Bird   123
10 The Good Egg   144

11 Happy Chickens   157
12 The Bird Explorers   180
13 Shopping   200
14 Cooking Cultures   219
15 Slow Chickens   238
16 Pet Poultry   253
17 Home To Roost   271

Foreword

Everyone who eats chicken should read this book. The spreading of her well chosen words would mean a great deal to the billions of birds that Hattie Ellis is writing about. And as you will see as you read, these poor creatures seriously need a break.

If you knew what I was up to only a few days ago, you might think me a hypocrite. I confess, I wrung a chicken's neck. A cockerel's neck, to be precise. I must have done it several dozen times or so, in the last few years, since I regularly started raising my male chicks for the pot. And although it's not a task I look forward to, it's not one I dread either. I know I can do it quickly, and efficiently.

The fact is, here in Dorset, my family and I enjoy our chickens when they are alive: we like to watch them scampering about in their grassy run, strutting their stuff and pecking the living daylights out of the grass, bugs and slugs, along with the corn and maize mix we scatter for them. And we enjoy them when they are dead: ideally roast whole, with a lovely crisp skin, tasty, flavourful meat (I'm a leg man myself) and irresistible, lip-smacking gravy. We enjoy them all the more for knowing how they have lived; and we understand that because they spend their lives doing properly chickeny stuff, they taste properly chickeny at the end of it.

The sad truth is, though, that not many people know what a chicken is meant to taste like. And that's a bitter irony, considering that chicken is the most popular meat on the planet. The problem is, that the majority of chickens consumed in the world (and an astonishing 97 per cent here in the UK) is factory farmed. You may find that term loaded, but in my view, it is the inclusion of the word 'farm' in the phrase that is open to question, not 'factory'. How could a corrugated steel and concrete shed, that houses 40,000 birds (called 'units'), who are fed, watered and heated by automated machines managed by a computer, be anything other than a factory? How could a system that permanently excludes daylight and has not a single blade of grass, or any other living plant on its floor be any kind of farm?

I would say it's hard, if not impossible, to enjoy eating one of these birds, once you know the full facts about what is has been through to end up on your plate. And that's why Hattie's book is such an important one. Although it's necessarily punctuated by some grisly revelations, it is a fascinating story that she tells: a story of ingenious science, dazzling entrepreneurship, and all-conquering economic advancement. And if these poor birds were only bicycles, or beans, we might all care to celebrate the story as a great triumph of human endeavour and ingenuity.

But at the heart of this remarkable piece of modern history are real live flesh and blood animals. In our complex and often fraught relationship with the other creatures with whom we share this planet, our dealings with the chicken are, in my view, the ethical frontline. We have pushed our greed and abandoned our responsibilities to a point of moral degeneracy.

A few millennia ago we evolved from 'savages' into farmers who nurtured their livestock, in an unwritten contract of symbiosis and respect, sometimes called 'good husbandry'. But the industrialisation of agriculture has brought us full circle. We have reduced, through mechanisation, the contact between 'farmer' and livestock, to a point where the sentience and natural inclinations of our farm animals is all too easily ignored. In the case of chickens, the process of disassociation is extraordinarily thorough, and almost complete. We are about enter an era where the first human contact with a chicken grown for food may be the moment when it enters the mouth of the consumer.

The anonymity of this process might be a little less appalling if it did not involve so much suffering. But suffering, as Hattie so forcefully reveals, is inevitable with this system. This is industrialised savagery, and for the sanity of our own species, as much as for the welfare of those animals we are so ruthlessly exploiting, this savagery has to end.

And it can end. Because those of you who read this book will be empowered to change the next chapter of the story. You can choose to be directly responsible for the liberation of those chickens – and not by any great assertion of energy, or noisy expression of outrage. You can do so quietly, and calmly, without drawing attention to yourself (though you may want to share your feelings with family and friends) by simply refusing to choose another bog standard, factory farmed chicken from the supermarket shelf, and opting for something free range, or organic, instead.

Hugh Fearnley-Whittingstall
January 2007

Part One

What We Are Doing

Chicken Pieces

The other day I went into a supermarket and smelt the air. As a child I was often told off for sniffing like this; it was considered impolite. But I have continued the habit and occasionally inhale my surroundings, in a discreet sort of way. Other cooks do the same. Your nostrils are far more sensitive than the tongue when it comes to flavours.

It was late November when I went into the supermarket. There was enough cold in the air to cut the edges of my face and I was glad to get past the sliding doors. In this snapshot of time there must have been around a hundred people waiting in line, moving through the sluice gates of the checkout and washing away goods that were being replaced even as their predecessors went out of the door. Trying to fix my eyes on this retail sea was like looking at ripples; everything stayed in the same place while moving infinitely onward.

The smell came to me after I'd stood by the door for a while. You get used to the fake scents in supermarkets: the artificial bread pumped through the ceiling pipes, the yum-yum odours that appear from nowhere. This was slightly different. It was hot and artificial, yet personal. At first, as I stood there watching the queues, it seemed like the smell of a crowd in a space just big enough to hold it. The tills would have to move quicker to get more in. It was the smell of a crowd backed up slightly where everybody – shoppers, staff – wanted to go further and faster. This smell of penned spending rose from the lines and became all the more powerful from the sheer push at its edges. Like the sea, it would win; it would go where it had to go.

Then I traced the source. It was the café just beyond the store's entrance. On a metal tray was some roast chicken. This usually delicious smell, the ultimate in family Sunday lunches and comfort food, was almost making me gag. It reminded me of my purpose that day. I headed for aisle thirteen.

There it was, between tea and coffee, fresh meat, and the ice-cream chest freezers: an end-of-aisle display of cheap chicken. At the side of the unit was the word CAGE. Inside were plastic trays of chicken rammed together in a wall of flesh. On the bottom shelf, where most eyes would fall, were the bargain whole birds, £6 for two, a saving of 98p each off their usual price of £3.49. Above them were three shelves of 'buy-one-get-one-free' bargains (the delightfully acronymed 'bogofs'). These variety packs of thighs and drummers were £2.99, in a two-for-one deal. The weight of each package, without exception, was exactly 825g. The weight of each whole chicken was 1.7kg. Exactly. It was as if the chickens were indeed bricks, made to precise speci-fications. Behind their tight plastic, the meat reminded me of the naked, shrink-wrapped magazine babes lined up on the top shelves of newsagents. There was something blandly pitiful about this commodification of flesh.

I went around the corner and saw a shop assistant shoving breasts into gaps on the top shelf. This was the posh chicken. At the top of the aisle was a piece of gastroporn food photography, soft-edged and with a crash focus on the centre of the browned bird. The visuals were mesmerizingly artificial, the food equivalent of daytime telly presenters. In a bid for dynamism, the whole bird had been tilted dramatically as if it had crash-landed on the unit. Scattered around were artful bits of fresh tarragon. If this were real life, the Kermit-green leaves would get stuck in your teeth for the rest of the meal, right into coffee and beyond. The meat was surrounded by a moat of uncooked lemon halves, suggesting abundance and sunshine.

Amongst all this glossy artifice, the supermarket had gone to great lengths to show just how real their chickens were. Every whole bird, free-range or non-range, bore a photograph of the real farmer and reassuring details of his real farm. We were introduced in matey fashion. This is one of our farmers, the label said, next to a black-and-white picture of a man. We learnt that Joe – or some such name – has been raising chickens at this farm in rural Lincolnshire for twenty years. Joe understands the importance of flock husbandry, I learnt, which makes him an ideal choice as a farmer for this supermarket. Coupled with his approach to bird welfare, the label continued, this ensures he maintains the high standard required by the company.

There were several real farmers to meet on the shelves that day. Frank had spent two years understanding the importance of flock husbandry on the edge of the Derbyshire Peak District. John had devoted ten years to the chickens on his farm in Norfolk, the land of rich soils (and Bernard Matthews). Oliver had a family farm, 'set within the fertile Cogher Valley, Co. Tyrone', whilst another farmer, Tom, lived in the same valley, perhaps further up because his label mentioned 'the hills of the Cogher Valley'. The association of these chickens with any sort of countryside felt rather odd. Would such birds even glimpse daylight, let alone fields, let alone the tourist sites of the Peak District or the hills or fertile land of the Cogher Valley?

It was all meant to be so reassuring. And we want so much to feel that everything is good and wholesome down on the farm. We want so much to feel that Farmer Chicken is looking after the birds, gathering them in at night to keep the flock safe from the foxes; throwing them handfuls of golden corn and hearing the contented clucks of the hens as they stay soft and warm within the arms of good husbandry.

But we are wiser these days. BSE, the disease that came from feeding cows ground-up cow remains, was a wake-up call. It told us we needed to care not just about what we ate, but about what the animals ate too. Salmonella and E. coli indicated how disease can be rife amongst the meat animals kept for our food. Foot-and-mouth disease showed how creatures were carted hundreds of miles around the country for a few people to make profit at a high cost to others. Many of us have developed an unease about how our meat is produced, and this was in the back of my mind as I looked at the chicken in the supermarket. By the time I walked out, it felt necessary to understand how this meat could be so cheap. I wanted to know the facts.

6

Bald statistics tell part of the tale. At any given moment there are about twice as many chickens as there are humans in the world; most of them are kept for meat and eggs. The average consumer will eat at least 550 birds in a lifetime. It is the meat parents most often feed their children; the healthy, convenient option. In Britain, we eat five times as much chicken as we did twenty years ago: it now accounts for nearly half the meat we eat. Translate this into the total number of birds produced and the numbers start to whirr into a blur. Upwards of a million tonnes of the meat is produced in Britain every year. Our big production lines can now kill no fewer than 9000 birds an hour. Take this on to a global level and the numbers get beyond boggling. In the United States alone, 24 million chickens are killed every 24 hours.

As if these numbers were not big enough, the sheer quantity of meat we eat is spreading from a mere sea into a vast ocean. Chicken accounts for the majority of the 50 billion animals eaten each year, and global consumption is now rising dramatically. The world is currently in the middle of what is termed a 'Livestock Revolution'. This is the animal equivalent of the Green Revolution of the 1960s, which spread chemically sustained crop farming around the globe. In this case, it is about the rise of industrially farmed creatures. The amount of meat the world eats is expected to rise by over 55 per cent in the next twenty years, and the chicken, as the most efficiently farmed animal, will be on the front line of this change.

How will these chickens be farmed? At present, more than 96 per cent in the UK are raised in 'factory farms'; that is, places that you could say 'manufacture units of meat rather than tending animals as livestock. The number of these intensive units has gone up by a massive one-third from what it was fifteen years ago. The Livestock Revolution, especially in rapidly developing and urbanizing countries such as those of Asia, means the push is on to produce more animals more cheaply. This means intensive systems. The chicken is already more highly industrialized than any other animal: worldwide, it is estimated that the majority of them are farmed this way for meat and nearly 75 per cent for eggs. The trend towards intensive chicken farming is set to increase even more with the arrival of bird flu. Lock away your birds: biosecurity is all – even if, as some believe, it was factory farming that helped foster the disease in the first place.

The scope of this story and the sheer size of the statistics are not a distant truth. Chicken is the planet's most popular meat; more specifically, it is what you or I might eat today. Humans become part of chickens' lives billions of times a day in the most intimate way possible. We eat them. We consume their bodies. They become part of us, flesh of our flesh.

You'd think you couldn't get closer to food than by putting it in your body, but there is a great deal to be learnt by visiting producers. It was meeting Richard Guy of the Real Meat Company that set me on the way to this story twelve years ago. A tall man with gleaming eyes that looked clearly through his glasses, Richard was direct, funny, and produced delicious chickens that were sold through a franchise network of Real Meat shops and by mail order. I was sitting in his farmers' kitchen, amidst papers, wellies, dogs and phone calls about the school run, when he summed up his view of the issues of poultry production bluntly: 'If you don't like factory farming, you've got two choices. Buy ours or become a vegetarian. You are in charge of a very short ethical chain. If you buy an ordinary chicken you know that it may have led a ghastly life, been transported terribly, lived badly, been killed badly. And you're responsible. Who else is?'

Put like this, it seemed a very straightforward choice. But if so, why is so much chicken of another kind eaten? Changing something as habitual as eating is very complex. Even after talking to Richard, I had to discover the truth of his words for myself. I had to look at what I ate and discover that I was responsible. Who else?

Not long after this, my encounters with chicken, and chickens, got personal. By a strange quirk of fate, I met the chickens I ate. I was testing chicken recipes for a book, and I was so busy that I could not manage to feed all the food to my friends. There is only so much chicken you can eat and, shamefully, I didn't always eat much of it. Some of it – well, quite a bit – went in the bin. Perhaps this was why Richard Guy's real-meat words did not always make it from my ears to my mouth.

There was a kind of chicken on sale at my nearest supermarket that seemed 'better-than-bog-standard'. Perhaps there was even a hint of a field on the label. It seemed okay; it was cheaper than the usual free-range birds I bought. I was buying so much of the stuff that this particular brand became part of my near-daily chicken run to the supermarket. Handling chicken, talking chicken, cooking chicken: eventually, I had to see inside a chicken farm.

Contacts got me in. I remember driving up to the farm with a nervous sense of anticipation. By this stage I knew what an intensive chicken shed looked like from the out-side: long, windowless buildings with conical feed contain-ers attached to one end. Once you know what they look like you notice them, and you start to wonder what goes on inside. I was about to find out.

The business was run by a man in his late middle age who seemed decent enough. He told me he was unhappy about the pressures on him to increase numbers in the sheds. Once bed-and-board had been deducted, he was left with so little that the whole enterprise was hardly worth-while. Everything was squeezed.

Then we went inside. The chickens were almost ready to go to slaughter and would shortly end up in the shops. At this stage, they filled the entire shed. I had never seen such a strange sight in all my life. Tens of thousands of birds stretched out in a layer at our feet. The whole shed was full of whiteness and dust and a motion that was a slight half-shuffle, muted and unreal. Many of the birds were almost immobile. I did not know why at this stage: later I would find out. It was almost impossible to see these creatures as individuals – as creatures even. They were a carpet of semi-animated matter. It couldn't be further from a storybook farmyard image. It was closer to an image from a spooky fairytale; a supernatural sight from another place, from Planet Chicken.

Then we went outside and talked. I asked the farmer where the chickens were sold. He said they were on trial at a particular supermarket in a particular part of London under a particular label. It was then I realized that these were the chickens I was getting off the supermarket's shelves. These were the very birds I had been eating – or chucking away. A strange quirk of fate had put the truth directly before me.

As I stood by the shed, with its tens of thousands of chicken-creatures, this fact had just started to sink in when there was an emergency. An alarm went off. The bell rang out, disrupting everything and scattering the songbirds in the trees outside the chicken houses. The farmer just ran. He hardly said goodbye – I think he flung a panicked 'Must go' behind him and I saw that his face was frozen in crisis. I went to collect my coat from his house and made my own way into the hall. When his wife came down the stairs I asked her what had happened. She said the electricity driving the fans had failed.

It was some time later that I realized the full extent of what this meant. The chickens 'grow', as they say, in one place and over time their faeces accumulate below them. Towards the end of their life, the heavy birds can spend much of their time sitting on the litter and this means they can get marked at the joints of the legs with what is known as 'hock burn'. It is easy to see this if you look closely at cheap chicken in the shops. There can also be blisters on their breasts for the same reason: their bodies too get burnt by the harshly alkaline ammonia. And gases rise from it, producing a burning, choking odour. These are removed by fans that circulate air into the sheds. If these fans fail the gas can get trapped below the animals' bodies, particularly if the shed is packed shortly before the chickens go to be slaughtered. The farmer ran because tens of thousands of birds were in imminent danger of dying from heat stress and being gassed by their own shit.

That was the meat on my table.

From Jungle to Farm

If a farmer from the first half of the twentieth century walked into a chicken house today, he would be profoundly shocked. What turned the husbandry of livestock into the management of millions of units of poultry-product? This is not a story from outer space; it is a recent part of our history and embedded in today's society. To understand where we are today, we have to trace this change as it happened. The first step is how a chicken became a chicken.

Today's chickens have so many hues and types of plumage that theories about the bird's origins have long included a bit of grouse, a bit of this, a bit of that, and at least four different kinds of jungle fowl along the way. DNA evidence now shows that the chicken we eat descended largely from the present-day red jungle fowl. In Asia today, this creature hops and jumps around under the protective shelter of the tropical canopy. These tough, hardy birds scratch through the carpet of leaves to find a favourite food, the small seeds of the bamboo plant, just as chickens pick their way around our countryside and back gardens. The wild jungle birds each lay around thirty eggs a year; the industrial chicken can lay more than ten times this number.

The male jungle fowl is a magnificent specimen of birdlife. His tail curves in a gorgeous green-black arc. His bronze mane flows from his comb down his back, the colour repeating lower down his wing-tips, alongside emerald-black and chestnut patches. His comb is scarlet; his earlobes white, echoed by the fluff of white feathers near his tail. The female, of quieter plumage, has subtler brown feathers highlighted with bronze. Looking at the appearance of this stately pair made me realize the essentially exotic origins of the chicken. The bird pecking around English pastures is not a creature on its native turf. Who knows, perhaps if we encountered the chicken's wild ancestors living happily in nature, without need or want of us, then our attitudes toward intensive poultry farming and its industrialized food products might be different. Robin-nugget, anyone? Blackbird-burger?

The jungle fowl came in from the wild as long ago as 8000 BC, in south-east Asia. Archaeologists picking their way through sites have found dusty chicken bones that suggest the birds had moved north into China by 6000 BC before following trade routes across the Russian steppes into Turkey and eastern Europe. These early birds were not kept for meat or eggs: the pugnacious male fowl, with its clarion crow, became popular through cockfighting. Battling birds went from China to Japan, and it is believed the Persians took them back to the Middle East after invading India in the fourth century BC. In turn, Persia was attacked by Alexander the Great, who took the warlike cock back to Greece and the ancient Mediterranean world. Roman soldiers wore the feathers of this warrior bird in their helmets: the rooster was an apt creature for these martial times.

The Ancient Egyptians may well have known about mass incubation, hatching ten thousand birds at a time, though it is uncertain whether this involved chickens or some other kind of fowl. The Greeks and the Romans certainly caught on to the edible aspects of poultry and farmed them with some professionalism. Pliny the Elder mentions chickens that could lay an egg a day, and the ancient world knew about caponizing (castrating males so that they grow to a large size), force-feeding and hybrid vigour. Varro in the first century BC mentions farms designed for forty to two hundred fowl, with such specialized features as places for roosting and trapdoors to keep out foxes and weasels.

When Julius Caesar invaded Britain he found chickens already here, commenting that they were for 'diversion and pleasures' – presumably cockfighting – and not for meat, though the eggs were eaten at this time; they were almost a useful byproduct of the sport. The Romans brought over meat chickens, including an unusual five-toed type (most chickens have four toes), leading to speculation that the Dorking, which has this feature, may be our most ancient breed.

Anglo-Saxon peasants had chicken yards; a percentage of what they produced had to be handed over to the landowner, as with many foods at this time. The Normans increased this tax to include more eggs at Easter. We can step amongst medieval chickens in Chaucer's *Nun's Priest's Tale*, with Chanticleer and his harem of seven hens including the gracious, courteous, discreet and debonair Lady Pertelote. Chanticleer is a lover, not a fighter, though he is fiercely beautiful, with his tall comb like a castle wall and his burnished feathers flaming bright. But despite such finery, for many centuries chickens were essentially 'dung-heap fowl', allowed to peck around the place, their eggs gathered up for the household and old birds killed for the pot. The young males, grown to a good size, provided more tender meat in the special treat of a spring chicken.

The Renaissance brought forth a fine scholar who studied chickens with a great breadth of enquiry. Ulisse Aldrovandi, born in Bologna in 1522, was the professor of natural history at the city's university. He was as affectionate towards his chickens as the keen modern amateur; one of his hens liked to wander around the house and sleep near the professor amongst his books. Aldrovandi wrote a book devoted to the chicken, covering everything from the biology of egg-laying to birds on coins, flock behaviour and medicinal uses. Among the illustrations were fantastical pictures of freak chickens, and he included a mouth-watering section on cooking. The chicken, we learn, was eaten in sixteenth-century Italy in many ways: flavoured with piquant sauces; stuffed with pine nuts and hazelnuts; braised with a bouquet of dill, leek, savory and coriander leaf; sauced with pepper, lovage, oregano and honey.

At this early stage, chicken breeding was still influenced by the popularity of cockfighting. The gamefowl, such as the Indian Game, looked like a prizefighter, with a broad, muscular chest and a squat, aggressive stance that looks ready to take on all-comers. It was a descendant of this breed that was to provide the modern meat bird with its prominent breast. Not all birds were there to fight, however. Regional preferences developed for different kinds of chicken, and some areas were more involved than others in the trade in meat birds. Londoners liked hens with white feathers and finer-grained legs, and this type of bird became a speciality of Sussex and Surrey. Egg production became more national. Scottish traders known as 'egglers' would, for example, take cartloads of eggs to sell in Berwick-on-Tweed, and from here the eggs would go as far as London.

It was not just farmers who were interested in chickens. The eighteenth-century artist George Stubbs, best known for his paintings of horses, spent the last fifteen years of his life – until just hours before his death – absorbed in his *Comparative Anatomical Exposition*. His subjects were the human body, the tiger and the common fowl, from which he removed the outer layer, be it skin, fur or feathers, to expose first the muscles and then the bones. To see the bird's internal structure in Stubbs's drawings, as if in motion and alive, is to reanimate what you see on your plate; to realize, again, that this is an animal.

This interest in chickens as creatures spread to the general population in the mid-nineteenth century with the phenomenon of 'Hen Fever'. It began with the large, productive and beautiful chickens that came off the boats from the port of Canton in Southern China, newly opened to foreign trade. Queen Victoria was presented with some Cochins from an early voyage. These buxom, fluffed-out birds with their feathered legs like pantaloons, caused a sensation. The young queen had a poultry barn built at Windsor and gave royal cachet to the newcomers. Chicken shows caught the public's imagination and spread the popularity of the Asian chickens and their novel brown eggs that were laid in the winter as well as the rest of the year. A Victorian chicken expert, S.H. Lewer, captured the excitement aroused by them when they were first shown in Birmingham. 'Every visitor', he wrote with enthusiastic exaggeration, 'went home to tell of these new wonderful fowl, which were as big as ostriches, and roared like lions, while gentle as lambs; which could be kept anywhere, even in a garret, and took to petting like tame cats. Others crowded to see them and the excitement grew and even the streets outside the show were crammed.' All this boosted the interest in different breeds; poultry keeping spread from farmers to the general population. The hobby chicken-keeper was born.

In their admirable poultry history, *The Chicken Book*, Page Smith and Charles Daniel describe the background of Hen Fever as the 'intoxication of inquisitiveness' of the eighteenth and nineteenth centuries played out in our own backyards. 'Chickens are certainly the most easily managed of domestic animals – they are smaller than goats or cows, and more practical than white mice,' they point out. Just as Stubbs stared into animals with his dissecting eye, the bird was a gift to the amateur scientist who was becoming increasingly interested in what we now call genetics. Breeding chickens is rewarding; it is possible for anyone to observe characteristics trickle down the generations.

Different types of chicken proliferated. When cockfighting was banned in 1849, the focus was no longer on just acquiring the butchest gamecocks. Feathers, facial features, colours, eggs, length of leg, breadth of breast: all became interesting. Today strict show organizers in Germany, a country keen on such matters, recognize 500 breeds of chicken; others have put it at more like an astonishing 7000, if you include all colours and forms of each sort. The fancy chicken world is a treat for the eye. Entire photographic books have been devoted to the subject, such as

Stephen Green-Armytage's *Extraordinary Chickens*. His images, in themselves extraordinary, capture this variety of life and how strange it can be. Chickens vary in their plumage, not just in colour but also in texture and form. Some of my favourites in his book are the Frizzles, which look like the sort of hat that female members of the royal family wore to Ascot in the 1980s, blow-dried by a fancy stylist so the swathes of feathers fall in choreographed drifts. Then there are the Silkies, the breed famous for its broodiness: the hens are happy to sit on eggs, their own or those of others, and the wonderful feathers make a parti-cularly soft covering for the clutch. Indeed, Silkies have such finely textured, fur-like plumage that you want to stroke them like cats.

The markings of many kinds of chickens are especially beautiful. The speckledy hen is just for starters. Sebrights and Wyandottes have feathers individually outlined in black, as if each and every one had been drawn in ink by Picasso. The terms for the types of feathers in them-selves show the range: barred, spangled, laced, cuckoo, pencilled, chainmail. The facial feathered plumage comes in many shapes and sizes. Some birds have muffs, some have beards, some feathery whiskers. The Polish became common in eastern Europe, though the name may also have come from their possible origins in Italy around the River Po, or from the old English word *poll*, for the top of the head: the head feathers sprout like a fountain from a small dome on the skull, looking like a poultry version of a Tina Turner afro. *Extraordinary Chickens* has a portrait of an Araucana, the Chilean blue-egg-laying bird, sporting a pair of facial side-feathers that look like a punked-up Victorian gentleman's sideboards. The variation continues with the rest of the chicken's 'head furnishings', as they are called. Under the bird's beak are the wattles and on the side of the head the ear-lobes, some of them huge and fleshy. The comb itself can rise magnificently like a crown, in many different shapes, in corals, in spikes, in a flopped-over breaking wave. They can look like brains, or molluscs, or mohicans.

All this specialist breeding was fine and dandy but it had its dangers. The purpose of this magnificent display, as far as the chicken was concerned, was mating. Once the breeders got going, the proliferation of fancy types backfired. Biology tends to dictate that the amount of effort going into plumage leads to less effort going in other directions such as good egg production. Some breeds were selected for such outré shapes that they had trouble mating at all. The French, a nation of canny farmers and gastronomes, always kept an eye on the economics and on the plate. Many regions in France developed their own kind of chicken that was good to eat and laid a reasonable number of eggs. In Britain, however, we let our eye dictate terms. Some of the fancy fowl were bred for looks more than the number of eggs they could lay, or their practical use as table birds. This matters. Strange as it sounds, it is through food that such creatures are most used and therefore perpetuated.

When the stock is of a reasonably pure strain, these fancy birds do have a use as a genetic pool. The older kinds have centuries of careful breeding in their genes. Fancier types can have more useful traits bred back into them. There are some efforts being made in this direction, but it is not the main focus of specialist breeding.

In the twentieth century hi-tech genetics were to take breeding in a radically different direction. For commercial purposes, types of chickens were to be developed that grew so fast and so fat that they were barely able to stand. All this variety became concentrated on one single economic purpose. The next step for the jungle fowl-turned-chicken was to be towards the broiler bird and the battery hen.

From Farm to Factory

In the first half of the twentieth century Britain was a nation of small-time poultry keepers, with commercial birds generally tended by farmers' wives who used the egg and meat money as one of their few independent sources of household income. This kind of production meant cooking a chook was a rare event. In a BBC Radio Four programme broadcast in 2000 on the evolution of intensive chicken farming, *Why Did We Do That?*, the former agriculture minister Lord Carrington described roast chicken as the sort of treat you asked your mother for on the evening before you went back to boarding school. For many families, such a dish was for high days and holidays. I've spoken to a number of people who remember only eating chicken on Christmas Day.

The pattern was similar, though less dramatic, for eggs. At the end of the nineteenth century we each ate an average of a hundred eggs a year; less than two a week. At the start of the twenty-first, we eat nearly double this in one form or another. Today most British eggs are home-produced. At that time, Russia sent us 75 million of them a year, France and Germany 71 million; 2 million more came from Portugal, and smaller amounts from Norway, Sweden, Morocco, Malta, Italy, Egypt and Turkey. An article in the *Evening Standard* in 1891 said that even Australian eggs were sent to Britain by ship; they were six weeks old before they reached our shores. The roots of our present international food system are long-standing and some of it, like the strange antipodean eggs, came about through the economic web of Empire.

The First World War made the British more aware of home food production. Initially poultry keepers were told to kill off their flocks to preserve grain stocks, but the order was rescinded and, after the war, ex-servicemen were actively encouraged to go into chicken farming. The idea epitomized the dream of the small entrepeneur. But many a rural idyll turned to ashes; it was ever a mistake to count your chickens before they hatched – or even afterwards. Newcomers were often sold poor stock of the sort that tends to be churned out to supply a booming market. Many of the chickens died of disease; there was widespread disillusionment and bankruptcy amongst the start-up farmers.

Perhaps this haphazard situation was allowed to develop because chicken farming was the Cinderella of agriculture, previously seen as 'women's work'. Production was about to get more organized. In 1921 a National Institute of Poultry Husbandry was set up and by 1922 there were ninety-three poultry inspectors around the country. By 1923 half the shell-eggs sold in Britain were home-produced. However, after passing through long and inefficient supply chains of egglers, retailers, wholesalers, and local and regional markets they could be less fresh than more efficiently organized imports.

Not all aspects of our chicken farming were so bad. At this stage, nearly all of the birds could range around. There are 1920s' photographs of chicken houses in the middle of meadows with cattle and sheep grazing alongside them. Keeping chickens in one place could lead to a build-up of disease and so these hen houses would be regularly moved about; this is a part of the system that some farmers are going back to today.

When servicemen returned home with their pay-off after the Second World War, a number of them chose to become poultry farmers just as their predecessors had done in 1918. But by this stage they were to go into a very different form of farming, thanks to techniques developed in the United States.

A US farm census of 1910 shows that the average size of flock then was around eighty birds. The vast majority of farms – 88 per cent – had chickens of one sort or another pecking around the place. All this was to change: the bird in the yard was set to become the unit in the factory. This ultimately sorry story unfolds with an inexorable economic logic. To have so many birds kept as an adjunct to other parts of farming was not efficient. As food systems became more centralized, each product was organized to work within bigger and bigger units, be it chicken, corn or tomatoes for ketchup.

One of the very first steps towards streamlining chicken farming was the incubator. This took the wayward element of reproduction out of the equation and enabled chickens to be bred in separate hatcheries. Chickens no longer had to waste valuable time sitting on their eggs. Strains were developed in these new laboratories that were ever better for food production. Breeding flocks produced chicks that were sent out to the farmers. 'Day-olds', as they are called, do not need food or water immediately after hatching; this is because they have absorbed the yolk into their body just before they emerge. Mother Nature bestowed this quality on them, originally, so that all the eggs in a clutch could crack open and the chicks crawl out over a period of time without the mother hen needing to attend to their needs immediately. In the modern industrial age it meant that newly hatched chicks could be transported long distances. The chick factories began.

Scientists had discovered that light stimulated chickens to lay eggs. If you kept the lights on for longer, the birds would lay more eggs. Looking back, the discussions on the manipulation of the birds in this way are a mixture of the sinister and the quaint. An author of a poultry manual, Professor Louis Hurd of Cornell University, wrote in 1928: 'The operator may use lights at any time of the day that is most convenient, and, according to his judgment, adds most to the comfort of the birds.' He remarks how the lighting makes life 'more pleasant' for bird and farmer alike.

Vitamin D, synthesized by the chickens in sunlight, is essential for good, strong bones. Once it was discovered that the vitamin could be added to feed, the birds no longer needed to be kept outside at all; everything could be done indoors. This was crucial. The less the birds moved around, the less feed they needed and the faster they grew, greatly increasing profitability.

It had been discovered that one particular breed, the

Leghorn, was the best layer of all; the incubation hatcheries began to mass-produce them. The Leghorn's reward for being such a good egg producer was, eventually, to be used to breed the hens that are put into battery cages all over the world.

All this was not, however, an exact science. While industry supporters say factory farming is more hygienic, there were immediate drawbacks to this form of animal production. The new breeds of specialized birds were susceptible to disease, a situation exacerbated by intensive rearing. The industrialization of the breeding stock meant that the chicks began their life in sterile conditions rather than acquiring immunity from natural exposure to bugs and germs in the farmyard. In California, where scientific egg farming was pioneered, the size of the flocks and the fact that they were increasingly kept together indoors and forced to produce more and more eggs, putting the birds' bodies under stress, meant that disease could spread like wildfire. Mortality rates could be as high as 20 per cent. The economically viable answer was not to reverse the way the birds were farmed but to develop vaccines that would prevent disease. The close connection between pharmaceuticals and farming had begun.

American flocks were increasingly separated and specialized into layers and broilers. In traditional farming, the meat birds were almost a byproduct of the egg layers. End-of-lay hens would be sold off for meat; as for the male birds, spring chickens would be killed young and tender, or caponized males would be kept to become bigger table birds. When egg producers increasingly turned to Leghorns this system no longer worked, for male Leghorns were not particularly good meat birds. Traditional farming had favoured hybrid birds that were equally useful for meat and for eggs. Now breeding became increasingly geared towards one kind of farming or the other.

The start of the industrialized farming of meat birds can be traced back to 1923 when a Mrs Cecile Steele of the Delmarva peninsula in Delaware ordered fifty chicks to stock up her small flock of laying birds. The order was misread, and five hundred baby birds arrived by mistake. Mrs Steele built a shed, raised the birds and sold them young for meat. Next year she produced a thousand with the help of her husband, who soon left his job with the Coast Guard to help out with the growing business. Her neighbours also caught on quickly; the peninsula and then the entire state rapidly became the epicentre of meat birds. It was not good growing land, but it was close to markets and was well sited for an industry based more on closed sheds than on open fields. In 1925, Delaware farmers collectively raised 50,000 birds; in 1926 a million (the Steeles alone were producing 10,000 birds at a time); 2 million in 1928 and 3 million in 1929. Before the 1928 elections, the Republican presidential candidate Herbert Hoover promised 'a chicken in every pot and a car in every garage'. Chicken was about to boom, and would stay that way; by the start of the twenty-first century the average American consumed a hundred times more chicken than at the start of the thirties.

To begin with, the meat birds were sold live into the nearby markets. The next big change came when the producers started to process (kill, pluck and cut up) the birds in the 1930s. This meant that the meat could be transported further and reach more people. A 'broiler belt' developed, stretching from Delmarva through the Deep South to eastern Texas. The Second World War then gave chicken farming a big push; the American broiler industry really took off in the forties and fifties. Under the pressure of war, beef and pork were rationed – but not chicken. Furthermore, the government set a high price for poultry meat, well above the cost of production, to encourage producers. A 'Food for Freedom' programme promoted the eating of chicken and eggs – the idea was that consumers should let the pork and beef, seen as nutritionally higher-value foods, go to the troops, according to Steve Striffler in his book *Chicken: The Dangerous Transformation of America's Favorite Food*. The question of status is revealing. The move was on towards cheap chicken and today's intensively produced broilers that grow from hatching to slaughter in six weeks and cost $3 or so.

Control of the birds operated at every level, from micro to macro. Fewer and fewer people owned more and more chickens in order to achieve economies of scale. Chicken farming is a business model that has been repeated with countless commodities. It is a story of 'vertical integration'; of bringing together different components into one single, streamlined system.

The best example is the meteoric rise of John Tyson, founder of one of the world's mega-chicken businesses. He began as a middleman, transporting chickens in the Southern States in the early thirties. His first innovation was to invent a contraption that meant the birds could be fed and watered en route and so taken to markets further away. From Kansas City and St Louis he moved to Chicago, Cincinnati, Detroit, Cleveland, Memphis and Houston. Such was his success at selling that he soon needed more birds. This turned out to be difficult. But wherever Tyson came across a glitch in the system, he moved in and fixed it himself. So he started hatching his own chicks. He started milling their feed. In 1958 he built a processing plant in Arkansas where the company killed and cut up the chickens. Others were starting to operate in the same way. Frank Perdue, also a well-known poultry entrepreneur, became especially famous when his company publicized its branded products through advertising campaigns. Frank appeared on a television commercial in 1971 telling Americans how 'it takes a tough man to raise a tender chicken'. Such were the men who set up the present system, in which everything is owned by the companies. The birds are contracted out to 'growers', as the farmers are called. Such operators have very little control over how the whole system works. The chicken magnates, along with the breeding companies, run everything 'from semen to cellophane', as the phrase goes.

Britain soon caught on to these new improved forms of chicken farming, both for eggs and for meat. For layers, the first prototype battery cages came into use in the 1930s. At this stage one bird was housed in each cage and records were kept of each chicken's egg production in order to select the best layers. Their tallies were put on a card in front of the cages, or recorded using abacus beads or with pegs moved along the mesh. The process of egg layers going into cages was slightly delayed by the need for metals for arrangements during the Second World War. The move then gathered pace from the mid-1940s, and no longer with a single bird in each cage; farmers began to keep several hens in one cage from the 1950s. Whatever the state of the birds themselves in this method of production (we shall come to that), the eggs rolled away from the cage looking pristine. The birds couldn't peck at their own droppings and this made the cages hygienic, as is often still argued by the industry. Chicken expert Fred Hams told me of a moment in the mid-fifties when farmers, including himself, began to think of investing in free-range flocks because they didn't believe the cages would be allowed to continue; they were simply too cruel. Retrospectively, it was a poignant crossroads; we took the wrong turning.

Our broiler industry too began to take off in the mid-1950s. Before that, British chicken farming was more like the French method, as still practised today in the famous *poulet de Bresse*. The chickens were left to range around for ten weeks or so, then brought in and fattened up with a mixture of ground oats, milk products and even mutton fat. This was not a kind form of farming: after ten days of this high-calorie mixture the birds had to be force-fed using a cramming machine. Following their success in the USA, the first broiler strains came to Britain in 1956. By the 1960s, they were the norm. These new chickens were given fancy names reflecting their sparkling new status, such as the Chunky Chic and the Silver Supreme. The Americans by this time had developed a form of bird that had its own internal biological patent. The highly specialized 'grand-parent' stock produced breeding birds. These, in turn, produced the meat chickens. But you couldn't breed from the broilers themselves: the profitable genetic stock was protected. Control of industrial chickens worldwide is now in the hands of just a few companies.

The modern broiler bird put on weight much faster and with less feed that before. The post-war priority for farm-ing – an entirely understandable reaction to austerity – was productivity. After fourteen years of food rationing the bountiful harvest of cheap meat, brought about by the appliance of science, was a beacon of progress. The government offered tax breaks that helped establish these new systems. Some farmers became millionaires. A new entrepreneurial type of business farmer had replaced the hen-wives of yore.

The techniques of farming, too, followed the American model. It was too time-consuming and labour-intensive to change their litter every day when the flock sizes became bigger. The birds were left on the same flooring throughout their life. When the sheds were not properly ventilated respiratory problems could develop, and the chicken, not good at regulating its own heat, could also become too hot or too cold. Ventilation systems had to be worked out to keep the chickens alive. If a certain number died but the 'crop' was still economically viable, the wasted birds were simply written off. They could go, for example, to maggot farmers who hatched fly eggs on the carcasses and supplied amateur fishermen with bait. It was discovered that feeding the birds antibiotics meant they both grew faster and did not become ill. Drugs became a normal part of a chicken's life. The lights were kept on day and night to keep them eating and growing. As for the feed, this also bore the mark of imports. Soya from across the Atlantic, in particular, became part of the chicken's staple diet, and this is still true today. The cheap chicken on our plates has been fed pellets made of 20–25% soya, mostly imported from Brazil. Some of this has even, in the past, come from deforested areas of the Amazon.

As chicken farming developed, it all seemed so scientific. In *Why Did We Do That?* industry executive John Archibold argued that the birds were now totally suited to their new dwellings and lifestyle: 'We have specifically adapted the birds which we are using today to the environment which we are keeping them in today so they can produce cheap, wholesome food for the human population at a minimum cost,' he says. It all made sense to the farmer. But what about the birds? We now recognize that the modern chicken's instincts and needs are remarkably similar not just to those of the old-fashioned birds, but even to those of the original jungle fowl. And what about consumers? Have we really changed so much that this form of meat production and eating is natural? How does intensive chicken farming work, and what does it mean for us and the birds in the early twenty-first century?

Meat and Eggs

Most people will never see inside a broiler house. But you can. The farm animal campaigning group Compassion in World Farming will send you a nine-minute film called *Live Fast, Die Young: The Story of the Broiler Chicken*. It is a video nasty; yet it is also an everyday scene that could almost be one of the old *Play School* 'through-the-window' items on factories, filmed for children. People are getting on with their jobs. Sometimes there is no commentary and you watch them working in silence, as in any workplace. Footage of production lines is transfixing, whether it is newspapers rolling off the presses, robots building cars, lids being screwed on to millions of tubes of toothpaste – or chickens becoming chicken.

The footage shows what the process is like at its worst; the camera singles out cases of obvious suffering. But the point of the video is more general than that. The film's argument is that the very basis of intensive broiler chicken farming is flawed.

Live Fast, Die Young starts with a picture of a man opening up a packet of cheap, ready-cooked chicken. He tears into the meat with his teeth. Cut to the high street and another man is eating fast food chicken from out of a box. He chucks away the bone, like a chav version of Henry VIII. 'How come', the voiceover asks, 'how come this chicken is so cheap?'

In the chick factory, the newborn's nest is a rust-coloured plastic crate. The birds cluster in a cheeping, fluffy mass. Next to them are egg shells, cracked open and discarded. It looks as if a cook had left the empty halves on a kitchen work surface. These eggs have just made animals.

Men in overalls reach down and take handfuls of the baby birds. Each grab lifts around eight small bodies. The chicks are placed on a conveyor belt that takes them to the next part of the process. Everything happens fast; too fast for the birds to do anything but be whizzed along. Dozens, hundreds, thousands, millions of yellow chicks flow on-wards on this mechanical river of creatures. They fall off the end of the belt – backwards, front-on, sideways – into a crate. The crate is loaded on top of another. The crates are stacked up in tall towers. The room is full of towers of crates. Each crate holds a hundred chicks. The chicks are going home. They are going to our homes.

We go into the factory. The white mass of birds is spectacular. There is a miasma of dust and bugs and dander rising in the air. You can see that some of the chickens are struggling to get to the feeders. As the sheds fill up, the voice-over says some of the birds will not be able to reach their food and water. They will die of starvation and thirst. This happens because they are crippled.

Then we go close up. There are birds with monstrous breasts, the Jordans of mass-produced meat, barely able to stand up. Other birds are trying to walk but their legs buckle under them. These chickens grow so fast that they can outgrow their skeletons and cardio-vascular systems. One lies, full-screen, unable to move, clearly dying. It is a pitiful sight. One leg is stretched out behind, splayed and awkward. It is hard to see this leg, this weakened, dis-located, pathetic leg on a dying bird, as the same sort of leg that you'd put in your hand and bite.

The video does a speeded-up version of the growth of two chickens. One is a meat bird; the other an egg layer. Whilst the egg-hen grows at a normal rate, the broiler swells up and up and up. Bigger and bigger it gets, soon towering above the egg layer's normal stature. At around six weeks of age, time for slaughter, it is a freakish giant. Yet this is still a young bird; a big-breasted baby distorted for our needs. We then see this bird grow through the factory process, from newborn ball of fluff – 'day-olds' – to the Incredible Hulk: the super-sized bird that forms prac-tically all the meat that we eat. We are starting to discover why chicken is so cheap, the voiceover tells us. The fast-bred chickens take half the time to grow that they did thirty years ago, saving on feed costs. They are packed into sheds, twenty, thirty or forty thousand deep. They do not live anywhere else in their short lives. They can have, instead, this 'fast and furious life of suffering'.

It is time for the chickens to die. Men come into the sheds. One kicks out at the chickens, which try to get away; not easy in these cramped conditions. Panic can cause 'piling' incidents when the birds suffocate in a terrified mass. The men are carrying sacks and wearing masks. Chicken 'harvesting' is widely acknowledged as being one of the worst jobs in the world. All you can say is that it must be even worse for the chickens. The men grab handfuls of chickens by their legs and swing them into crates, shoving them in and slamming the crates shut like the doors of the Tube in the evening rush hour. The birds' fragile bones break.

We see two trucks of piled crates, neat as Tonka Toys. You may well pass such a cargo on the road. Chickens are not able to sweat and are vulnerable to temperature changes. The voice tells us that many chickens every year die in transportation in Europe alone.

The final section of the video is in a processing plant. The chickens are taken by the legs and hung upside-down. A macabre Busby Berkeley chorus line flows along an endless repeat of apparently precise procedures. Except it does not go like clockwork, we are told. The birds' throats are taken past a revolving blade, but some will not be cut properly. The upside-down chickens' eyes gleam and so do the beads of blood on each white neck. The pre-stunning may not work. Some can be conscious as they bleed.

The deathly chorus-line, shorn of its feathers, comes around the corner and a blade cuts the body from the feet. The feet continue onwards – perhaps all the way to China, where there is a market for eating them – and the chicken bodies drop down. Now they look like the chickens you buy. There are no extremities; nothing to tell you that each one was once a creature. Nothing to tell you how it was born, raised, snatched, transported, killed and plucked. It is as anonymous as an egg. Or a piece of innocent white chicken, wrapped in its little plastic tray.

Here are the problems you can get with intensive chicken farming. Let's start with a simple fact. The average broiler bird is now ready for slaughter at thirty-eight to forty days, and weighs 2kg before plucking. Thirty years ago, it took twice that time to reach that weight. Put another way, over the thirty years between 1976 and 2007 the birds produced via this system will have achieved what is said to be an industry target of living an average of one day less every year. Most chickens today are mere babies when they are killed, forced at an unnatural pace through an industrial system.

The young chickens are bred to have the huge breasts that the public like and are fed high-protein feeds to make them grow big quickly. As the video says, feed is the main cost of chicken production and so the less time and feed it takes to 'grow' your birds the better. The amount of feed needed has halved in twenty years. In some countries (mostly not the UK these days) almost constant dim lighting discourages the birds from moving so that they put on more weight. For a short period of time the light may be turned off, but this is only so that the birds would not panic in the event of a power cut.

The bones of a chicken can be put under tremendous strain. The legs may be bent inward or outward or twisted. A condition called tibial dyschondroplasia occurs when the cartilage does not form properly and the bone does not calcify as it should; one study showed that this problem affected nearly half of a heavy commercial strain of broiler birds. The bones of a proper free-range bird and a rushed-through broiler are different. A bird's bones are fragile and light in any case; they were designed to be so in order that the creature can fly. When put under the pressure of a fast food, fast-growth factory, it is harder for them to grow properly and to cope with the strain of their now vastly inflated breast muscles. Instead, they go 'off their legs', the unforgettable phrase commonly used by chicken farmers.

Bacterial infection can attack the top of the leg joints, causing lameness and hot, swollen joints and tendons. Such problems increase as the birds get bigger, putting ever more strain on their already painful legs. Around 6 million birds a year die from the infectious leg disorder bacterial chondronecrosis (BCN) is the figure quoted in a recent government-funded study, Leg Health and Welfare in Commercial Broiler Production (2006).

Because of these problems, and their unnatural weight, the birds become even more inactive. At six weeks, most of their time can be spent lying down. This is one of the first things you notice in a broiler house. In the shop, you notice something else. When the birds are sitting in wet litter they get breast blisters and hock burn. In the course of writing this book I would periodically go down to the cheap chicken stand at one of my local supermarkets, and on some days it would be hard to find many that did not have hock burn: most of them would have the tell-tale, bruise-like markings. Hock burn is easier to see than breast blisters, occurring for the same reason but often covered by the label until you get the bird home and take off the plastic.

The chickens may certainly be in pain, and may die in the sheds. One reason the mortality rate of broilers is so much higher than that of laying hens is heart failure. Overall mortality is estimated at around 3–5 per cent a week. That is quite a number when you consider that an average chicken shed contains tens of thousands of birds: in total around 45 million of the 900 million birds hatched in the

UK each year. These birds are simply written off as wastage.

There are two main ways in which these chickens can die of heart disease. Ascites, also known as 'water-belly' or 'leaking-liver', affects a significant number of birds worldwide. According to Karen Davis, who runs the organization United Poultry Concern, it used to cost the US broiler industry $100 million a year. The victims are found dead, their bloated stomachs filled with yellow fluid and clots. Before they die, their hearts have been frantically trying to pump enough blood through their arteries to supply their bodies with oxygen. In order to achieve that the blood becomes more viscous, and the heart chambers dilate in an attempt to force the thick blood through. When it simply can't be pushed on, blood begins to go backwards. It fills the veins, the organs swell and blood leaks from the liver. Eventually the abdominal cavity fills with fluid as the bird suffocates. The second major cardio-vascular problem, Sudden Death Syndrome, is also known as Flip-Over Syndrome. Male birds, which grow faster than females, flap their wings frantically and then suddenly keel over.

It is not uncommon for a single person to look after all the thousands of birds in a shed. They will walk through, supposedly checking on the birds and picking out the dead ones. When you look at the sheer number they are dealing with, to what extent could anyone, even if they were skilled and motivated, care for the birds as birds?

The quantity of birds kept in too small an area can contribute to a number of the problems in chicken farming. In an intensive broiler unit, for reasons already given, the birds' litter is never changed. In a smaller operation, new bedding is put on the ground every day. In the large sheds the faeces build up on the unchanged bedding, which can cause air pollution as the pungent ammonia burns the birds' eyes and lungs. The filthy floor can cause sores to form on the chickens, especially as they get older and spend more time squatting down on the ground because of their painful legs. The sores can become infected with bacteria. One disease, deep dermatitis, causes the skin on the birds' backside to become hot, swollen and yellow. Their breasts and hocks can become blistered, as explained above. And the birds suffer from foot-pad dermatitis, or foot burn.

The stocking density of chickens is measured in kilograms of bird per square metre. A panel of experts reporting to the European Commission* concluded that major welfare problems could be reduced if the stocking density was no more than 25 kg to the square metre. Since each bird grows to about 2 kg in weight before slaughter this would be the equivalent of about $12\frac{1}{2}$ birds per square metre. The UK government's advisory body of experts, the Farm Animal Welfare Council (FAWC) recommends that it should be no more than 17 birds. But a large number of poultry units still contain up to 19 birds per square metre. In Denmark farmers used to be able to stock at 21 birds per square metre – nearly twice the density advised by SCA-HAW. By 2006 this should have been reduced to 20. Well, lucky chickens!

But progress is being made on stocking densities, thanks to the pressure put on the industry by the report. A new broiler directive proposed pushing the recommended density in the UK down to about 15 birds per square metre. But

* From the Scientific Committee on Animal Health and Animal Welfare (SCAHAW), 2000

picture that in your mind and see if you feel comfortable with it. Chicken factory farmers would be able to stock at around 19 birds, but in the processing plant their birds will be inspected for indications that the litter is in reasonable condition. Swedish systems show that stocking density is not the only factor in the birds' welfare.

The chicken industry claims that improvements have been made to leg problems through breeding programmes. But an important government-backed study carried out at Bristol University shows that, despite years of pressure from campaigners and pressing words from FAWC the serious issue of leg disorders has not been solved. The study, published at the end of 2006, showed that 27.3 per cent of broiler birds had moderate or severe leg and walking problems. In one of the companies surveyed this rose to nearly 72 per cent. Relate these figures to the size of the national broiler flock and you get 200 million birds a year suffering for the price of cheap meat in the UK today.

John Webster, Emeritus Professor of Animal Husbandry at Bristol University, wrote an authoritative and influential book on animal welfare, *A Cool Eye Towards Eden* (1992), in which he did not mince his words on the situation of the broiler chicken. Approximately a third of the fast-growing, heavy breeds were in 'chronic pain' for around a third of their lives, he said. And because of the scale of chicken meat farming the broiler industry was, he judged, 'in both magnitude and severity, the single most severe, systematic example of man's inhumanity to another sentient animal'.

This is a terrible story, and nobody is going to enjoy reading about it. In the second half of this book I turn to what has been done, so far, to address the conditions of the mass-produced meat chickens, and what we can do about it ourselves as consumers. But first there is yet one more aspect of factory farming to address that is even more hidden than the broiler sheds: the breeder flocks for the broiler birds.

Broilers are now bred to grow so fast that they can have severe health problems if they are not killed at around six weeks old. But this is before they reach sexual maturity. The broiler breeder birds therefore have to be fed unnaturally in order to reach their reproduction age without keeling over and also to avoid reproductive problems if they survive. Their food is restricted. A breeder broiler hen at times is said to be fed 60–80 per cent less than a bird would eat if left to its own devices. Critics say they are fed in one go, and can rush at the food and eat it in less than ten minutes. Because they are hungry, they can drink a lot and this can cause their litter to be runny, causing problems with the bedding. The pedigree birds have the worst time. In order to see what their genes are like they are fed to their maximum growth rate for six weeks, after which their food is suddenly severely restricted so they can go on to breed. Some of the unsavoury aspects of the chicken industry came to the public's attention when two members of London Green-peace were taken to court over statements made in a leaflet criticising McDonalds.

The judge in the McLibel trial in 1997, Mr Justice Bell, was certainly critical of the practice in his judgment: 'My conclusion is that the practice of rearing breeders for appetite, that is to feel especially hungry, and then restricting their feed with the effect of keeping them hungry, is cruel. It is a well-planned device for profit at the expense of suffering of the birds. The birds may be healthy but there is no ground for supposing that the birds are compensated by awareness of that fact, as a man or woman who restricts an overindulgent diet would be.'

Furthermore, the breeder cockerels can have the ends of their beaks removed and their spurs can be cut to stop them damaging the hens. Because this is mating in a highly unnatural situation. One PhD thesis, from the University of Guelph, Canada, showed that many of the hens struggled when mated; about 50 per cent of these observed matings were forced and in the process the hen could get deep lacerations on her head and torso and under the wings*. Hidden this may be, but it is large-scale. At any one time there are many millions of broiler breeder hens in the UK. They are an integral part of the process that produces the cheap chicken we eat.

I have focused so far on meat chickens; their situation is less well known than that of caged egg layers. But even if a large number of people now buy free-range eggs, we must never forget the existence of the battery cage system. It is interesting that we hear some welfare scientists talk of this method of production as 'scientific'. Such systems should be judged according to how the birds themselves feel, and not how we feel about them, they say. All the same, it is hard to be a human being and not to respond to the image of birds crushed together in a cage and used as egg machines. The nitty-gritty of the conditions of these creatures seems to be even more

* (Millman, S.T. An Investigation into extreme aggressiveness of broiler breeder males (1999))

unspeakable than even this powerful image conveys. Discovering the details of the life of the caged egg-bird is like looking under a clean white tablecloth and discovering a cesspit.

The male chicks that are not going to be fed into the system are thrown away. On reflection, they are the luckier ones. The females are reared so they will lay as early as possible. Shut up in barren wire cages that give each hen less space than a piece of A4 paper, they are unable to stretch their wings, scratch about, dust-bath, groom themselves or do any other of the activities that make a chicken a chicken – except, of course, to lay eggs. The way they have to do so is totally unnatural. In nature, a hen will find a private, warm spot to lay her clutch. The founding father of ethology, Karl Lorenz, compared forcing a chicken to lay its eggs in cramped conditions, alongside other chickens, to making humans defecate in front of each other. In his opinion, it violates a very powerful internal sense of what is right and wrong.

In this confined space, the chickens can become frustrated and their pecking order instinct gets out of hand. They peck each other viciously, and the victims are unable to escape. This is why, around the world, many are debeaked, or beak-tipped; a sad 'solution' to a problem we caused in the first place.

The speeded-up life of the birds is entirely focused on their egg production. They are stimulated by light to lay continuously. By the end of a year or so, exhausted – or, as the poultry industry phrase goes, 'spent' – they are taken off to the slaughterhouse with few of the niceties that broiler birds are given. The spent laying hens may have broken bones. In the past, their claws could be twisted to the point that they got trapped on the wire floors; now, at least, there is a regulation that each cage should have a claw-shortening device. Their legs can be painful, with conditions such as osteoporosis which leads to broken bones and chronic pain. These chickens become the meat that goes into extra-extra-cheap products.

If a laying hen is not killed after a year, there is an extra painful indignity for her to undergo. In nature the birds moult, or shed their feathers, once a year and at this point stop laying. If the birds are going to be kept for a second season, the normal practice used to be to turn off the lights and stop feeding them; this would stimulate them to moult so that they could start laying again quickly. Such severe treatment has now ceased – apparently – replaced by merely giving them feed that is hard to digest. More are just killed as 'spent' hens.

And so this is how very cheap chicken and eggs are produced. What is grisly reading for many consumers will just be a fact of production for others. Factory farmers say that breeding programmes and improvements to the housing have solved the health issues, and that the breeding birds continue to put on weight and so are not 'starved'. They say that examples given by campaigners such as Compassion in World Farming show the worst cases. But how can we be certain that this is not the chicken that ends up in our mouths? And how much have conditions improved? Is there an inherent problem in keeping huge numbers of birds in such unnatural conditions and making them grow so phenomenally quickly and to such proportions? Not if you look at it from a purely economic perspective. Ruth Harrison, in her seminal book *Animal Machines* (1966), sums up one of the biggest obstacles to change: 'If one person is unkind to an animal it is considered cruelty but where a lot of people are unkind to a lot of animals, especially in the name of commerce, the cruelty is defended, and once large sums of money are involved, will be defended to the last by otherwise intelligent people.'

Drugs, Bugs and Poo

Chickens, like any living creature, are full of microbes. Most of them are harmless; some are quite the opposite. Food poisoning, as sufferers know, is agonizing and dangerous. It is said to cause around five hundred deaths a year in the UK. In 2000 the UK's Health Protection Agency estimated there may have been 1.3 million outbreaks of such food-borne illness in just one year. And the number one culprit is chicken.

Salmonella bacteria cause the most well-known form of food poisoning from poultry. Around the world, salmonella affects 1.3 billion people a year. It is a notoriously awful illness. One sufferer described it as 'even worse than divorce'. Another man I spoke to was hospitalized after eating salmonella-infected food. He managed to tell a grimly entertaining story about what had happened – in hospital he had hallucinated films he had never seen – but it had clearly been a horrendous experience.

Normally you need relatively large amounts of salmonella to cause illness in healthy adults. This can happen if infected food is left out of the fridge, perhaps on a buffet table on a summer's day, in warm conditions in which the bugs can multiply rapidly. Vulnerable people, such as the very young, the old and the immuno-compromised, can be attacked by smaller quantities of the microbes. These are the groups that tend to die. You get a sudden headache, acute tummy pain, diarrhoea, nausea, vomiting and fever, all of which can last from four to seven days. Poultry meat is one source of salmonella food poisoning, but in 1988 Edwina Currie, then a junior health minister, notoriously put salmonella-in-eggs on the front pages. 'We do warn people now that most of the egg production in this country, sadly, is now infected with salmonella,' she said.

Since this scandal broke, vaccination has reduced the incidence of salmonella considerably – at least in British produce, both meat and eggs. It costs the industry £4 million a year to inoculate 2 million birds a month. Eggs bearing the Lion label – around 85 per cent of those produced in the UK – are from vaccinated birds. There are problems, however, with imported eggs. The latest figures given out by the European Food Safety Authority (EFSA) in 2006 show that the incidence of salmonella in eggs is highest in Poland, with 77.6 per cent infected, followed by Spain at 73.2 per cent. UK eggs have the seventh lowest infection rates in the EU. Luxembourg, Sweden and Slovakia have managed to eradicate the problem altogether, so it can be done. The UK industry complains that, after cleaning up its act, it is suffering because of cheaper imports from countries that save money on food safety. In the last couple of years twenty people have died from salmonella from imported eggs. An estimated one in eight Spanish eggs – and eggs from Spain make up a significant percentage of foreign eggs brought into the UK – was infected with salmonella. We now import 10–14 per cent of our supplies, and most imported eggs are used in the catering trade. Egg-fried-rice in Chinese restaurants is one dish to watch out for in particular.

The most common form of chicken food poisoning today is campylobacter, a nasty bacterium that causes severe abdominal pain and often bloody diarrhoea. Rare but serious long-term effects can develop, such as Reiter's Syndrome, a type of arthritis, and an estimated one in a thousand people struck down with campylobacter go on to suffer Guillain-Barré Syndrome, a neurological condition that can be fatal. Whilst the incidence of other kinds of food poisoning has gone down, the number of campylobacter cases increased by 46 per cent in the 1990s. In the 1999 scandal when dioxin-contaminated feed got into the Belgian farming industry, there was a withdrawal of chicken from the Belgian market – shortly followed by a decline of 40 per cent in human campylobacter cases.

How much of our chicken is infected? A 2001 study by the Food Standards Agency showed that half the samples of raw and frozen chicken they found on the UK high street contained campylobacter microbes. Chicken is the main cause of this kind of food poisoning, of which there are an estimated half a million cases a year. Some 82 per cent of the people admitted to hospital for food poisoning have been struck down by this nasty spiral-shaped microbe. About 100 of these patients die. The bacteria spread easily around the birds in the barns, and then in the killing process when the birds' guts get sprayed around. The bacteria are killed in cooking – but will the bird be cooked properly? Just a few hundred microbes counts as an 'infectious' dose.

There are macabre peaks of campylobacter infection at festival times, such as Christmas and Easter. There's even a St Valentine's Day massacre, when restaurants are under pressure and more inexperienced cooks take to the home kitchen.

The Food Standards Agency has a target of halving the number of campylobacter-infected chicken carcasses by 2010. In order to do so, they are working with the industry to improve biosecurity on farms. But as is so often the case, some problems arise for economic reasons. One way infection spreads is through the practice of 'thinning' the flocks. This involves a percentage of the birds, generally the males, which grow quicker than the females, being taken out and slaughtered slightly earlier than the rest of the 'crop'. This offers the market different sizes of birds and makes the most amount of money for the farmer, who can keep more chickens in a house. It is estimated that the chicken houses would need to be 10 per cent bigger to make the same money if thinning was not practised. But thinned flocks, unfortunately, have double the campylobacter infection rates of non-thinned ones. One reason for this, given in a 2006 essay by leading food poisoning expert Tom Humphrey, Professor of Veterinary Bacterial Zoonoses at the University of Bristol, is that 'social stress increases susceptibility to bacterial and viral infections in chickens'. Not only does thinning introduce human catchers and possible contamination into the flock, it can also distress the birds which causes them to excrete more and so further pathogens are spread. Professor Humphrey's message is that happy chickens can be safer chickens. 'Animals are more susceptible to infection when they are in a poor environment, fed a poor diet and/or under physical or psychological stress.' This can happen in all systems.

Professor Humphrey believes British chicken has never been safer. In 1989, around 80 per cent of chicken carcasses tested positive for salmonella; by 2001 this was down to 5 per cent. The latest figures given out by the Food Standards Agency in 2006 for the number of people suffering from campylobacter and salmonella have both fallen by more than 20 per cent. The main problem is now imports, he believes.

Every year in the UK there are around 60,000 reported cases of salmonellosis and campylobacteriosis, but these infections are estimated by the government to affect over ten times that figure.

Over the same period, a huge number of cases go unreported. At a domestic level, it is important that people understand the basic rules of food hygiene: food should be kept in the fridge to stop bugs multiplying and should be properly cooked to destroy them – that is, until meat comes easily away from the bone and the juices run clear. Most importantly, people need to know how to stop bugs spreading from raw meat to food that will not be cooked before being eaten. The Food Standards Agency ran a graphic television campaign that used an ultraviolet glowing substance to show how bugs can spread around the kitchen from raw food to cooked with a dab of the hand or a cut of the knife. It is crucial not to cut raw chicken and then food that will be eaten uncooked, such as salad, without cleaning the knife and chopping board in between. There's no need to be frightened of food poisoning once you know the basic rules; but the FSA clearly takes the view that it would be better if the risks were lower in the first place, in every kind of chicken.

Resistance; residues; regulation: these are the three Rs to grapple with when it comes to the murky business of drugs and chicken farming. It comes as no surprise that infection can easily become rife in packed chicken sheds. It's not just a question of the number of birds and their close proximity; the stressful conditions of the birds' lives means their immunity is compromised in the first place. Soon after the start of factory farming it became routine to give the birds disease – preventing antibiotics in their feed and water. Farmers soon discovered that the drugs had a highly beneficial side-effect, as they did on other livestock: antibiotics increase growth rates. It is not known exactly how this happens. It could be because the antibiotics destroy bacteria competing for nutrients and that they affect the animal's metabolism as well as stopping disease. Whatever the reason, it was all very handy: you could cram birds into a shed, worry less about infectious disease and get a faster-growing 'crop'. The situation developed to the point that, of all the antibiotics used in the United States, an estimated 70 per cent were put in the food and water of farm animals that were not sick. In the UK, by the 1990s some 450 tonnes of antibiotics a year were being used on farm animals.

Why does this matter? The bugs that survive these antibiotics are the ones that are, by definition, not killed by them. By giving millions of animals low dosages of these drugs, concerned scientists argue, farmers are creating an incubation system for antibiotic-resistant microbes. Such resistance has certainly increased at an alarming rate, and it has done so alongside the spread of the use of antibiotics in factory farms. To give one example, resistance to more than one kind of drug by some kinds of salmonella microbe grew from 5 per cent to 95 per cent in twenty years.

This worrying situation was allowed to develop even

though questions were raised right from the start about the possible risks of using antibiotics in this casual way. After the deaths of a number of children from antibiotic-resistant salmonella, a government-appointed committee of experts was set up under Sir Michael Swann, reporting in 1969. It recommended that types of antibiotics used in human medicine should no longer be used for growth promotion purposes on healthy farm animals, though they could still be used on sick creatures, under veterinary prescription, and their use actually increased. Other closely related kinds, termed 'digestive enhancers' or 'performance enhancers' by the industry, continued to be used without prescription and for growth promotion. But science now shows that antibiotic resistance can spread from one type of microbe to another in the digestive system of animals and humans. This is why it is hard to feel reassured by the argument that there is nothing to worry about because the drugs used on animals are different from the human ones.

Consumers these days are much more aware of the issue of medication routinely given to animals, and with good reason. The importance of antibiotics to human health is enormous. 'If sanity prevailed in this world this egregious deployment of antibiotics would beggar belief,' summarizes Colin Tudge in his thought-provoking book on farming *So Shall We Reap*. 'The stakes are extraordinarily high.' The industry may say that the amounts fed to the animals are in dosages too low to be significant and that antibiotic resistance is not down to what happens in farms. But their confidence is no longer shared by legislators. Governments are starting to wake up to the problem. In 1997 the antibiotic avoparcin, routinely fed to chickens as a 'digestive enhancer', was banned in the EU because it was similar to the antibiotic vancomycin. Vancomycin is a crucial pharmaceutical weapon in human health; a drug of last resort against, for example, the deadly *Staphylococcus aureus*. The incidence of vancomycin-resistant enterococci is another serious worry in modern medicine. After the Danish governments veterinary laboratory showed a link between avoparcin in animal feed and resistance to vancomycin in the treatment of humans, Denmark and Germany banned its use in feed in 1995. When this was discussed at EU level, Britain was one of only two countries to vote against the ban, on the grounds that more research was needed. Our chicken-farming lobby, it seems, was stronger than the urge for the best possible human health protection.

More than half a century after it began, routine feeding of antibiotics as growth promoters has – at last – been phased out in the UK and the rest of Europe. Farmers are still allowed to feed their chickens such drugs under veterinary supervision as a prophylactic measure – that is, to prevent disease. But this could easily be a loophole. It is all too easy to say you need to give the chickens medication in order for them to survive conditions that make them vulnerable to such disease in the first place. And antibiotics of all kinds are still routinely fed to meat chickens in the United States. According to a 2001 report by the Union of Concerned Scientists, more than half the 10,000-plus tonnes of anti-microbial drugs fed to farm animals are of the type now banned for routine use in Europe – the ones that are directly relevant to human medicine – and chickens are fed three times as many drugs, of all types, as they were twenty years ago.

Within the industry, the switch away from growth-promoting antibiotics can be a headache. One of the problems is that gastro-intestinal disease causes wet litter, which the over-heavy birds then sit in. You can see why medication continued for so long. It is, ultimately, one of the props on which this kind of farming has depended. Some critics think the practice will end, eventually, because the drugs won't work. Sir Richard Body, the farmer and former Green-Conservative MP, and a stern critic of factory farming, is one such believer. 'It's going to come to an end in due course because of antibiotics losing their efficacy,' he said in the Radio Four programme *Why Did We Do That?* 'They can't have these hen cities, or fowl cities, or whatever they are going to call them with these millions and millions of birds looked after by just a few people – it's not going to be possible without the use of antibiotics on a tremendous scale.'

Another condition against which British chickens are routinely medicated is coccidiosis. This is a disease caused by a protozoan, a small single-cell parasite that passes through the bird and develops on wet ground, such as can be found in a faeces-littered intensive broiler house. The chicken eats the waste on the ground and ingests the developed organisms, which multiply and pass out of the body to develop some more, and may then be ingested again. As the cycle continues the disease builds up and starts to cause a problem. The chicken becomes listless and hunched, its comb pale and its eyes closed. It eats less. This is all very bad news for chicken farmers plumping up birds as fast as possible; the death rate can be over 50 per cent. Organic and amateur chicken keepers try to avoid coccidiosis by making sure the chickens do not stay continually on the same piece of ground and by clearing up damp areas of chicken mess. For the large-scale producer such individual, watchful care is not even a possibility. And so they find another solution.

Richard Young is a policy adviser to the Soil Association with a particular interest in the drugs fed to farm animals. He has co-written a number of reports on the medications known collectively as coccidiostats that are used to control the problem. *Too Hard to Crack* (2004) looked specifically at one coccidiostat, lasalocid, and the residues of it found in eggs. Young's general point about this and other veterinary drugs routinely fed to chickens is that these are highly toxic substances: too toxic for use in human medicine; so toxic that every year there are incidences of animals dying from them. Yet the controls for them were set in less scientifically rigorous times and in some cases, he says, without adequate testing. These drugs are fed to food animals to make it possible to keep them in overcrowded conditions, and unacceptable levels of residues are getting through.

Lasalocid is not meant to be fed to egg-producing chickens at all. Residues accumulate in the yolk, and this is a drug that can cause heart problems in susceptible people. Yet in 2003, the government's monitoring of eggs discovered that more than 12 per cent had residues of lasalocid. How come? Various theories have been put forward. The drug could have got into the hens' feed through a mix-up in the feed mills. Or there could have been a mix-up in the feed hoppers at the farm. Successive loads of feed are put into the conical feeders you see at the end of chicken factory farm buildings. Remnants of the medicated feed can cling to the sloping sides and come through later, mixed in with a subsequent load of non-medicated feed. Drugs can also be spread from the chickens pecking at the faeces on the floor, a phenomenon known as 'faecal recycling'. Or the residues may come from young hens which are given the drug and produce eggs earlier than expected, before they have gone through the legal withdrawal period for the drug. After the report came out, the egg industry pointed out that these figures are high partly because the government targeted places with likely problems. Does that make one feel safer? Is enough testing done in the first place? Another Soil Association report, *Too Hard to Swallow* (2001), points out that in that year the regulators tested just 250 samples; we eat 10 billion eggs a year. Even though there are serious issues with residues, the Soil Association says that fewer tests are conducted now than were done ten years ago. But at least we do test for lasalocid; other countries do not. This is a matter for concern in a world of international supply chains. The concern is that as legislation is tightened in Britain and the rest of Europe, cheaper imports from countries with less stringent controls, or even less monitoring of controls, will increase.

Because of concerns about lasalocid, the British egg industry decided to place a voluntary ban on its use in all egg layers. It can, however, still be found in chick-crumb of the sort bought by the domestic chicken keeper or smallholder (and it is still being given to meat chickens). Coílín Nunan, co-author of the Soil Association's report on lasalocid, bought such a bag by mistake for his own flock. He says it is easy to imagine how the feed could be inadvertently given to hens and quantities of it eaten. 'When you have your own chickens you tend to eat lots of eggs because they taste nicer than factory farm ones, and there are times of year when you have a lot of them,' says Nunan. 'So you get a double whammy of lots of eggs and very high residues and no idea that is happening.' It seems strange that a drug with such a high level of toxicity should be sold off-the-shelf like this. Lasalocid, like all these toxic coccidiostats, is available without prescription, put into formulated feed that anyone can buy.

Other questions have been raised about residues of another coccidiostat, nicarbazin. This is the active ingredient in feed that is routinely given to broiler chickens in their first four weeks of life. A 2003 survey of the broiler industry as regards coccidiostat residues, done by the Irish food safety promotion board *Safe*Food, showed that 100 per cent of the participants – representing 90 per cent of the island's industry – were using a narasin/nicarbazin mixture amongst the twelve drugs or drug combinations they used to control the disease. There is a nine-day withdrawal period for nicarbazin, such is its toxicity. Campaigners are concerned it may be mutagenic. Whilst the drug has been given to animals for some fifty years this does not mean it is safe, though this is an argument put forward in its defence. The Soil Association and others have raised questions about its use, again due to concerns about human health and inadequate regulation.

The UK government acknowledges that consumers do not want avoidable residues of veterinary drugs in their chicken and eggs. The drugs, in theory, should be given under strict controls. The medicated feed should be withdrawn a stated number of days before slaughter. The feed mills, bins and pipelines should be thoroughly cleaned between batches of feed. Guidelines have been issued to farmers on how to avoid nicarbazin residues. But in 2004 residues of nicarbazin above the permitted amount were found in 17.6 per cent of broiler livers. In November 2006 consumers in Queensland, Australia were outraged to discover that 49,000 birds had died from eating feed containing nicarbazin and that the meat from the rest of the flock had gone on sale after being isolated for a week. Some of the birds had survived just because they were stronger than the ones that had been struck down by this overdose of toxic chemicals.

In a better world, the whole issue of coccidiosis in poultry farming would be sorted out by using vaccination. But according to Richard Young vaccine costs 6.8p a bird whilst coccidiostats in feed cost less than 0.5p. With the profit on a bird currently at around 2–3p, or less, you can see why it doesn't happen. The *Safe*Food coccidiostat report said that vaccination tends only to be used for breeding stock and birds in organic production. And there's another reason, too. Farmers responding to a subsequent *Safe*Food report, in 2005, said that vaccination does not give the indirect benefits associated with coccidiostat use, including 'improved performance'. We are back to economics.

You may take the view that the risks inherent in using these drugs are worth taking for the economic advantages of this sort of medication; that tests and regulations are properly in place and that they provide us with an adequate safety-net; that producers will switch feeds correctly and everything will tick along like clockwork. Producers say the drugs are present in 'pinprick' amounts. Or you may choose to buy your meat from a clearly identifiable and trusted source that puts a higher premium on safety and does not use routine feed drugs of this type.

You may also decide, on a broader level, that your meat should come from the UK. There is certainly evidence that poultry containing residues of banned veterinary drugs does go on sale in the form of imported meat. In 2004, chicken pieces and whole birds sold by supermarkets and other shops were found to be contaminated with nitrofuran, a substance that was banned by the EU in 1995 (and the USA in 2002) because it is carcinogenic and genotoxic (causes damage to the genes) after long-term exposure. Since the ban, nitrofuran residues have been found in Brazilian, Portuguese and Thai poultry. The Food Standards Agency, for example, reported that Brazilian chicken imported through Belgium and Germany had tested positive. Tests have been developed that pick up the metabolites, or break-down products, of the drug so that it can be better detected. In March 2003 the FSA tested some Portuguese poultry and found 34 out of 37 samples positive for nitrofuran residues. Then again, the problem drug was also found in British organic chickens in 2004, when whole birds and chicken pieces with nitrofuran residues were recalled from such brand names as Moy Park, Waitrose, Tesco and Morrison's.

It is not exactly easy to get information about the drugs in chickens. Transparency is hardly the name of the game when it comes to drugs used on livestock. There is a comedy of errors in the Soil Association's *Too Hard to Swallow*, which offers a rare insight into the way even the government must grapple with industry secrecy. A senior toxicologist advising the government wrote a letter complaining about the pharmaceutical industry's continued reluctance – after being asked for data on several occasions – to provide details about the safety of nicarbazin. This is a drug, remember, that is routinely fed to vast numbers of the broilers we eat. What jumped out at him, the expert wrote, was the inadequacy of investigations for mutagenicity. Furthermore, two different committees had set different allowable residue levels. 'As there have been gaps identified in the toxicological data on nicarbazin and as there are inconsistencies between the decisions on the two committees that have seen these data, I feel uncomfortable when asked to comment on the consumer health significance on any residues of nicarbazin found in food,' he wrote. His letter was inadvertently faxed to the report's co-author, Alison Craig, who happened to have the same surname as a member of a regulatory committee. The concerns raised would never have come to light but for this mistake.

Organic farmers are fond of poo. It is part of a system of farming that recycles nutrients and works with nature to produce fertile soils. But what is a beneficial and thrifty part of small-scale farming becomes a nightmare of waste disposal on a factory farm. The enormous number of chickens 'grown' for meat in such places also produces mountains of manure. The nitrogen in this soiled poultry litter is useful for the land – up to a point. There are laws about how much can be applied to the land before it becomes a pollutant that risks contaminating our water sources. Then there is the issue of bodies in the muck. Cattle grazing on pastures spread with chicken fertilizer have been infected by botulism from diseased carcasses left in the mess, though there are supposed to be strict guide-lines to stop this happening and new legislation means that every farmer in the EU has to have a permit from its national environment agency.

The shit is really hitting the fan in the United States. The US government estimates that in excess of 335 million tonnes of animal manure is produced every year by farms, making up nearly a third of all municipal and industrial waste. In the case of chicken mess, some of it goes into useful fertilizer pellets and some of it pollutes. In 2005 the Attorney General of Oklahoma, Drew Edmondson, filed a suit against the chicken industry as part of a bid to get it to clean up its act. 'It all comes down to pollution,' Edmondson said. 'Too much poultry waste is being dumped on the ground and it ends up in the water. That's against the law. The companies own the birds as well as the feed, medicines and other things they put in their birds. They should be responsible for managing the hundreds of thousands of tons of waste that comes out of their birds.' After spending three years trying to negotiate a way through the problem he turned to the law, alleging that poor dumping and storage of poultry waste was damaging the state's streams and lakes. The waste contained such unpotable substances as microbial pathogens and the arsenic used in chicken feed. Arsenic is fed to at least 70 per cent of American broilers, according to a recent survey, *Playing Chicken: Avoiding Arsenic in Your Meat*, carried out by the Institute for Agriculture and Trade Policy, which found detectable traces of it in 55 per cent of samples of uncooked chicken taken from supermarket shelves and 90 per cent of samples from fast food outlets. Whilst the amounts were below Federal levels, the report questions why such a toxic material is in the food we eat at all. Arsenic is added to chicken feed in the USA to counter coccidiosis, to help weight gain and improve the colour of the birds' flesh. In other words, it props up the inadequacies of intensive farming. It is banned in feed used in the EU. You do not want it in your food and you do not want it in your soil.

There have been grass-roots protests against chicken pollution. If you live in a chicken-producing area you may well have millions of birds and their byproducts on your doorstep. The US environmental group the Sierra Club, founded in 1892, has taken up the issue, and in

1999 employed a dedicated campaigner, Aloma Dew. Her road trips around the poultry-producing areas of Kentucky, a 'Tour de Stench', raised awareness about the pollution of poultry waste. One woman joined the campaign after she found herself with ninety-two chicken houses within three miles of her home. Faecal dust, chemicals and sheer stink keep her indoors most days. 'Welcome to Chickenshitsville: Follow Your Nose to Our House' greeted the guests on the first tour. They went on to stop by a school where children often vomit from the stench of the chicken houses near by, and to hear about issues such as nitrate pollution of water sources.

There are moves to make chicken poo more economically productive. In Britain, a company called Fibrowatt now has a series of incinerators in East Anglia, Lincolnshire and Scotland that burn chicken waste to produce power. Their plant at Eye in Suffolk was the first in the world to be fuelled by chicken shit. The company is now expanding into the USA. Critics say such power stations are expensive to run and there are concerns about pollution; they object to the idea as a whole because it supports factory farming, making it more a 'brown' than 'green' source of power.

Technical advances can be made. Researchers at the University of Nebraska are investigating the possibility of making a natural, biodegradable fabric out of chicken feathers. Four billion pounds of feathers are produced worldwide each year and could be put to use in replacing fabrics made out of petrochemicals.

Chicken mess needs the latest technology to clear it up. But the issues of chicken litter are to do with quantity and the way the birds are farmed. The more birds we eat, the more waste there is – if you buy factory-farmed chicken.

You have to ask yourself whether we want such quantities to clear up in the first place, and whether we really need all this cheap chicken and its resulting stench and its power to pollute our environment.

Killing

On 10 September 1945 Lloyd Olsen, a farmer in Fruita, Colorado, took an axe into his yard, planning to get a young Wyandotte rooster for dinner. He wanted to keep the neck whole; it was his mother-in-law's favourite morsel. So he aimed high. The head came off. But the cockerel did not die. The axe had missed the jugular. A blood clot formed and stopped the bird from bleeding to death. The head was gone but there remained an ear and the brain stem where most of the animal's reflexes were stored. The rooster continued to operate like a normal animal, albeit one with an avian version of phantom limb syndrome. He 'pecked' and 'preened' and slept with his 'head' under his wing. He was, Olsen said, 'a robust chicken – a fine specimen of a chicken except not having a head'. The farmer discovered that he could use an eye-dropper to feed his bird through the neck. He drove his farmyard miracle –

64

now called Mike – to Salt Lake City University where the bird was displayed to scientists. Then commerce moved in. Mike-the-Headless-Chicken became a showground attraction and featured in *Time* and *Life* magazines. Insurers valued him at $10,000. Fed through his neck, he even gained $2\frac{1}{2}$ lb in weight. It was on the celebrity circuit that Mike finally succumbed to fate. Olsen stopped at a motel in Arizona and noticed that his chicken had begun to choke. Eighteen months after the axe fell, the chicken – finally – died.

Mike now has his own website and annual festival. He is a celebrity example of our fascination with the freakish. But while the headless chicken is funny, in a macabre way, the humour is of a complicated sort; a gallows humour with the slightly strained 'ha-ha' that is close to an uncomfortable grimace of fear. This is revealing. Even though we happily chomp our way through wings and legs and thighs of chickens, modern Western society is uneasy about the subject of meat eating. And this is centred on the almost taboo subject of killing.

The Scottish anthropologist Nick Fiddes argues in *Meat: A Natural Symbol* that the carnivorous diet has powerful meanings that exist even when – indeed, especially when – they are not discussed. We may not acknowledge killing, and buy small, anonymous pieces of meat in supermarket trays, but he thinks meat eating is significant precisely because blood has been shed. A family will gather round as a special occasion for a Sunday roast or the Christmas turkey because of the high status of eating an animal. Where does this status come from? Fiddes argues it is because meat eating symbolizes humans' domination over nature: the point of death dramatizes the bloody moment when we take this life in order to eat. 'Killing, cooking and eating other animals' flesh provides perhaps the ultimate authentication of human superiority over the rest of nature, with the spilling of their blood a vibrant motif,' he writes. Blood is life, kinship, power. And blood is at the heart of eating meat. Meat provides us with nutrients and it tastes delicious, yes, but it is ultimately a food with a strong, underlying force for other reasons. 'Meat is a curious thing . . .' are the starting words of Fiddes' book. 'In Uganda, plantain that would feed a family for four days exchanges for one "scrawny" chicken with less than a twentieth of the nutritional value.'

In the past, killing was more explicit. Chickens used to be sacrificed for religious ritual. Cruel as this seems now, it at least put the matter of death before us in a context that underlined the importance of taking a life. We no longer have a priest to sever the jugular at the altar, divine the future through the birds' entrails and throw precious spices in the fire and on to the animal, their fragrances transporting the deed to the breath of the gods, before we share the meat of the roasted creature. No. We go to the curry house on the way back from the pub for a cheap chicken tikka masala. Meat eating has become casual.

One traditional view of eating is that the bloodier the food, the higher its status, with beef at the top and bloodless animal products such as dairy foods and then non-animal foods such as vegetables at the bottom. This was not a simple hierarchy – the expensive and the rare and the delicious (like the truffle) don't fall neatly into order – but on the whole it held true for many centuries. Part of the problem with chicken has been that, even when it was scarce, it never had quite the cachet of a filet of beef or a haunch of venison. We respected it less for being 'unbloody'.

Now we have also become more uncomfortable about eating animals, and squeamishly distant from the process of killing. Amongst the other factors behind the rise in chicken consumption – health issues, economics – is the fact that people prefer white chicken to blood-red beef partly because it distances them further from killing. There are even 'vegetarians' who eat chicken; ironic, given the welfare issues of mass poultry production.

We don't like to think about taking the life of an animal for our food and so we don't think about it. We have sent the act away to large buildings we don't know: slaughtering is out of sight and out of mind. The irony about this distanced attitude is that it allows everything to happen behind even more firmly closed doors, and this, like the rest of factory farming with its anonymous, windowless sheds, has enabled practices to become normal that should be examined and improved. Living as we do in a culture that values the humane, it is important that we know, in some basic way, the facts of death if we are to share in its products.

Poultry processing plants are, for the most part, huge assembly lines. They need to be when the UK dispatches 860 million broilers and 30–35 million end-of-lay hens a year. But what seem like huge, streamlined systems are not quite as straightforward as we would wish. Like anything else, they are subject to error. More worryingly, the very design of the killing method has been shown to be imperfect. The survival of Mike-the-Headless-Chicken is certainly not a laughing matter when you consider the reality of endless production lines that collectively dispatch millions of chickens a day. Far from being a laughing matter, this is the stuff of nightmares.

Welfare campaigners believe the end of a broiler chicken's life has the potential for the worst abuse. It starts when the catching teams go to clear the sheds. In ideal circumstances the animals would be picked up individually, but of course this would take for ever. And so they are carried by the handful upside-down. There are not meant to be more than three birds in each hand but it is not unknown for this number to be as high as six. The Humane Slaughter Association is an important organization that is working steadily towards better welfare for chickens and other animals at the killing stage. In 2006 it produced a DVD to promote high welfare standards in the industry. One section on the catching process advises: 'If any bird starts flapping during capture, gently rest its breast against the side of your leg for a few seconds.' Somehow this is hard to imagine amidst the pressure of removing tens of thousands of birds in as quick a time as possible. The DVD advises workers removing end-of-lay hens from battery cages not to hit the birds' heads against the metal as they carry them in bird bundles through the narrow canyon between the cages. All the advice is sound; unfortunately it makes you imagine how the opposite can happen.

There are now automatic chicken catchers that hoover the birds up with a giant nozzle and take them into the machine's belly. When operated correctly, this system may be a better welfare option; certainly better than bad manual catching, though one wonders whether human hands, operating on a smaller and less hurried scale, wouldn't be the best option of all. One chicken industry insider told me he'd seen better catching in Brazil and Thailand where labour costs are lower than in Europe. The whole process can be done well; it is appalling to think of it being done any other way.

In the poultry shed the birds are packed into plastic modules, perhaps 12 birds per unit. A book written in the 1990s said that an estimated 3 per cent of them lost claws in the process of being shoved in and out of the crate (N.G. Gregory, *Animal Welfare and Meat Science*, 1998). These drawers of chickens are layered up so a single lorry can take six thousand. You see such vehicles on motorways, bombing along towards the slaughter lines. Their living freight may be completely covered with a tarpaulin, or there may be open panels on the side. The birds are given no food and water prior to travelling. Hunger, thirst, acceleration and vibration, noise and social disruption can all cause stress at this point. The birds find it difficult to regulate their body temperature and this is one reason why transportation can cause suffering and death. In hot weather, especially if it is humid, they can over-heat. They get some relief as the lorry moves and circulates air; the nightmare comes when this is not the case. Imagine being stuck in a jam on the M1 in mid-August. Now imagine it if you were one of six thousand birds packed into crates. In winter, the birds can shiver with cold-stress, huddling together to keep warm and in the late stages of suffering becoming lethargic and drowsy before collapsing. Whatever the weather, a number of birds die from shock due to wings and legs being dislocated in the catching and loading process.

Because of temperature-stress, the birds are meant to wait at the slaughterhouse for as short a time as possible. But because such places operate, like the industry as a whole, on small margins there can be no glitch in the continuous line. The birds must be stacked up ready to go as soon as there is capacity for them. So they are put in a holding area, or lairage. Let us hope they are not left for too long in hot or cold conditions; that the logistics of freight run smoothly. Even at the last stage of movement, there is the possibility of suffering. The birds are lifted from the lorry by forklift trucks driven by people who are, technically, stockmen. Their jerks and driving and drops will affect the birds' lives.

Once inside the plant, the aim is to frighten the chickens as little as possible. There is an economic reason for this. Wing flapping and crushing damages the meat; too much of it and the carcasses will be downgraded. To minimize this risk the lights in the large processing rooms are toned down, perhaps to a blue dim. Noises, such as the pressure release of pneumatic equipment, are supposed to be kept to a minimum.

The birds are hung upside down on a long, moving unit. To do this, workers grab them at great speed and slot their legs into the metal shackles of the production line. They may be imperfectly shackled, putting even more pressure on legs that may have grown faster than their skeleton can deal with. It is bound to be especially painful for such birds to be strung up by the legs.

From this point, the chickens are supposed to be hung upside down on the moving unit for no more than two minutes. Even if this time is never exceeded, two minutes is a long time if you are hung upside down in pain. The birds are whisked on to the stunning bath. This contains a salt solution through which an electrical charge is passed, but not so much as to kill the chickens. Doing so at this stage could affect the quality of the meat by sometimes causing little blood spots to appear on the pure white breasts. The aim, instead, is to stun the chickens. They should not, in theory, be conscious when their throats are cut in the next part of the process. However, a number of chickens are not stunned by the bath. Some lift their heads to avoid it, as well they might, perhaps after being partially shocked by water splashing off the previous birds. The birds are not all one size and will not equally fit this dip into the stun-bath; these are not tubes of toothpaste, but animals.

The Humane Slaughter Association is critical of the water-bath stunning technique because the birds are not stunned individually. Ideally, they would prefer to see a water-bath that kills each bird rather than stunning them. This would eliminate the risk of the birds being conscious when they are killed by neck cutting. The judge in the McLibel trial verdict in 1997, Lord Justice Bell, agreed that the incidence of birds going to the blade conscious was 'frequent'; on a national level it could be that 40–50 birds an hour were conscious when their throats were cut, he said. Has this situation improved? I asked Dr Mohan Raj, Senior Research Fellow in the Department of Clinical Veterinary Science at the University of Bristol, and a leading scientist in the welfare of poultry at the slaughter stage. He thought it could have got worse, especially in the USA, because the speed of the killing lines there has increased, exacerbating the problems. In the USA there are killing lines operating at a rate of 220 birds a minute (13,200 an hour).

The killing is done by passing the line of birds before a rotating blade. The long line of shackled broilers passes before the whizzing wheels that are supposed to sever the vessels carrying blood between the brain and the heart. In an ideal world both the carotid arteries, one on each side of the neck, and the jugular vein would be cut as this is the most rapid way of causing death. Mr Justice Bell accepted that nine in every thousand birds were not actually killed by this process. In the UK improvements have been brought about through installing double blades or even cutting the head off altogether. There is now a person on the line whose job it is to make sure all the birds are dead. You certainly hope they are not conscious when they go through the bleed tunnel and pass on to the next part of the unit, the scalding tank. A welfare-orientated meat producer told me how he had been taken on a show tour of a conventional killing line and, embarrassingly, the death checker was not at his post. Animal welfare scientists are also concerned about decapitation because it can be used to mask inadequate or poor stunning.

The scalding tank contains hot water to loosen the feathers and make the birds easier to pluck. There are other implications of this immersion in a communal water bath, known to some in the trade by the appetizing term 'faecal soup'. The birds have been shackled and shocked. No wonder that the contents of their intestines can spill out. All this can go into water, the perfect medium for bugs to thrive in. It is in the water baths that most of the cross-contamination of carcasses occurs. This is the breeding ground for food poisoning microbes such as salmonella and campylobacter.

Then the birds go through the plucker where rubber fingers flail off the feathers. Then off with the head and the feet; then rapid chilling; then on to factory floors of hi-tech processing machines and the low-paid battery chicken workers who, like the chicken factory worker played by Margi Clarke in the 1985 film *Letter to Brezhnev*, spend their lives 'stuffing chickens' arses' and working with knives or machines to get all the portions and processed products we love so much. Then off to the retailers. We are back to the supermarket shelf and the meat that we eat.

Slaughtering is seen as distasteful; nobody wants to dwell

on the subject. But if we buy something, we are part of its production. The Humane Slaughter Association and others work towards making technical improvements to a necessary trade and should be supported. Instead of wanting to stop eating chickens, we can eat them in a more responsible way. A simple acknowledgement that eating meat involves a life – and a death – is an important step towards seeing chicken not just as a cheap, under-valued commodity but as real meat from a real animal to be valued and treated with respect at all times in its existence.

The UK industry clearly realizes that all is not well in large-scale killing because it is starting to turn to the alternative system of gassing the birds. Crucially, the birds are not strung upside down on shackles for a production line but kept in their catching boxes and taken into the room where they are killed; they are shackled only for further processing once they are dead. One large egg company has already converted to this method. Mohan Raj says around three-quarters of turkeys are killed this way and around a quarter of meat chickens. In Europe and further afield there is some debate amongst welfare scientists about the right kind of gas to use. There are two methods: the inert gases argon and nitrogen, which are extracted from the air; and carbon dioxide. Mohan Raj led a team that investigated which method was better for the chickens. They found that, in high concentrations, carbon dioxide causes suffering to the birds. The 1995 Welfare of Animals during Slaughter or Killing Regulations allowed inert gas or inert gas mixed with up to 30 per cent carbon dioxide. Opponents of the inert gas method say it causes the birds to flap their wings and, even if they are dead, this causes some damage to the meat. Since carbon dioxide is a byproduct of the fertilizer industry one suspects there will be pressure for its use in smaller or larger quantities: it is cheap if not cheerful.

Mohan Raj is glad to see the shift towards gas starting to happen, even if it has been long coming: it was first recommended by the government's Farm Animal Welfare Council in 1982. He feels the shackle slaughter method is 'inherently flawed'. Alongside the pain caused to the birds by being hung upside down, the amount and quality of the electrical current passing through the bird at the stunning stage is too variable. 'Eventually someone will have to really point out to the industry that enough is enough and let's move away from this: it is not appropriate to this century,' he says. Raj believes the shackle system is 'Stone Age'.

At least in the UK the birds are legally meant to be unconscious before cutting. In other countries there isn't even a requirement for that. In the United States, poultry are actually excluded from the Humane Methods of Slaughter Act of 1958. This means they have no legal protection at all in terms of welfare, and if you include ducks, turkeys and other poultry this situation affects all the one million-plus birds killed there every hour. The Humane Society of the United States (HSUS) has filed a suit against the US Department of Agriculture to get birds included in the Act, and urges a move towards gas. Spokeswoman Sarah Uhelmann said, 'Of all the commercial slaughter methods, CAK [controlled atmosphere killing] causes the birds the least distress, and an industry shift toward it would result in a massive reduction in animal suffering.'

A UK industry spokesman told me there was some confusion about which was the best system, and that while legislation caught up with the latest technology and scientists disputed the best methods, people awaited a forthcoming EU directive on the matter. The cost of changing the systems was great, he said, and people were reluctant to change until it was finally decided which method was best. Welfare scientists feel there is an answer already available. Meanwhile the birds keep on rushing down the line, strung up by their legs and suffering so that we can eat cheap chicken.

How many slaughter houses are there for chickens? Fewer and fewer. Most chickens now have to travel to the large processing units that fit into large-scale industrial supply chains. Bob Kennard runs Graig Farms, an organic meat company in mid-Wales, and has fought for more than a decade to try to keep the small processing plant going in the face of ongoing legislation. Whilst he agrees, wholeheartedly, that every slaughterhouse must work to the very highest standards, he thinks that many good small places have been frightened into closure by regulations that are usually far too onerous for the less-than-giant operator. 'It's horrendous,' he summarizes. 'We've been fighting for ten years and it's supposedly getting better, but they keep wiping plants out. It's the death of a thousand cuts. People get fed up and throw the towel in. The government has a schizophrenic attitude. They say they want local food but put in legislation that closes down the abattoirs that make it possible.'

Here is a classic example of what Bob and his fellow campaigners in the UK have to fight against. By law, a vet has to be present during slaughtering at operations licenced by the Meat Hygiene Service. Originally, the vets were to be paid an hourly rate whether they were working in a large industrial unit or a small artisanal one. Clearly the burden of this not inconsiderable cost was far less per animal for a large unit than for a small one. This hourly rate would have included travelling time. If you were a small unit deep in farming country, down a set of country lanes, this highly expensive milometer would tick up much more than if you were close to a motorway, as is the case for big processing plants. In such ways the local loses out to the large-scale industrial, and goes under. Luckily, in this case the legislation was changed so that costs were calculated by numbers of animals, not hours of the vet's time. But this only happened after a long, hard battle. The mindset of government does not appear to be to help the small and local to survive. Quite the opposite. As a result of the problems besetting them and increases in imports, Kennard says, the number of UK poultry slaughterhouses has dropped by 25 per cent since 2000.

If you want to kill chickens for sale, you now have to operate at one of two levels. You can have 'exempt' status and run an operation that is licensed by the local authority. This means you cannot export your chickens, or even sell them in this country beyond a limited distance: 'local food' is seen as coming from your own county and neighbouring ones. It also means you cannot kill other people's chickens; only your own. This discourages small cooperatives from forming. Your total output must be under 10,000 birds a year, or no more than 40 killing days a year. Otherwise you must go for a full EU-licensed plant, operating under the Meat and Hygiene Service [CK], that has bells and whistles and a hundred other box-ticking details. This is prohibitively expensive for the smaller operator. As a result the small must keep very small and the large must be very large.

The closing down of small and medium-sized abattoirs

means the chickens have to travel further and further. Death rates in transport double if the journey is longer than four hours. The Humane Slaughter Association mentions in particular its concern for spent laying hens which are usually killed after the first laying season, when the quality of their eggs may not meet supermarket standards. About 35 million of these birds are killed every year in Britain, and the lack of facilities for them means they have to travel further than they used to. This is particularly cruel because their bodies are especially frail after the forced rigours of battery egg production. There is also no economic incentive to keep their flesh free of bruising when they are going to go into pet food, not on to the meat shelves.

In a traditional farmhouse, a chicken would be plucked straightaway as its feathers come off more easily when the body is still warm. But then the bird might have been left to hang until required by the household. In this way, it would have been discovered that hung meat tastes better. A recent taste test study at the Harper Adams Agricultural College in Shropshire showed that panellists preferred chicken that had been hung for ten days. This is interesting, as it is certainly not the industry norm. Indeed, factory birds cannot be hung for long. One reason for this is revealing.

Most birds are 'wet-plucked' – that is, as already mentioned they are dipped in a tank heated to 52–62°C in order to open up their skin follicles for the rubber plucking fingers to do their work more easily. But critics argue that this also takes off the outer layer, the epidermis, of the skin, and this is nature's barrier against contamination. So the chicken has by now not only lost this protective layer but has been sluiced in warm, faeces-ridden water in which vast amounts of cross-contamination can take place. This is why the birds are whipped off to the chiller immediately. But they will never recover their ability to keep out microbes.

The alternative to this system is dry-plucking. Paul Kelly, an East Anglian farmer who is a great advocate of the method, reckons it costs him £3 a bird and thinks it worth the money. At no stage is the bird put in water. Instead, his chickens go into a pheasant-plucking machine that removes 60 per cent of the feathers; the rest is done by hand. 'It looks a bit stubby and tatty and a bit cottagey,' he says. 'But you can't hang a bird properly unless you dry-pluck it.' You have to go to high-quality, small-scale producers to find chicken that has been dry-plucked and hung. It costs Paul as much just to pluck an artisanal bird as it does for a shopper to buy a whole factory bird. Whether you want to spend this money depends on whether you see chicken as a special food rather than commodity protein.

Various methods can be used to make wet-plucked chickens 'cleaner'. The EU's food safety regulators, the European Food Safety Authority (EFSA) plans to allow chickens to be washed with one of four chemical solutions: trisodium phosphate, acidified sodium chlorite, chlorine dioxide and peroxycid solutions. There is concern in the British industry that this will enable producers operating to lower standards to get away with bad hygiene. Furthermore, it could have implications for imports. The US poultry industry regularly uses these 'antimicrobials' as they are called. This change in European law should ring a loud warning bell to anyone concerned about where their chicken comes from. It could be a further step down the globalization of meat supplies. Even as British chicken producers make improvements, the market will be taken over by cheaper imports that do not even come up to the current standards of the British industry.

The American documentary maker Fred Wiseman turned his camera's eye on animals and death in *Meat* (1976). As with all his work, Wiseman was producer, director, editor and distributor. The film-maker's apparently blank eye is cast upon the scene of a meat-packing plant for cattle and sheep. There is no commentary, just a simple journey from the cowboys on the plains to the steaks in the cellophane. We see the animals become meat in an ordinary place of work. Events have the flow of the conveyor belt: endless, endless. The point of death is very quick; almost insignificant. The flayed heads of the cattle emerge slightly twitching. Their tongues loll. The enormous guts seem to have a life of their own. The meat packers half-watch American football on TV as they deal with these roiling stomachs. Splatters are wiped off the screen. Amidst office discussions on phones, a salesman talks of the international potential of tubes of packaged eggs. There are faces eating in the canteen; there are carcasses moving on hooks like flying ghosts. The horses on the feed-lot work with the men and, as such, are given respect and affection; the cattle are meat animals and treated as a commodity.

The film is in black and white, with no colour or smell and little feel of the miasma of the slaughterhouse. It is non-sensational, very different from the footage shown by campaigning groups. There are no words, apart from what is spoken in the plant, and the viewers must play their part by creating their own commentary. I found myself noticing, from a post-BSE perspective, that the confrontations between management and workers had sinister implications. Everything was being squeezed; it meant that corners would be cut and that these changes would become institutionalized – and then, no doubt, there would be further cuts. Ground-up cow remains would be fed to cows. Millions of chickens would be killed every day in a flawed system.

The film made me face up to a truth. The forces that take a bird and turn it into a cheap commodity are not from another planet. Killing plants, as much as factory farms, are simply part of the way society operates. Are we, as consumers, prepared to take responsibility for all parts of a chicken's life and death?

Frozen, Fast, Processed

There are a number of reasons why we eat so much cheap chicken. One of the most important is convenience. This sounds reasonable; certainly understandable. But bit by bit, our need for ease has climbed its way up the shopping list: above a wish for quality, above ethics – above price, even. And it matters. The growing demand for convenience and fast food is linked directly to the boom in factory chicken farming. The nuggets that children eat, the ready-meal that's handy in the freezer, the sandwich at the station, the ready-cooked bird from the supermarket deli counter, the post-pub curry: all these play a part in the impetus to push the birds hard and fast. The rise in poultry consumption came about over the last four decades of the twentieth century with the ability of the food industry to slash the price of production. Alongside this, and entirely connected to it, have been developments in food technology and retailing that make this bargain form of protein ever more available and ever cheaper. Welcome to the world of processed poultry.

All this has been part of a general shift in how we live and eat. At the same time as chicken was getting cheaper, women moved away from the stove and into the workplace. We have seen the rise of the cash-rich, time-poor. Domestic de-skilling has taken place on a serious scale: life isn't just too short to stuff a mushroom; it has become far too rushed to peel a carrot, let alone roast a chicken. Then came the rise of the fast food joint, which popularized industrial chicken in a way that appealed to children, who took to chicken nuggets like birds to worms. Manufacturers copied the success of the junk food giants of the high street; the nugget invaded the home kitchen.

This decline in fresh home food seems set to grow. It can hardly fail to do so when many children don't learn how to cook at school, or, far more importantly, at home. It can hardly fail to do so when children don't even eat fresh food in either place, a phenomenon given its own grisly poultry icon, the Turkey Twizzler, by Jamie Oliver's TV programme *School Dinners*. If the next generation of young eaters fails to get a taste for freshness, then the processed food industry will have well and truly got its fangs into our diet. Which came first, the nugget or the non-cook? It doesn't really matter. Either way, the two undoubtedly encouraged each other. And both are bad news for good food and good health. How did it happen?

Novelty always has a particular sheen. Strange as it seems now, even the first frozen chickens had some sort of glamour. It wasn't too long, however, before consumers wised up to the way water was added to the birds, legally, in the freezing process. The practice was allowed – so it was said – in order to keep the bird's 'succulence' in the oven. But when the chicken reached the table, the flesh had often lost taste and texture. There were problems from food poisoning. People put unthawed meat in the oven and didn't cook it through properly. The traditional roast came with a gravy of bugs.

The emerging fast food chains were somewhat sexier. I remember the first moment, in the early eighties, when my hand went deep into a bucket of Kentucky Fried Chicken. It was as exciting as a lucky dip. The appeal was the Americanan-ness of being allowed to eat with your fingers – in front of the television, even! Fast food broke the boundaries of the table. This was the pleasure, more than the 'special blend' of eleven herbs and spices.

Kentucky Fried Chicken emerged from a colonel who wasn't a military colonel: that's authenticity, fast food style. Harland D. Sanders was enterprising from an early age. He had to be. His father had died when he was five and the boy took on the role of household organizer and cook. In later years, Sanders' can-do attitude was applied to many trades. A head-down, wheeler-dealer story of American entrepreneurship took him from farmhand to army private in Cuba to fire-fighting to selling tyres to, eventually, catering. He put his special blend together when he was running a gas station in Crobin, Kentucky, and had the bright idea of filling up the drivers alongside their automobiles. The Governor of Kentucky, Ruby Laffoon, made him a colonel – a standard form of political favour. One biography, *The Colonel* by John Ed Pearce (1982), says this was in return for Harland helping a local man to get prison parole; the official KFC website says it was 'in recognition of his contributions to the state's cuisine'. When Sanders started styling himself as 'the Colonel' in 1950, there was a certain amount of sniggering around town. But the Colonel was an early discoverer of the power of the brand image. To make the picture complete, he went to Lo's Beauty Shop in Crobin to bleach the reddish tinge out of his beard.

Then the Colonel went on the road to sell the secret of his recipe, in return getting a nickel for each chicken sold. His franchise restaurant business began. The first Kentucky Fried Chicken outlet opened in 1954 in Salt Lake City. By now a bespectacled man in his mid-sixties – you've seen the picture on the packaging and the hoardings – Sanders promoted his image as 'Colonel Sanders' by donning a black string tie and a white Palm Beach suit. He would get through eight of these a year, such was his work rate, wearing a heavy white cotton one in winter and a lighter type in summer. KFCs snaked their greasy path around the States and then around the world, arriving first of all in Britain in 1964. Advertising hoardings were graced by this cheery, grandfatherly figure (who in reality was clearly a hard-headed operator). The KFC outlets helped to popularize cheap chicken; the broiler sheds boomed.

There was an even bigger step to be taken in the chicken's conversion into fast food. In 1979 Fred Turner, the chairman of McDonald's, was a man heading a beef-based industry. As he watched consumer trends he saw the bird racing up behind the lumbering cow, so he asked a supplier to develop an ultra-convenient way of eating this cheap meat the McDonald's way. They got to work with all the wizardry of food technology. A chef can have an idea, tinker about in the kitchen and serve it up the next night. A multi-national corporation, with its army of technologists, accountants and marketeers, takes four years to launch a new product. And lo, it came to be. It came big. Seldom has such a small piece of food had such a great impact on the way we eat.

Within a month of launching the McNugget in 1983, the company was the second biggest purchaser of chicken in the entire USA, second only to KFC. According to Eric Schlosser's industry exposé, *Fast Food Nation*, the McNugget was such a hit that McDonald's chicken suppliers, Tyson Foods, developed a special large-breasted bird nicknamed 'Mr McDonald'. These chunks of engineered food – pulped meat held together with stabilizers, coated, fried and reheated – are part of the global story that has seen McDonald's go from the six thousand restaurants it had when this contemporary chicken product was launched to thirty thousand worldwide today. It is hard to understand why, in terms of food and pleasure. To eat a chicken nugget is to encounter an alien object. It has a weird, bouncy texture that offers no resistance to your teeth and no sensory impact other than the outside, which is nothing more than hot and fried-tasting.

None the less, chicken fast food started as an American story but soon spread. McDonald's corporation has a creepy phrase for their conquest of the world: 'global realization'. Somewhere in the world McDonald's, Burger King and Yum! Brands (the last the name of the organization that encompasses KFC, Pizza Hut and Taco Bell), open a new outlet every two hours. The global service-sector food market is worth more than a trillion and a half dollars. Up to half of the money expended on food in developed countries is now spent outside the home, not least at places like these. One in three American children now eats fast food once a day. This is big, big business; no wonder it is an engine that drives the chicken industry. Following on from the arrival of KFC and the success of the McNugget, there are now multiple chains of fried chicken shops in Britain. You smell and see them on pretty much every high street. They sell the likes of 'chicken poppers', which sounds like the latest clubbers' drug but is in fact a product from a chain with the bucolic name of Chicken Cottage. At all such places, chicken is the bargain basement meat: cheap cheep, any time, everywhere.

Adversaries of broiler factory farming have now taken the fight to the high street. A campaign against KFC was launched in 2003 by People for the Ethical Treatment of Animals, PETA. The 'Kentucky Fried Cruelty' campaign (subtitle: We Do Chickens Wrong) highlights the conditions in which they say the company's chickens are farmed, caught and killed. The website drops the company in boiling oil: 'PETA is asking KFC to eliminate the worst abuses that chickens suffer on the factory farms and in the slaughterhouses of its suppliers . . .' The campaigners say chickens killed for KFC suffer in ways that would result in cruelty-to-animals charges if cats or dogs were the victims. They conclude, 'As the leader in the chicken industry, KFC has a responsibility to ensure that the chickens raised for its buckets are protected from the worst cruelties.'

In the first year of the KFCruelty campaign, the *Sunday Mirror* ran an article by journalist Martin Coutts and the campaigning group Hillside Animal Sanctuary about a UK factory farm supplying KFC. Some birds were so lame and deformed that they could only drag themselves to the food and water troughs by their wings, Coutts wrote. 'In one shed where chickens had been taken away for slaughter there were dozens of carcasses littering the floor. In another – where scores of birds had died – their remains were being picked over by other chickens.' An undercover investigation in 2003/4 of one former KFC 'Supplier of the Year' slaughterhouse in the USA has captured footage of workers throwing birds around and slamming their heads against walls as if they were mere objects rather than sentient creatures. Much of the footage on the campaign's website is simply sickening.

Kentucky Fried Cruelty subverts the company's famous branding. The logo at the top of the website shows the Colonel with his famous suit splattered with blood, wielding a crimsoned knife on a shocked chicken. Multiple celebrity endorsements reach out to many groups. There's the Reverend Al Sharpton, the African-American preacher-activist, urging customers to boycott the company until they introduce such practices as mechanically gathering the broilers from the shed instead of using catching gangs. He says the company should be 'putting the chickens to sleep' with gas rather than using the standard shackle slaughter techniques. The KFC name is repeated over and over: how KFC doesn't like to spend money just out of the goodness of its heart; how KFC is acting as if it knows more than God by giving the birds such an unnatural life. 'KFC', he says. 'That's foul.'

The poet Alice Walker wrote a Mother's Day poem for the Kentucky Fried Cruelty campaign, addressed to David Novak, the CEO of Yum! Brands (parent company of KFC). She writes: 'The animals of the world exist for their own reasons. They were not made for humans any more than black people were made for whites, or women for men.' Sir Paul McCartney included an open letter to Novak in the programme for his concert tour. Pamela Anderson's video is advertised as 'explicit'. Playboy Playmates in bikinis carried placards complaining that 'KFC tortures chicks'. The musician Ravi Shankar, *The Office* actor Martin Newman and many other well-known figures have all added their voice to the campaign to spread the word as widely as possible. In the UK, there was an ad campaign on the London Underground, and stunts which included a giant crippled chicken crossing and recrossing the road outside branches of KFC.

PETA is taking the fight to the sort of people who eat the fast food that forms a significant slice of the chicken profit-pie. The attitudes of some of these people towards animals can be gauged by Burger King's www.subservient chick-en.com. The website is one of a number of campaigns in the USA, including a heavy metal band called Coqrock and other such concepts, aimed at the 18–34-year-olds, mostly men, who apparently account for nearly half of BK's customers.

I logged on. The words come up: 'Get chicken just the way you like it. Type in your command here.' Well, there's plenty of strange stuff on-line, but this must be one of the most bizarrely masochistic. The airless room has a soft white carpet, a red sofa and chair. There is a bookcase, a telly and some breakfast-bar stools. The lighting is discreet. Then BK has dressed up a person as a chicken complete with kinky red suspender belt. The chicken fills the centre of the room. I typed in a couple of simple commands: 'Sit on the sofa.' Then: 'Do a cartwheel.' The message flashed up: contacting chicken. And the chicken obeyed. It then returned to the centre of the screen, ready for the next order. The pre-programmed human-bird is meant to be funny. Instead it's disturbing.

The food industry has some very unpleasant tendencies. Take one of the insidious ingredients in convenience and fast foods: trans fat. People are waking up to the presence of this nasty substance in our food, not least in the most convenient forms of the chicken we eat. This machine-made fat was first created a century ago, when it was discovered that hydrogen could be used to solidify liquid vegetable oil. This long-life fat became popular after the Second World War when it was taken up by the booming processed food industry. It goes into baked products such as biscuits and pastries, replacing more expensive and spoilable animal fats; and because it is cheap, has a high flash point and resists oxidation and rancidity it is also popular with fast food joints for frying. Unfortunately some of the fat molecules change shape when they become trans fats, and these mess up your body.

It is now believed that these trans fats are not just as bad for you as saturated fats, but actually worse. The Food Standards Agency cautiously states: 'Trans fats have a similar effect on blood cholesterol to saturated fats. They raise the type of cholesterol in the blood that increases the risk of coronary heart disease. Some evidence suggests that the effects of these trans fats may be worse than saturated fats.' In fact, considerable evidence has been accumulating for some time about the evils of trans. Right back in 1975, a group of Welsh scientists raised questions of a link between trans fat and heart disease. In 1993, the *Lancet* published one of the papers coming out of the huge Nurses' Health Study conducted at the Harvard School of Public Health, showing that trans fat consumption was directly related to coronary heart disease. Walter Willett, the epidemiologist who helped set up the study, estimated that these fats probably caused around thirty thousand premature deaths a year in the USA alone. What was more, the evidence was that trans fats increased the risk of heart disease more than saturated fats. The reason was suggested by other studies, such as one at Wageningen University in the Netherlands, published in the *Lancet* in 2001, which showed that trans fats lowered 'good' (HDL) cholesterol as well as raising 'bad' (LDL) cholesterol. Some of these findings were disputed, but a 2006 review of the trans fat evidence, in the *New England Journal of Medicine*, found that a 2 per cent increase in the energy intake from trans fats was associated with a 23 per cent increase in coronary heart disease. The Danish Nutrition Council estimates that, gram for gram, trans fats are ten times worse than saturated fats for cardiovascular health. The problems they cause are probably not just to do with cholesterol. A report by the council suggests that trans fats in nerve sheathings in the heart may cause the heartbeat timing mechanism to malfunction, leading to arrhythmia and sudden cardiac arrest. The World Health Organization is now so convinced that it is considering urging governments around the world to phase out trans fats in food if labelling alone doesn't work.

The labelling on food packaging in the UK is currently inadequate. You will spot the presence of trans fats in the form of 'hydrogenated fat' or 'partially hydrogenated vegetable fat', but it cannot legally be stated in the nutrition section of the labelling unless a claim about low levels of trans fats has been made on the packaging; otherwise, it is actually illegal to state its presence or otherwise. In the USA, specific labelling of trans fats became mandatory in 2006 – at least on packaged goods. Crucially, it does not have to be declared at all in fast food. Yet, as Dr Nicole M. de Roose, the leader of the Dutch trans fat study, has said: 'The major sources of trans fats in our diet are the ready-made baked goods and fried fast foods. These foods are not labelled, so the consumer does not know how much trans fat he gets.'

US activists are targeting the trans offenders, and high on their list are the Chicken Barons. In 2006, the Centre for Science in the Public Interest filed a suit against KFC for using trans fats in its frying oil without giving a clear warning to consumers. CSPI executive director Michael F. Jacobson said KFC was recklessly putting its customers at risk of a Kentucky Fried Coronary. The plaintiff, a retired doctor from Maryland, Arthur Hoyte, said: 'If I had known that KFC uses an unnatural frying oil, and that their food was so high in trans fat, I would have reconsidered my choices. I am bringing this suit because I want KFC to change the way it does business. I'm doing it for my son and others' kids – so they may have a healthier, happier, trans-fat-free future.' In a statement, KFC said it was considering using an alternative cooking oil but there were 'a number of factors to consider including maintaining KFC's unique taste and flavor of Colonel Sanders' Original Recipe, supply availability and transportation, among others'. However, trans fats have now gone from their fryers.

There are strong signs that consumers are getting angry about the dodges used by the food industry – with results. The Centre for Science in the Public Interest took out a full-page advertisement in the *New York Times* in 2004 complaining that McDonald's had failed to keep a promise to eliminate trans fat from its cooking oil. The company subsequently settled a class-action suit by donating $7 million, admitting it had not followed through. In the UK, in 1998 the company halved the amount of trans fat in its cooking oil from 30 per cent to 16 per cent, and in 2006 was reported to be lowering this considerably. Interestingly, McDonald's has managed to go trans-free in Denmark, where the fats were effectively banned by the government in 2003, and the undesirable fats have also been taken out of the friers in Germany. Canada too is set to impose legal limits after getting a report from its Trans Fat Task Force in 2006. New York City is moving in the same direction after a voluntary ban did not work.

In the UK an anti-trans campaign, TFX (Campaign against Trans Fats in Food) got going in 2004. Its website, *www.tfX.com*, contains the startling estimate that, if UK death rates are based on those in the USA, up to twenty thousand people a year could be dying prematurely because of these 'stealth killers'. Oliver Tickell, the campaign's founder, is highly critical of the UK government's lack of action on trans. Now that the British food industry is removing trans fats from food, he thinks the main area of concern should be their use in the catering trade, such as fast food outlets, pubs, fish and chip shops, high street bakeries, work canteens and even in school meals: he believes that the presence of trans fats in school dinners is putting our children's health at risk. Processed chicken, for instance, is often coated in a cheap catering crumb that soaks up the trans fats in the partially hydrogenated cooking oil favoured by many caterers for its long life and low cost. But there is no label present to declare it.

But is labelling, in any case, a bit of a side issue? The highest consumption of trans fat is amongst people who eat lots of junk food – people unlikely to spend hours scanning labels even if they were there in the first place. Why don't we go the same way as the Danes and the Canadians and set limits on trans fats? asks Tickell. When questioned on the issue in 2006, public health minister Caroline Flint said UK average consumption of trans fat is falling, and is now within guidelines – guidelines that Tickell points out have not been revised for more than a decade despite the plethora of new medical evidence. But the problem is people who eat fast food as part of their regular diet and whose consumption of it is way above average levels. The government has no plans to assess the feasibility of putting a legal limit on trans fats in food. Chicken nuggets and drumsticks and countless other processed poultry products are being sold on high streets all over Britain. They continue to contain this unnecessary and damaging substance; and some people – often those whose diet is already nutritionally poor – are eating trans fat in dangerous amounts.

In Britain, as well as adopting American fast food with gusto we developed a processed chicken trend of our own, the ready-meal. This particular form of food came about because of our supermarkets. No other country has a retail sector dominated by so few players. The sophistication and overall monopoly of modern supermarkets means they have very good supply chains. This enables them to develop own-label products such as ready-meals, using 'cook-chill' technology which means chicken can be cooked, then cooled, then be ready to sell quickly on the supermarket shelf as 'fresh' even if it is ten days old. It is an ideal way for the supermarkets to make money from the cash-rich, time-poor. These were 'upmarket' products, unlike the US frozen TV dinner, and they had an upmarket price-tag to match. The beauty of the ready-meal, from the super-markets' point of view, is that they can get more profit from them than by selling the chicken as fresh meat. Farmers have a saying: 'Everyone makes money out of food unless you grow it.' This is especially true of ready-meals, where the producer of the chicken can get just pennies of the final shelf price of the product.

But what are the advantages for the shoppers? What goes into these 'fresh' products? At each step down the line of further and further processing we lose control of what goes into our mouths. Just take a look at all the additives on the ingredients list that are supposed to impart flavour and give the dish a longer shelf life. And what about the chicken in these ready-meals? Whilst the labels on whole chickens and chicken pieces often trumpet the British origin of their meat, do you see the same sort of detail about sourcing on the ready-meal packet? The mysterious omission of this information suggests that the further shoppers are from the raw material, the more likely they are to be getting cheaper imports. Should consumers be worried about this?

In 2004 a book came out that made consumers far more alert to the food politics on their plate. Felicity Lawrence's *Not on the Label* began with an alarming chapter on chicken. She tells the David and Goliath story of environmental health officers (EHOs) on tight resources following the squalid business of chicken laundering. They discovered that meat condemned as unfit even for pets was going into human food. Six men were eventually convicted of conspiracy to defraud. The scam involved taking unfit poultry, bleaching and cleaning it, and passing it back into the food chain through wholesalers and retailers by getting it an illegal health mark. The trail the EHOs uncovered linked the Derbyshire business Denby Poultry to a thousand food businesses, showing just how far dirty meat can spread.

Unsavoury shenanigans are rife in the meat trade, which has been called the third biggest source of dirty money after drugs and guns. In 2003 a *Panorama* programme called *The Chicken Run* filmed Dutch catering companies – suppliers of the sort of trade chicken that goes into our cheap meals – boasting about how they could add beef proteins to chicken meat to enable it to hold more water. And it was not just an isolated case: twelve companies were using the same trick. Furthermore, they were doing it in such a way as to make it undetectable. Coming at a time when there are still cases of BSE, a disease caused by the recycling of cheap beef proteins, the idea of chicken bulked out by a process that involved cattle remains is, to say the very least, unappetizing. In November 2005 the Food Standards Agency chased after hundreds of tonnes of frozen poultry, beef and pork that had come into Northern Ireland illegally from China; such imports were banned because of concerns about bird flu and veterinary drug residues.

If your supply chain is a local one, from farm to butcher to consumer, and you are cooking fresh meat yourself at home, there is a far greater level of trust. If your lunch or supper is based on catering chicken that has been produced in Holland, frozen, exported, cook-chilled and carted around from pillar to post, with the potential for each person to cut corners to make more profit, you might start to wonder if the price of convenience is worth the underlying insecurity.

As for the chicken nugget, popularized by the fast food joint and quickly copied by processed food manufacturers, some of them include mechanically recovered meat, the slurry produced when the carcass is pushed through a sieve and turned into malleable protein pulp. Trading standards investigations have shown that nuggets can contain as little as 16 per cent meat. Convenient? Yes. But high in nutrition, taste, value, trust?

One reason for eating fast food is that it can fill you up on a low budget – it is a cheap form of hot fodder. Chef Barney Haughton has tackled this particular argument head-on. At his cookery school in Bristol he runs a workshop on cooking real food at home on a budget. The first ingredient he focused on was chicken.

Before starting up the workshop, Barney and his family lived on income support for two weeks in order that he could understand some of the realities of a low income. Could he eat well on this money? 'It was tough, but not impossible,' he says. 'It was educational for me and for my children in how you could be more careful with food.' His aim was to find a way to stretch an organic bird to feed a family of four. He discovered that, with some cooking knowledge, making dishes like soup and risotto that used all the bird, the family could get five meals out of a chicken costing £16. The total price of ingredients, including the meat, was £22. The price per person per meal worked out at £1.10.

Barney is a chef deeply concerned about the environmental and social aspects of eating. He sources locally and organically in both his restaurants, Quartier Vert and Bordeaux Quai. When he walks his dog in a nearby valley he sees the factory broiler barns and he knows what they contain. He has been inside one, in Yorkshire. Immediately, he was struck by the stench of ammonia. 'It was pretty dreadful,' he says. 'I asked [the workers] how they put up with it. It was infinitely worse than a nasty loo – not choking, but it made me shallow breathe. It was not an atmosphere I would want to stick around in for any longer than fifteen to twenty minutes. There were long lines of chickens all looking in the same direction. There didn't seem to be any walking around at all. They were sitting down. Afterwards, I realized how dreadful it was. It was quite shocking. I don't think anyone could go in there and ever eat them again, even if they didn't want to spend £16 [on a chicken].' He summed up his reaction to the experience. 'The moribund quality of life was really powerful,' he said. 'Even the bit with all the tiny baby chicks, sweet as they are under their lamps, is a brief window of freedom.'

Barney thinks that none of the forty chefs who have worked with him at Quartier Vert would ever cook a cheap broiler again. 'Once you understand the gastronomic differences, you could never go back,' he says. The texture and taste of a good organic bird are completely different, and so is the quality of the bones: 'You can't get decent stock out of a battery bird.'

In workshops for single mums on income support, Barney got the participants to taste two birds: a cheap broiler, price £3.20, and a proper, organic chicken. 'We cooked the thighs of both in the same way. The difference in taste was immediate. It was an epiphany for these women. They'd never thought there was a difference – a chicken was a chicken was a chicken. They weren't trained tasters or chefs. But there was no comparison.'

What was stopping people from eating real chickens, Barney thinks, was only partly the fact it was more expensive. It was also basic food skills. His courses cover shopping, storing, preparing, looking after food and making it work for you in a cost-efficient way while keeping it based on fresh ingredients. Junk food was not actually all that cheap, he said, but it did save time. That's the big challenge, he thinks. Time.

The major problem with our attitude to chicken is not just the specific details of the meat in the ready-meals and the fast food and the frozen food. The problem is the fact that we eat so much of them at all. Take the ready-meal. It is presented as an appetizing, no-hassle option. But any cook knows you could make a far more delicious dish yourself for the same price or less. Sticking a whole chicken in the oven to roast is easier (well, okay, apart from washing the pan), and far more rewarding, than wrestling with the packaging of ready-meals and pinging them correctly in the microwave.

Behind the frozen, the fast and the processed lies a chronic lack of knowledge about cooking. This has to be the missing link in the food chain. In 1980 the average meal took an hour to make. This went down to twenty minutes in the early 2000s and is predicted to be eight minutes in 2010, according to the campaigning food journalist Joanna Blythman. If you shop well, you can eat well without much cooking; but on the whole this will not be the case with the eight-minute meal.

What is the result of a nation eating a diet of processed food? What is the price of convenience chicken? Serious for all of us. Even if you don't eat this stuff yourself, you pay the taxes for the hospitals that will cope with the fall-out.

The latest figures on childhood obesity are stark. A soaring number of British children – 30 per cent of those aged two to fifteen – are now so overweight that it could affect their health. This has massive implications for life-threatening conditions such as diabetes and heart disease, and health experts warn of a time bomb waiting to explode. Poor diet currently accounts for around a third of deaths from cancer and heart disease, the major killers in the UK. Not all of this is down to diet, of course: lack of exercise contributes to an overweight population. But the hidden fats in processed foods and the general lack of care that goes with not cooking and eating fresh food are a large part of the problem.

We have to get back to fresh food. If you cook for yourself and your family and friends, you know what you are eating. You don't need to add chemicals to make your chicken curry last as it is shunted around the country on articulated lorries and sits on a shop shelf. You don't need to wonder what happened in Brazil to make this chicken so frighteningly cheap.

If you don't cook, you are in danger of being ripped off. Ripped off in price. Ripped off in quality. Ripped off in terms of health and nutrition. Ripped off in value. Ripped off in taste. Ripped off altogether. And this is why the front line in the chicken battle isn't just about organic and free-range and so on. It is much broader than that: it is the fresh versus the processed. Are we prepared to get back to basics and get closer to our ingredients by cooking chicken ourselves?

International Chicken

I have seen the future of chicken. It looked like a 15-foot pink-brown squiggle of digestive tract. This was an up-scale model of a 'chicken tender ribbon', and it was next to a machine boasting a production rate of four thousand per hour. The super-sized artificial snack was part of a display stand at the International Poultry Expo, the biggest chicken industry trade fair in the world.

Step right up! Some eight hundred stands and seventeen thousand visitors had gathered here in Atlanta, Georgia. People responsible for the lives and deaths of millions of chickens a week were making deals here for millions more. There were Chinese visitors, a whole Latin American section, processing giants from California and a gas-killing executive from Diss in Norfolk. The taste level of the whole event could be gauged by a metal cage near the entrance. Some fluffy chickens were stuffed inside to advertise a raffle. The birds were crammed into the small space, their heads sticking out through the bars and with no room to move – just like real life! It was weird, if hardly surprising, to see so much cartoon, cuddly chicken branding in the Expo hall, given the true nature of the goods on offer.

Here were companies with names like ChickMaster, and slogans like 'Moving Forward Faster'. Two plastic roast chickens whizzed round and round and round on a conveyor belt, to show just how much faster they could go without falling off. There were DVDs used as selling tools that were almost worse than those produced by campaigning groups like Compassion in World Farming. In one, packed-in broilers sat on the ground in a factory farm in South America, too fat and crippled to do much more than sit there and pant. I saw day-old chicks spewed out of a machine like pieces of popcorn as the seller boasted to a prospective client of 'the spread', and another machine that counted sixty thousand chicks per hour. There were stalls of rubber plucking fingers, gels for holding water in breasts, and give-away display charts of yellow, like a paint-shop colour swatch, showing how you could put additives into chicken feed to get different hues of yolk, from pale primrose to free-range gold.

In two days of walking around and getting more and more boggled by the contents of the International Poultry Expo I counted one pair of dungarees and two lumberjack shirts. Everywhere else were suits and spotless chinos, gym-buffed bodies and copious hair products on lush locks. Occasionally there were the sort of bellies that come from eating chicken nuggets at the rate of potato crisps, but the crowd wasn't exactly down-home. This was agribusiness at work.

Looking at aisles and aisles of hardware, all clean and

shiny-new amongst the shiny, clean people, I tried to visualize exactly what these goods were used for. There were, for example, the metal cages in which American chickens are taken to the slaughterhouse, here layered up, neat and tidy and empty. In reality the birds are packed into them, transported for many miles, and then unceremoniously tipped up through the 'easy-motion' doors, so they slide out together, all over each other, into the killing room. The RSPCA would not approve.

There was a chicken bus made by the same company that made such vehicles for schools. The salesman explained how much better it was than the standard truck. The top was made of a single sheet of steel so that the thousands of birds inside would be better protected in an accident. It had plenty of air vents that could be conveniently opened by the driver to relieve the overheating birds and save them from dying of heat distress. He told me about his competitors, with their closed-up trucks that packed in even more thousands. To change the airflow drastically meant taking the trouble to alter the machinery. 'The trouble is,' he said, 'when it's ninety degrees and the alarm goes off [to indicate that the birds are too hot], if the driver has twenty minutes left he may as well just get to the end of his drive and give up a certain percentage as wastage.'

One display caught my eye in particular: a glass case with an elegant fern on top. Inside were five layers of raw chickens on a poultry cake-stand. The chickens had been cut about two-thirds of the way along their bodies, so the cross-section showed off the thickest part of the breast. The birds sat on greenery and grapes. One of the chickens was called an 'ultra-yield Extreme'. The longer I looked at it, the more disgusting it got.

Super-sized breasts. Maxed-chickens. There must be a word to sum up so much of what I saw during those two days in the International Poultry Expo. It's a word that would express how a mere human can feel about this ruthlessly expansive urge. It would describe the weird sensation I felt, for example, at the top of an escalator going into the event. I felt uneasy even walking towards the Expo. Atlanta is corporatesville; Coca-Cola has its HQ here. It is not a place in which you feel comfortable as a pedestrian. The World Congress building, where the Expo was held, was so large that you would only see its form if you were flying over in an aeroplane. Even a blockbuster like Versailles has some sort of outline for the earth-bound human eye. I entered this triple stadium of a building, then walked on for ever and ever, finally emerging down an escalator into an atrium of a vastness I had never seen before. I felt sick. It was not vertigo, nor agoraphobia. It was fear at the sheer scale of everything. The place made me feel so very, very small; and that nobody and no creature existed as an individual. What word could describe this? 'Gigantaphobia' has been the best suggestion so far. I still struggle for the right term; it was so far from my own scale of reality.

The fear in the conference halls that day was from a different source: bird flu, or avian influenza (AI) as it is known in the trade. The angle taken was a predictable one. Foreign birds, invading US boundaries, were the new terrorists. Biosecurity was all. At a talk on a recent outbreak of a less virulent form of AI, requiring the killing and disposing of a mere 4 million or so creatures, the question of what had caused the outbreak was quickly raised. Was it those pesky *backyard birds*? These were hard-headed businessmen and they did not like the vaguest threat from irresponsible, half-baked amateurs who let birds roam so dangerously. The speaker had made a disparaging reference to the free-range. 'I'm concerned about the proliferation of backyard birds of various kinds,' he said, darkly. But the latest outbreak of bird flu, of a less dangerous type than the feared sort, H5N1, was thought to have been spread by equipment and people taking their 'dailies' (the birds which die before slaughter) to a rendering plant. The suggestion that disease and its spread might be increased by intensive systems would be seen as heresy in this hall.

In the whole vast trade fair, I had found only one other reference to less intensively reared chickens. It was towards the end of the last day and the stallholder had pushed off. But I read the literature of the Certified Humane meat label with much interest. It focused on animal welfare and finding a middle ground pricewise, at a lower level than organic meat. The price comparison was impressive. A whole commodity chicken cost $1.29 per lb; a certified humane one was $1.89 per lb and a certified organic was $4.99 per lb. The promotional booklet quoted a survey by the United Egg Producers showing that 50 per cent of consumers rated animal care as 'important' when deciding what to buy and where to shop. More than this, 75 per cent said they would buy animal welfare goods. But only 51 per cent said they would pay more. As a result, just a tiny percentage of meat sold is actually from such better systems. People seem to value convenience and price higher than the birds' conditions. Price and convenience aside, they would buy 'kind' meat. Those two stumbling blocks again: price and convenience. And what about the concerned consumer? If we pay more for an organic chicken, what are we getting? If we pay less for another kind of certified system, will that mean our meat is safe and the chickens are well cared for? This will be part of my quest in the second half of the book.

The International Poultry Expo showcased the trends behind the chicken sold around the corner from you, from me, from most people in the industrialized, globalized world. In Britain, where does our chicken come from? In the late 1980s, 97 per cent of it was home-produced. Just a few years later this figure had dropped by nearly 10 per cent, and it has continued to fall. In late 2006, the amount of imported chicken meat eaten in the UK was standing at 50 per cent for breast meat. As welfare improves in the EU, buyers turn to cheaper imports. This trend is set to grow; and no wonder when the cost of production in the UK has been estimated at a whopping 60 per cent higher than in Brazil and Thailand, two of the major sources of our imported chicken.

There are trade tricks that encourage this trend. Brazilian and Thai meat can attract lower import tariffs by being sprayed with salt; apparently this means it is a preserved meat rather than fresh. As regards Thai meat, in 2002 there was much clucking in the industry of a confidential 'bullets for pullets' deal in which Thai chicken imports were raised in exchange for trade with the British defence giant. BAE Systems. It's hard to imagine that your chicken supper could be linked to the arms industry, but that's global horse-trading for you.

In response to concerns about the safety of imported poultry, the British government claims that imported meat has to be of the same standard as home-produced. This is certainly not true in terms of welfare regulations. As far as global trade law goes, fairness to the animals is seen as a nicety rather than an international necessity.

Food miles are often defined as the distance between source and mouth. They roll much further if you count up the carbon that goes into making the packaging and the petro-chemicals in the fertilizers for the chicken feed crops. But even at a basic level, food miles are a useful marker of how globalized our food supplies have become. Once you start watching the food-milometer, some strange practices emerge. When researching fish, I discovered that a sizeable quantity of fish landed in Grimsby was going on to China to be processed before coming back to be sold in Britain. Even more bizarrely, the delectable Morecambe Bay shrimp, beloved regional food, could go from Lancashire to Norfolk, to Holland, to Africa (to be shelled) – and back to Morecambe Bay again to be put, finally, in a rustic little butter-covered pot. It all makes sense to somebody's bottom line, often because of the subsidies and tax breaks that artificially support the food business. In this crazy world, chickens fly around as if they had wings. The wings themselves may whizz off to China and other parts of south-east Asia, along with the feet. Russia is another place that likes dark meat and the gizzards. Meanwhile, the Americans and Europeans prefer white meat, to the extent that the University of Georgia has even got a grant to develop a way of turning dark meat into white. This is why in Britain, around 50 per cent of our breast meat is imported, and as well as imported whole eggs, we get processed eggs – liquid and dried – from all over the world, including the United States.

Chicken production has been concentrated in the hands of a few, as with most foods. Did you know, for example, that 70 per cent of dog and cat food worldwide was in the hands of two companies? I learnt about this in an American magazine called *Renderer*, a fascinating read that divulged the fact that in the States the ground-up remains of chickens represent up to 45 per cent of all rendered animal byproducts. Ground-up chicken carcasses, pushed and pulverized into goo, were, it said, still fed to other chickens in the USA and elsewhere – a practice now a total no-no in Europe – along with ground-up pork and beef. American meat has many practices that are different from those in the UK. But US meat gets around. An economist told me that when cheap frozen chicken parts get near the end of their freezer life they are exported and dumped in places such as the Ukraine at rock-bottom prices, wrecking the livelihoods of local chicken farmers. World trade is supposed to help developing countries; more often it seems to be about opening markets for richer ones.

The American meat industry has a global reach. In the USA, four companies control 56 per cent of the chicken meat industry. Tyson, the biggest, calls itself 'the largest provider of protein products on the planet' and operates in Argentina, Brazil, China, India, Indonesia, Japan, Mexico, the Netherlands, the Philippines, Russia, Spain, the UK and Venezuela. Worldwide, two American companies own more than 80 per cent of the world's breeding stock for meat chickens.

The American trend for vertical integration – the ownership of the entire process – has become the industry structure in Britain. Here, five companies process around 70–75 per cent of all the UK's chicken meat. According to a survey published in the trade magazine, *Poultry World*, in July 2006 they are Grampian, which produces 3.8 million broilers a week in the UK, and has factories in Thailand; Moy Park, based in Northern Ireland (3 million-plus a week); Faccenda Group, a large family firm based in Northamptonshire which pioneered chilled chicken products in the 1970s (2 million-plus a week); Sun Valley, the Herefordshire firm that supplies McDonalds (1.1 million a week); and 2 Sisters, based in Birmingham (1–2 million a week). As for the eggs, the situation could become even more concentrated with the two biggest players, Deans Foods and Stonegate, announcing a planned merger in 2006 to form Noble Foods, which would take a 46 per cent share of the UK fresh egg industry.

The individual farmers contracted into the chicken meat companies say that business is bad. They have the threat of cheaper imports on the one hand, and higher, costly welfare standards on the other. Some are getting out of chickens and going into other lines, such as biofuels. But you only have to spot the presence of poultry magnates on the *Sunday Times* Rich List to see that there is, for some at least, still a great deal of cash in chickens.

A large proportion of the money and the power behind UK chicken is, however, in the hands of the sellers: the supermarkets. It is they who can tell the farmers what production methods their customers would prefer. It is they who control the prices that put pressure on standards. There's a startling statistic from a paper presented to a conference in 2003, that all purchasing decisions in Europe go through just 110 buying desks*.

* Grievink, J.-W. 'The Changing Face of the Global Food Supply Chain, presented to the OECD Conference on Changing Dimensions of the Food Economy'.

The number will be far smaller than this for meat. Think of the farmers at one end of the food chain and all the consumers at the other. The supermarket buying desks are the gates between us. Most consumers are affected, every day, by decisions made by these few gatekeepers.

The supermarkets' concentration of this power could also make them vulnerable. Surveys on animal welfare show that the majority of people want good animal welfare in the food that they eat. When they go into a supermarket, this may not always translate into paying more for a product that has higher welfare credentials. But could this be because we trust the supermarket to sell us food that is basically okay? And what will happen when consumers start to realize that the chicken sold to us in supermarkets is *not* all cluckerty-cluck? When we start to visualize that some nineteen birds are kept in a square metre of space. When we think of birds that can barely walk below vastly over-inflated breasts. When we think of the diseases and drugs. When we think of birds shackled by their sore legs for a crude form of killing. When we know about the starvation of breeder flocks. When we discover that chicken sold in ready-meals and sandwiches comes all the way from Brazil and Thailand.

Will these consumers blame the farmers? In 2006 UK farmers make at most just 2p per bird, down even from a couple of years ago when it was 3p, and often less than this; some say they are now operating at a loss. There is very little wriggle room for them. There is even less wriggle room for the birds, who have always been at the very, very bottom of the pile in this rush for profit.

The question arises: who does make the money? Part of the answer is clear for the British consumer: the super-markets. And it has to be the supermarkets, those few meat-buying desk owners, whom we can hold partly responsible for the way the chickens we eat are produced.

Real differences are starting to emerge between different supermarkets' attitudes towards meat chickens. If this continues, we could have a race-to-the-top that will make a difference to the way chickens are farmed. Compassion in World Farming has held a biannual award ceremony, marking companies on a number of strict criteria for welfare. In the 2005/6 report, Waitrose won the most recent gong for chicken, with 49.3 points out of 60. Marks & Spencer was just pipped to the post, but won the award for investment and innovation in farm animal welfare research for developing its slow-growing Oakham chicken. The Compassion in World Farming initiative is a useful audit and one that encourages the supermarkets to compete for better animal welfare. Anyone who is interested should obtain a copy of their Compassionate Shoppers' guide.

The vast majority of chickens in the data for this report were still reared at densities that exceeded even the guidelines of the UK government's panel of experts, FAWC (criticized by welfare groups as being too high) of around seventeen birds per square metre. Waitrose and M&S insisted that all their suppliers meet at least the experts' guidelines. Sainsbury's allowed the upper level of around eighteen birds to exist on a temporary basis but were heading in the right direction. In Asda, Co-op, Somerfield and Tesco, the maximum stocking density for intensive birds was higher than FAWC's guidelines.

The welfare issues arise not just from stocking densities but, crucially, from the type of bird. It is the fast-growing chickens, the maxed-chooks, that suffer the most problems. Marks and Spencer's were 100 per cent slower growers; more than 80 per cent of those sold by Sainsbury's were of this type, as were about 30 per cent of the chickens sold by the Co-op and Waitrose. In Tesco, this figure plummeted to just 8 per cent. They now sell the Willow Farm brand chicken, advertising itself as slower-grown 'for flavour and succulence' so it seems that production is heading further in this direction. As of late 2006, 13 per cent of their fresh chicken was from slower-growing strains. At the bottom of the pile for slow-growing breeds, according to the CIWF survey, came Asda with 3 per cent and Somerfield with 1.5 per cent.

In the report these trends were mirrored in the kinds of eggs that the various supermarkets sold. As mentioned earlier, M&S no longer sells any battery eggs at all, either whole or in its processed foods. The Co-op's shell eggs are now free-range. Waitrose has managed to do the same for its whole eggs and those in their own-label processed foods. But, according to CIWF's report, 75 per cent of Somerfield's whole eggs were still battery, as were 42 per cent of Asda's and 41 per cent of Tesco's. As for own-label products, the bottom scorer was Asda with 99 per cent battery, closely followed by Somerfield at 96 per cent. Tesco came in at 74 per cent (it is now 70 per cent, and 38 per cent for whole eggs) and Sainsbury's at 80 per cent, still quite a way off the 0 per cent of the two supermarkets competing for pole position, M&S and Waitrose.

There have been improvements since the appearance of CIWF's report. Supermarkets are susceptible to customer opinion and pressure; that is something we must never forget as citizen-consumers. We can make a change. The supermarkets are always supposed to reflect what we want, though to what extent this happens and to what extent we are fobbed off is open to question. In the second half of the book, I look at how we may choose to make this change. The particulars of what we buy relate directly to the big picture. The international chicken business is not an abstraction, a distant truth like a satellite photograph of the world. It is part of the chicken we take off the shelves.

We and the chickens are living and eating in the midst of the biggest biological experiment of all time. Genetic engineering, for good or ill, is the most phenomenal box of tricks ever created. Its possibilities and problems, depending on your point of view, are exhilarating or terrifying. The Nobel-winning biochemist George Wald, of Harvard University, outlined the broad sweep of the technology in its early days in the late 1970s: biotechnology, he wrote, meant that society would have to face problems unprecedented not just in the history of science but in the existence of life on earth. 'It places in human hands the capacity to redesign living organisms, the products of some three billion years of evolution. This is the transcendent issue, so basic, so vast in its implications and possible consequences that no one is as yet ready to deal with it . . . I fear for the future of science as we have known it, for human kind, for life on the Earth.'

Many scientists believe genetic engineering offers opportunities that far outweigh the risks. But nobody can say with certainty what these risks are. Few consumers fully understand the detail of biotechnology, but we do have a sense of how the food system works. This is part of what makes us cautious. Genetically modified foods do not exist in a world of pure theory; we want to know how they will be used. Breeding, so far, has been used by the chicken industry to produce bigger birds, to produce them faster, and to keep them in more and more intensive conditions. So what is next for the GM chicken? The chicken is involved in biotechnology in two ways: through techniques on the bird itself and, more pressingly, through feed.

Cloned chickens have already been produced. In an early development, genetically engineered chicken sperm has been used to produce transgenic hens by a US company. The scientists irradiate one cock's testicles to destroy his sperm and implant transgenic sperm produced by another bird. It was a highly invasive technology and very expensive. Transgenic hens can now produce biomedication in their eggs.

As this science develops, a vast amount of genetically modified (GM) feed is already being pecked up by chickens all over the world. Animal feed is the money-spinner for the GM industry: if people won't eat it, give it to animals. Whilst there are strict rules about the labelling of GM foods in the UK, milk, meat and eggs from animals fed with GM are not covered by these restrictions. Campaigners see this as a major loophole in the law, and one that will allow GM to creep through the back door into our food system. We cannot object to the use of GM if we don't even know what is happening.

The soyabean is the boom crop of the moment, often backed by government subsidies, especially in the USA. Around 90 per cent of the world's soyabean production goes into animal feed, and about two-thirds of this is fed to chickens. A Friends of the Earth survey in August 2006 estimated that 56 per cent of global soya production is now

GM. This subsidized crop is a large part of what makes chicken so cheap. It used to be thought that such feed was not given to our chickens, but this is changing. A Soil Association investigation in 2006 discovered that GM feed was going into feed for egg layers. The egg giant Stonegate admitted that its feed for caged egg birds could come from any kind of soya, and this could be a mixture of GM and non-GM. Only customers who insist on non-GM – such as the Co-op and Waitrose – would get that guarantee of non-inclusion. The SA report states that most of Stonegate's non-GM feed is for their free-range birds. Other major egg companies, when questioned by the Soil Association, were distinctly coy about what went into their feed. It is worth noting, the report adds, that Lion Quality Eggs, which includes about 85 per cent of the industry, does not require non-GM feed in its members' standards.

There is a new development: GM feed is now apparently going into UK broiler birds. The chicken giant Grampian told the SA that it did use some GM feed, even if 'by far the vast majority' was non-GM. In the past, most of the super-markets would not guarantee that the feed given to their pigs and dairy cattle was GM-free; now chicken could go the same way, though supermarkets are still wary of GM feed.

Even some organic production could be tainted by this problem. The European Commission has revised its regulations to allow 0.9 per cent of organic feed to be GM. The Soil Association and Organic Farmers and Growers, the two main UK organic bodies, objected strongly to this loosening of standards. The Soil Association pointed out that it meant that one in a hundred mouthfuls could be GM. The 0.9 per cent threshold is about global politics, the SA argues. It makes international free trade more possible and takes away consumers' right to know what goes into their food. If consumers want a non-GM guarantee, and it were backed by strong laws, then feed manufacturers would have to make it a priority.

In Britain there was a wariness of GM foods amongst a wide cross-section of shoppers. When such foods first appeared, unexpected people staged their own polite British protest against biotech products. Little old ladies took their baskets to the checkout, then asked the till assistant to remove any GM produce. 'Don't worry, dear. We're not in any hurry,' they reassured, kindly, as flustered shop managers saw the queues mount behind this highly respectable revolt. And so British supermarkets issued their own ban on GM produce. This is a major victory for consumer power: we can make a difference. 'Don't be depressed: be angry and be organized!' urged the campaigning Alan Simpson, MP for Nottingham South and one of the few who raised their voices in Westminster on the issue, at a Brighton screening of Deborah Koons Garcia's anti-GM film. *The Future of Food*. His mole in the biotech industry has told him to keep passing on the message about the real fear in the industry: that having won the battle on food people will start getting active on feed, which he said was propping up the industry.

As feelings grow in Europe that we do not want or need GM, or certainly don't want to be rushed into it, around £100 million a year of British public money goes into biotech research compared with the £3–4 million that goes into developing organic and low-input farming methods. But consumers mind about how food is produced and its effect on our world. It is a long, slow process, but the seed has been sown that what you put in your basket has direct consequences, for good or ill.

There are problems, too, with non-GM soya crops. Brazil is now the second largest producer of poultry after the USA, and European imports of Brazilian chicken meat are growing apace. The country is also a major supplier of the feed that goes into chickens all over the world. Brazil initially decided to hold fire on planting GM crops, fearful of what might happen to its export markets. Some GM soya did infiltrate the southern part of the country; it was nicknamed the 'Maradona' bean, because it got there 'by the hand of God' and also, the joke continued, because the plants are 'small, fast and dependent on drugs'. Brazil now allows GM to be planted, and it could become more difficult to separate out the two kinds – another way the new plants can creep into our mouths.

Meanwhile, a major Greenpeace investigation revealed that in 2005 some 25,000 square kilometres of Brazilian Amazon forest were cut down, largely under the greedy chainsaws of non-GM soyabean agribusiness. Greenpeace tracked the way some of the soya grown on the deforested land was exported by the feed magnates Cargill to the UK and fed to the chickens of the Cargill-owned company Sun Valley. According to Greenpeace, around 25 per cent of Sun Valley's feed soya was Brazilian, and whilst only a small percentage of this came from the Amazon it was still contributing to the threat to destroy the forest's ecosystems. There was another twist. Sun Valley produced up to 50 per cent of the chicken used by McDonald's in Europe: deforestation was now directly linked to the Chicken McNugget. McDonald's and other companies including Cargill responded to the campaign by setting up a zero deforestation plan to try to prevent soya monoculture farming, mostly for livestock feed, eating into Amazon forest. It was a victory: McDonald's has huge buying power. But it was still only one part of the international story of animal feed.

In industrial countries we eat an average of 80 kg of meat per person a year; in developing countries the statistic is still well under half of this at 30 kg a year, but rising rapidly with prosperity. The boom in meat eating is mirrored by urbanization and growing incomes. A report on global meat eating by the environmental group Worldwatch showed how in south-east Asia income grew at a rate of 4–8 per cent per year between the early 1980s and 1998; in the same time urbanization grew by 4–6 per cent per year; and meat consumption grew by 4–8 per cent. At present, farm animals occupy a third of the world's surface but use two-thirds of the agricultural land for their feed. Between a third and a half of the world's entire crop harvest goes into farm animals. The shift from eating plants to eating animals encourages a trend that is worryingly inefficient even as we are waking up to the finite nature of the earth's resources. It is said that chickens have a relatively good feed conversion compared to other animals, of about 2kg of feed to 1kg of meat. This does not, however, include all the feed that goes into the breeding flocks, and of course it is less efficient than eating the plants directly. The amount of meat we eat, in the developed countries in particular, is not good for us, for the animals or for the planet. Concerns about world hunger could focus far more, especially in richer nations, on the issue of eating less but better meat.

International capital is pushing out to expand intensive chicken empires. At the very time when bird flu was first hitting the headlines, it was announced that Tyson – 'the biggest protein provider on the planet' – was buying a stake in south China's largest chicken company, with a current output of 120 million birds a year. Bird flu is a terrible threat; it is also a business opportunity for those who want chickens brought inside and farmed in intensive systems in ever greater quantities.

As I was writing this book, bird flu cast a long, dark shadow. Every day, new updates would arrive over the internet charting its course. There were appalling pictures of birds being buried alive; there were disturbing rumours of infected carcasses being disposed of in lakes and other places that were part of the human drinking water supply. Chicken faeces was used to feed farmed fish; could the disease spread that way? And of course, quite apart from the way the chickens were treated, there was the terrifying spectre of this virulent strain, H5N1, passing to humans, unleashing a lethal pandemic on the scale of the 1918 flu that killed tens of millions of people. To begin with, I felt scared that few people seemed to know about this danger-ous development in east Asia; when it hit the UK headlines, I became scared of the scare. How would it all play out? There was a nasty moment when it looked like all wild birds would start to seem suspect; that people would no longer take bread to lakes to feed ducks and would welcome a silent spring, when birdsong would be absent from the sky and no longer threaten us with disease. As for chickens, it looked as though free-range birds might be brought inside.

Bird flu has swept through flocks of all kinds since the end of the nineteenth century. It has done so many times before, and will do so again. Advocates of intensive systems say the risk of H5N1, this especially worrying and fatal strain, can be controlled by biosecure houses; that is, factory farms. Opponents say that it is precisely these intensive systems that encourage disease to spread quickly through the flocks and build up more drug-resistant strains.

It looks likely that this type of bird flu, like others before it, will become endemic in the wild and will need to be managed in farmed birds. It is essential that this is done within good welfare systems. It would be a tragedy if we lost the time-honoured methods of less intensive farming in order to patch up a problem which needs intelligent insight and more fundamental change. The long-term solution is not to make chicken rearing yet more intensive but to eat fewer animals and to farm them better.

Do we want world production to move in the direction of the International Poultry Expo's 'chicken tender ribbon'; to go faster and faster, get bigger and bigger, to be controlled by fewer and fewer people who are further and further away? Or can we regain respect for chickens; for the way that we farm them; for the way that we cook and eat them? How do we move forward to get what is fair for the fowl and good for mankind?

Part Two

What We Can Do

The Whole Bird

Picture a small flock of chickens, pecking around: a cockerel and his seven lady hens. They glean food by foraging: tugging up a worm here, spotting a bug there, gathering in a spill of grain, tearing at tufts of grass. Some may select useful herbs for an ailment; there is evidence that chickens know how to self-medicate. At night the birds are shut into their house to be safe from the fox. Some will go happily and others take more time. Chickens have different characters. Some cockerels like to see their hens safely in the hut before going in themselves; others, frankly my dear, don't give a damn.

Inside, the chickens hop on to their perches, each head tucking under a wing for a sleep or bowing down slightly towards the feathered breast for a doze. The rooster's eyes, more sensitive to ultraviolet light than a human's, perceive the new day creeping in long before we do. He takes long gulps of air and crows, the loud sound startling the empty silence. The day begins.

As for the humans, every morning they collect the eggs from the nest, pulling them out of the henhouse even while they are still warm from the hen. They are used to bake a cake, golden with yolks and good butter. It will rise and hold; the whites are firm and the yolks are rich. For Sunday lunch, a fattened-up young cockerel may be taken, his neck pulled and his body, plucked of feathers and gutted, placed in the oven alongside some crisping roast potatoes. Outside, the other birds continue to peck, cackle and crow.

The chicken is part of the household. Wild birds are part of nature beyond the home – sparrows whirr in and out of the garden, swallows come and go with the seasons – but humans and chickens are close. We use the eggs, we eat the meat. More than a quarter of a million people in Britain are thought to keep chickens as a backyard hobby. For most of us, whether we keep a flock or not, chickens remain a powerful symbol. These farmyard images are part of a continuing folk-understanding of chickens. The cock's crowing, noisy and disruptive, is an ancient sound that signals to humankind another day of being alive. The hen's fluffed-up broodiness and care of her chicks makes her the mother of all mothers. The just-hatched chick and the Easter egg mean nothing less than the springtime renewal of life.

But such lives are not just folklore, or childhood stories. These scenes continue today, in reality, all over the world. Whilst these most domestic of farmyard animals have come to be regarded both as cheap bits of protein or as an image from some storybook past, they still remain creatures. In order to get back our respect for this much-abused bird we must see it again in this light. And so after the unnatural history of the world's favourite bird comes the natural one: how a chicken is a chicken. This is the basis for the fightback for better welfare and quality food that forms the subject of the second part of this book.

In the beginning is the egg. Apparently whole in itself, the flawlessly smooth surface breaks open to let an entirely new life emerge. This fresh life begets more eggs; these eggs open up into further lives. There is an endless completeness of the chicken and the egg. Which came first? The technical answer is the egg. They were produced by reptiles long before birds evolved. The more philosophical answer is that neither came first: they are one inseparable roll towards infinity. A chicken, as the Victorian author Samuel Butler said, is just an egg's way of making another egg.

Many creation myths start the world with this miraculous object. Long before it was known that the earth was round people found a symbol in the World Egg. In Indian cosmology, Shiva let a drop of blood fall into the primeval water. It made an egg. From this hatched Purusha, the Supreme Soul. Then heaven and earth came from the two halves of the opened shell. The corporeal yolk became the earth and the ethereal white the sky. The yellow yolk also symbolized the fiery sun, the giver of life. A sixth-century BC inscription relating to the ancient Egyptian sun god Ra reads: 'Thou didst raise thyself from the waters out of the secret egg.' An egg, such a commonplace object, is easy to overlook. Six objects in a box; a breakfast; a lunchtime sandwich; an omelette for supper. It seems too ordinary to be special. The egg's connection to myth makes you look again. So does the sheer beauty of its natural history. In the beginning was the egg; but what is an egg?

Much of what is so special about the egg can be appreciated by its use in the kitchen. Like milk and honey, an egg is exceptionally nutritious because it is designed to be nature's own food. Harold McGee, in his classic book on food science, *On Food and Cooking*, goes so far as to say that it is unmatched as a balanced source of the amino acids, the building blocks of life. What we see as good food is created to be just that – for the developing chick. How the egg is itself formed, and how it builds a bird, is an extraordinary everyday story that takes us beyond our encounters with the egg on the plate. To see one close up is to find the cosmic in the domestic.

In the beginning is the egg, and in the beginning of the egg is the germ egg-cell. Even as the female chick emerges from her own egg, she has thousands of microscopic seeds of future life stored within her. You can see a developed germ cell if you crack an egg into a pan. At the top of the yolk is a tiny cloudy-white circle, surrounded by a clearer pool of yolk. These few square millimetres of material are the original package of the hen's DNA. From the time the hen is sexually mature and ready to start laying, aged four to six months, each germ cell in turn gains a yolk as it develops deep within the bird. This yolk provides three-quarters of the calories in the final egg, and is rich in the proteins, mineral and vitamins needed to nourish and build the developing embryo for the twenty-one days it takes for the fertilized laid egg to become a baby bird.

The egg yolk's colour depends upon the hen's feed, but a deep yellow does not necessarily come from Mother Nature. Producers may add marigold petals to the feed to obtain a consistent golden colour and there are other additives, as shown in the little Chinese booklet I found in the International Poultry Expo that showed how you can get your chicken's yolks to range from deep carrot to a pale primrose yellow.

In its natural state, Harold McGee calls the egg 'the sun's light refracted into life', a description that for ever puts a different slant on the phrase 'sunny side up'. The yolk looks like a sun, but its relationship to solar energy is slightly unexpected. The word 'yolk' comes from the Old English for 'yellow', and McGee points out that this is related to the Greek word for 'yellow-green', the colour of new plant growth. The gold of the yolk derives from pigments in plants which actually protect the plant and its process of photosynthesis from being overpowered by the sun's rays, acting somewhat like nature's sunscreen. So the yolk has both the sun's energy from the plants it eats, and their guard against too much of it.

More than half of the egg's calories – about 60 per cent – come from fat. Eggs contain a large amount of cholesterol – four times as many as in the equivalent weight of meat – because it is an essential part of all of our cell membranes, and the egg's job is to make an animal. Since a high level of cholesterol in the blood is associated with a risk of heart disease, at one time it became common for the recommended number of eggs in our diet to be restricted to just a couple a week. But recent studies of moderate eaters show that the dangerous form of blood cholesterol is raised not so much by eating eggs as by eating saturated fats – and only a third of the egg's fats are of this kind. Eggs, mercifully, are back on the menu.

Once the yolk – this enormous single cell, the largest single cell in the animal kingdom – has been formed, the egg starts its long roll towards life. From this point, it takes twenty-five hours to be ready to lay; just longer than a single revolution of the earth around the sun. The newly completed yolk, a naked, fatty globe, is gently gripped by the oviduct, the conveyor belt of the hen's internal egg-making factory. The oviduct is a very long tube, neatly folded up in the hen's insides. At the top of the oviduct, the germ cell and its yolk may encounter the cock's sperm, which can stay alive in the hen for some time after mating. If the two meet and fuse, the egg is fertilized.

For the next couple of hours, whether fertilized or not, the outside of the yolk is slightly thickened and then, as it travels onwards, gains four viscous layers of white, alternating in texture – thick, thin, thick, thin. The first thick layer of white spirals in the oviduct to form two twisted cords, or chalazae. These connect the yolk to the two ends of the egg and keep it centred, protecting the developing chick from knocking against the sides of the shell. When a cook separates an egg into yolk and white – as, for instance, when making meringues – the chalazae are the obstinate globs that refuse to fall away easily. This can be a pain if specks of fatty yolk get into the white, making the business of whisking the whites much more tricky. You might chase the speck around its viscous pool with a hapless teaspoon – but it's no good, and you may as well start again. Only pure whites whisk properly, since the fat molecules in the yolk make it much harder for the egg white proteins to bond and form those cresting snowy peaks.

Once cooked, these proteins in the white provide one of the cook's most useful tools. They will bind to make a thin, strong pancake. They will rise to make a cloud-like soufflé. They will form the stable light foam of a meringue. The yolk, in turn, will emulsify with butter to make a velvety hollandaise, or wobble into a mayonnaise when combined with oil. Give a cook a meagre store cupboard, a few odds and ends in the fridge and a pot of herbs. Then give the cook a box of eggs, and shortly there'll be a good meal for four.

Two membranes surround the white. They cling to each other everywhere except at the blunt end of the egg. Once the liquid white pushes these membranes to their limit, the egg is full and ready for its outside. The shell takes fourteen hours to form and is a tenth of the whole egg. Beloved by artists and sculptors for its beauty, and by engineers for the strength of its endlessly curved form, a bird's egg is a miracle of nature. An egg is robust enough to be thrown and caught; yet it is also fragile enough to be broken with a tap on the edge of a bowl or the pressure of a baby chick's egg-tooth. Hens' eggs are more delicate than those of other birds because of the way we have bred them. The eggs are two or three times bigger than those of the hen's ancestor, the jungle fowl of south-east Asia; yet the amount of material in the shell is the same, just stretched over a larger surface area. Made of protein and calcium carbonate, this material is porous to enable the developing chicken to breathe. The holes are tiny. According to McGee the ten to seventeen thousand microscopic holes would, if clumped together, only make a gap two millimetres in diameter. Eggs are so porous that if, for example, they are kept in the fridge next to truffles they take on their sexy feral scent. The Wallace Collection in London contains a piece of Sèvres porcelain that demonstrates this property of gaseous absorption. The piece is in three layers. At the bottom is a small pot to hold burning pastilles. The scent drifts up to the next chamber, containing the eggs. On top, as if brooding the whole operation, is a hen with a hatched chick.

The shell's colour, genetically determined, is added by pigments put on in almost its last layer. The range of hues found in the world of birds' eggs is astonishing, from deep olive-green to a translucent white that is blushed with the body within. Some are scribbled with marks like Japanese calligraphy, and others are mottled with bumps. As for the chicken, some hobby (and indeed professional) keepers choose a selection of birds to get different coloured eggs, from the dark chocolate-browns of Marans and Welsummers to those of the South American Araucana, which are the fine blue of a December morning sky. Most British laying breeds these days produce brown eggs, somehow seen as being more wholesome than white. The British are unusual in this preference. In other European countries, white is perceived as best. Our odd liking may stem from the novelty factor of brown eggs when they first appeared, laid by the Asian breeds imported in the mid-nineteenth century. To put a different spin on it, a chicken expert, Fred Hams, told me that he preferred white eggs because you could see when they were really fresh; within a few days small grey dots start to appear, and so it is easy to tell whether the eggs are anything less than super-new. 'It wasn't just for the housewife that brown eggs took off,' he said with a wry chuckle.

The final layer on the egg is a cuticle that covers the pores to keep out bacteria and stop the water evaporating even as the air comes in. It is best not to wash eggs, even if they appear to be dirty, as it removes this final protective layer.

When the egg has been laid, the change of temperature from the hen's body to the outside world makes the two layers of skin inside the shell pull apart at the blunt end. Air comes into this gap through the shell to form the first oxygen supply for the new chick when it is ready to hatch.

From the human eater's point of view, the air sac serves another purpose: the longer the egg is outside the hen, the fuller it gets, and therefore it indicates how old an egg is. The homespun method of testing this is to put the egg into water. A new-laid egg will stay horizontal. After a week the air sac will have filled up enough to make the blunt end tilt upwards. At two or three weeks it will stand upright, blunt-side up. If the egg floats, it is inedible. A more finely-tuned test is to put the egg in well-salted water. The food writer Tom Stobart recommends a 12 per cent solution that can be kept in a bottle and reused. He says an egg that is even just two to three days old will start to tilt.

Why is it so special to have a really fresh egg? Anyone who keeps hens or has immediate access to their eggs knows there are few foods so good. The white is firm, the yolk perky. The properties of the egg – all the ways in which it is so useful in the kitchen – are stronger. But from the moment the egg is laid, it starts to change chemically. The white starts to look clearer, not as cloudy as in a new-laid egg, and becomes more runny, whereas a fresh egg has a proud viscosity and stands to attention, ready to perform.

To get back to the hen's point of view, there is a practical reason for laying an egg. Chickens do not fly so much as flap around, or loft up on to a perch. In the jungle where they evolved, they did not need to fly far. But the instinct is still there, and as with all birds the hen's biology means she needs the developing egg to be outside her body and not weighing her down. Like all birds, the hen needs to lay the egg in order to fly.

Even in the first day of development within the hen, the germ cell has developed into an embryo of sixty thousand cells. Once outside its mother's body, this tiny embryo develops into a baby bird over the next twenty-one days. Its heart beats from day 2. On day 14, the embryo rolls over to lie lengthways in the egg. On day 19, it starts absorbing the yolk into its body and soon occupies the whole of the egg space. It is almost ready to hatch.

When the embryonic chick is in the egg, it starts to make peeping noises. The mother hen responds. It could be that mother and chick become familiar with each other's noises, and when the new chicken emerges it is mother's cluck that matters. The chick breaks through to the egg sac and takes its first gulp of air. For the final stage, it uses the special egg-tooth on its beak to saw a hole anticlockwise in the shell. And so the chick emerges to its first day.

What, then, of mother hen? The very word 'hen' calls up immediate affection. A Lancastrian might call you 'ducky', Bristolians 'my lover', burly bus drivers in plain-spoken Leeds are even known to say 'love' to another bloke. In Scotland, and elsewhere, a regular term of everyday good-will is 'hen'. There's a maternal warmth to the word, a fluffing around of comforting feathers, the softest of pro-tections.

The fluffing-up is a sign of broodiness, which means a hen wants to 'set' or bring her eggs to fruition. In short, she wants to hatch. Modern birds tend to have had the trait bred out of them, but backyard hen-keepers may still have to be wary: the pecking and protectiveness of a broody chicken can be fearsome. Some broody hens simply return again and again to their nest – to be taken out, again and again, by the owner, who sometimes gives up and puts a plastic egg underneath as a sop to nature. The more determined free-range birds may sneak off and lay in secret, in due course emerging proudly with their offspring from behind some shed or bush.

But whilst the hen has become a byword of maternal instinct, in reality this is not always the case. The degree of broodiness varies from breed to breed. Fluffy Silkies look bound to brood, and indeed are often put on to the eggs of other breeds, such is the softness of their plumage and their will to sit endlessly on eggs. Some hens make good mothers; others are careless. With chickens, as with people, gender stereotypes don't always fit. Backyard chicken keepers report that their hens can change sex, develop masculine traits and crow like a cock. Martin Gurdon, author of the entertaining *Hen and the Art of Chicken Maintenance*, had one such she-he chicken. Nature abhors a vacuum, he says, and his cockless flock took matters into their own hands when one of the hens, Yvette, started crowing and strutting. You can hear the phenomenon of the transgender chicken on one of the websites run by a devoted chicken owner: The Other Side of the Chicken (on www.angelfire.com) has a section on Chicken Noises. One click takes you to 'Susan turns into a man' sounding as strangulated as a teenage boy with his voice breaking; another takes you to the triumph of 'Susan's first crow'.

It is difficult to tell male and female birds apart until the cock's wattles and comb start growing properly at around six weeks, although there are 'auto-sexing' breeds that produce different colours for the two sexes, or special markings on the feathers to show what's what. One folk tradition says that if you throw a hat in the air the males will look up and make chirruping warning noises, displaying their genetic destiny as guardians of the flock, whilst the hens will lie low and keep quiet. I've also heard of a keeper with a medal that he swings over the birds, as if dowsing for gender. In the mass-production of egg layers there are ultra-specialized people who peer at the vents of day-old chicks, rejecting the males and keeping the females as future layers.

In the farmyard and the backyard, the traditional mother hen gathers together a clutch of eggs. She sits on them for the full twenty-one days, leaving only for a fifteen- to twenty-minute food-and-water-break each day. She only starts sitting once there are enough for a brood, and the fertilized embryos only start growing when she starts to incubate them all together in her nest. This means that, even though the eggs are laid at different times, the chicks are all ready to hatch at once, enabling the hen to tend them together when they emerge. The job can also be done in a mechanical incubator. This has to be precisely managed, ensuring that the humidity in the chamber is correct; in nature this is controlled instinctively and efficiently by the hen.

A hen starts laying at four to six months and most of her eggs are produced within her first two seasons, though she can lay for six or seven years, and birds have been known to live for as long as fifteen years. Egg laying takes an enormous amount of effort. A quarter of her daily energy goes into her eggs, and the 'reproductive effort' of a chicken is a hundred times that of a human. In a year, she lays eight times her own weight in eggs. But taking away the eggs is not cruel. A hen is naturally triggered to lay when longer daylight hours stimulate her pituitary gland to secrete the hormones that make her germ cells mature, and this is why some breeds have a laying season that roughly spans the time from when the clocks go forward to when they go back in the autumn. The connection of light to laying is a part of the chicken's biology that has been exploited to the maximum by the chicken industry.

Once she's ready to lay, a hen will go off to find a nest. Backyard chicken keepers talk of the secretiveness of a laying hen. This is all part of a sense of safety. They like a quiet, darkened area where they can be left alone. This may be under a bush or in the laying box so thoughtfully provided by the person who will take their eggs. A soft surface is good, such as wood shavings.

The hen has a special nesting call she makes when ready to lay, which may be so the rooster can help her find a safe spot. There is another sound, a sort of triumphant cackle, once the deed is done. One suggested reason may be so that the ancestral jungle fowl can find her way back to the rest of the flock that have wandered off into the jungle, as they answer her call. A hen will respond to her mating cockerel and stay close to an alpha-male. One study even suggests that she immediately ejects the sperm of lower-rankers in order to leave room for preferred males. These rejected cocks can become less fertile in what is effectively psychological castration. It is not true, however, that hens lay better when a cock's in town. For a start the cockerel can represent a hazard, for example by scratching her with his sharp spurs as they mate.

When the first chick hatches out, the hen will stay on the nest for as long as it takes for all of them to emerge. At the end of hatching she leaves the nest, doubtless tired and hungry. Over the following weeks, she and the chicks stay close. She calls to them and from the number of replies knows if they are all present and correct. The small battalion is learning how to feed, perch, roost and keep clean – a process called imprinting which, with variations of detail, is undergone by most birds and mammals. With chickens, it can be done by other means too. People who have hatched chicks in an incubator may dip their little beaks in water to introduce them to drinking, and the birds soon pick things up from their fellows and do other things from instinct. Roosting is more complex. People who rescue battery-cage birds often talk of the poignancy and rewards of encouraging the birds to learn how to hop on to a bar.

Whilst the instinct to feed is natural, there are many tricks to the trade. Chickens are great scavengers. They will peck and scratch their way around a farmyard hoovering up everything: tender greens such as grass, young leaves, your favourite flowers and all the other plants that give a proper barnyard egg its natural gold. Then there are the morsels of insect protein such as worms, grubs and ants. Amongst all this they will eat hard nuggets such as pebbles. These collect in their gizzards and allow the birds to start digesting their food by grinding it up. In factory birds this part of their anatomy is half the size it is in free-range hens with their internal waste disposal units. Chickens need this milling system because they have no teeth; instead, their horny beaks provide a cutting edge as well as being full of sensory nerves for exploring their surroundings. Beak tips are routinely trimmed in factory egg-laying birds, and indeed in free-range and barnyard birds, to prevent the birds in these industrial systems from attacking each other.

Back in the garden or the farmyard, the newborn chicks will see the mother hen do all the other things that chickens do. She will 'dust-bath' to clean her feathers. This involves her ruffling down in a dry patch of dust or soil and letting the particles spread down through her plumage, removing any mites on the feathers or her skin. The sight of a hen having a right old dustbath is hugely satisfying. It seems to be something they need and want, and yet is impossible in an industrial unit.

Because chickens don't have a system of preening oil running through their feathers to make them waterproof, they need shelter. This is partly why they perch. In the wild this would be on a tree, to give them shelter and, more importantly, safety from predators. The chicken's feet lock on to the branch or pole so that it does not fall off when asleep.

Hens naturally establish a system, or 'pecking order', with different degrees of dominance over the others; this can result in bullying, though not if the hierarchy is established. Introducing new hens to a domestic flock is a tricky business. A bird of a different colour, or just a newcomer, can be attacked. Once chickens see blood, they go for it. The end result is not a pretty sight for the hen-keeper. Aggression is lowest in small-sized groups where a chain of command is established so that each hen keeps the hen below her in check. Humans find the submissiveness of hens useful when picking them up – or indeed when keeping large numbers of birds in cages.

In nature, a mother hen tends her chicks for around five weeks. Then, abruptly, she leaves. They are ready to be independent. In a modern industrial meat-producing system, they would shortly be dead. The meat sold in supermarkets is generally from birds not much more than six weeks old.

If the hen is the folk-image of the mother of all mothers, the cock is the *capo di capi* of masculinity. The cockerel is a bird of great beauty, and his proud strut and erect carriage help display his fine feathers; his comb stands tall as a castle battlement and his wattles shake vigorously as he paces.

The cock announces his presence by the loudness of his crow. He doesn't just sing just before light; he also crows at dusk, to call the hens in to roost, and during the night. Since each rooster can recognize the cry of at least thirty others, these noises are partly territorial. By crowing at the earliest, imperceptible light the cockerel gets the advantage of dominating the early-morning airwaves; the rest of the dawn chorus occurs slightly later. Sound travels further in the tunnel of cold night air that clings to the ground before day breaks – but the cock scarcely needs the advantage of getting in first as he has an especially loud call. There are cock-crowing competitions held in Germany with the noisiest bird winning, and a breed called the Bergse Kraaier has been specially developed for its vocals. The cock's calls and crows vary from the familiar dawn announcement to warning cries that signal whether a predator is above or at ground level. He will tell his hens that there is food to be had and how good it is. He can even be seen calling his favourite hen to a choice morsel.

The cock's dawn call links him to the powerful sun and to hope of the new day. But it is not an altogether welcome noise, as many living near one will agree, and in classical mythology its origins have an association with punishment. Mars put the god Alectryon on guard outside the door while he indulged in his adulterous passion for Venus. But Alectryon fell asleep and was then turned into a cockerel that must evermore announce the dawn.

Whilst the hen is the subject of many cosy folk traditions, the male has been associated with more complex ones. It was said that if you wanted to make a good flute you should gather your material from a wood far from the noise of a cock's crow so that the trees would not have been damaged by the sound. The cock also has a more mysterious and potent magic, though again there is an ambivalence in the symbolism, as with many powerful forces: they can swiftly turn destructive. One such powerful image is of the cock crowing thrice in the night of Peter's betrayal of Jesus.

Stories of the cockerel's power have been collected in one of the best books ever written about a creature and the food it produces. In 1972 two Californian academics, Page Smith and Charles Daniel, ran a course on the chicken at Cowell College, University of California, Santa Cruz. In the post-sixties climate of breaking down barriers, part of their purpose was to study this bird and its eggs from many angles. By combining their respective disciplines of history and biology they were taking a bold step out of narrow specialization. Even to study something as 'ordinary' as a chicken caused a stir and some mirth at the time. Page Smith used to go to august history conferences wearing a chicken T-shirt underneath his suit. When ribbed by his condescending colleagues he would flash his fowl defiantly. He was right. The range of research collected in *The Chicken Book* makes it feel modern today. Quite apart from being a good read, the book both illuminates the chicken and shines a light on the way over-specialization can dangerously reduce life to technicalities. Smith and Daniel saw that, for students as for farmers as for anyone, you can become so specific that you lose the essential nature of your subject. The joyful, engaged and broad approach of their book represents the opposite of the over-focused.

One of the many observations in *The Chicken Book* is that the cockerel's power as a life force is founded on his sexual power. His swaying, thrusting pride, strutting around the farmyard, is unmistakably phallic. His beautiful physiognomy is linked to sexual function – the cock's proud wattles and combs brighten in colour during amorous events. The ancient Greeks and Romans celebrated the sexuality of the cock in literature, myth and custom. Older men would give a cockerel to a boy as a seductive love token. Parts of its body were used as aphrodisiacs; Pliny the Elder recommends the right testicle. As early as Anglo-Saxon times, the word 'cock' meant penis. Coy Victorians took to calling male chickens 'roosters' to avoid this sexual term. Religious leaders were apparently less prudish: the Vatican contains a bronze statue that combines wattles and comb with an erect penis. (Smith and Daniel point out that this is a celebration of life-force as a form of divine power rather than an erotic symbol.)

If two cockerels are put beak-to-beak in a ring, they may fight to the death. This fact is exploited in cockfighting, often claimed to be the world's oldest sport and still practised in many countries, most prominently in Asia and also legally, still, in some of the states of America – New Mexico and Louisiana – and illegally elsewhere.

Many ruses are used to encourage the birds to become aggressive. One concern about bird flu spreading is the fact some owners suck and blow into the holes on their cockerels' beaks in order to get their birds going. Metal spurs used to be, and can still be, attached to the cock's natural spurs to make them more deadly. The earliest known British spurs were those given by Charles II, a keen cocker like all the Stuarts, to his mistress Nell Gwynn. Sometimes the cock's natural spurs were left sharp and naked for prolonged and less predictable fighting.

The British cockfighting breed was the Game Cock. Its broad-set breast and the four-square stance of its strong legs make it look like a heavyweight boxer. Cockfighting, indeed, is the origin of the terms 'bantamweight' and 'featherweight' used in the human fighting sport. Such is its aggression and bravery that a game cock will go for a cat that is after his hens; he can kill a rat and there are even stories of them chasing off foxes. Any cocks that ran away, that 'showed the white feather' in the defensive ruffling of their tail rather than raising their hackles, got eaten.

Cockfighting in Britain reached its zenith in the vicious, grimy times of the eighteenth century. A 1716 map of London contains no fewer than ten Cock Alleys, nine Cock Courts, eight Cock Yards, four Cock Lands, a Cock Hill, Cockpit Alley, Cockpit Buildings, Cockpit Street, Cocks Rents and Cockspur Street. Amongst the many pits (the term was to continue in theatres) there was a royal one at Birdcage Walk and another famous one in Pickled-Egg Lane. Fights took place all over Britain. The founder of Methodism, John Wesley, delayed one of his sermons in Gwennap, near Redruth in Cornwall, until a noisy cockfight had finished; the pit later became a famous natural cathedral that could hold a thousand people.

Cockfighting was as popular then as football is today, with contests between towns and even counties. In Queen Anne's time the Gentlemen of Essex took on the rest of Great Britain, in a show of this county's strength – not unfamiliar today – that can only be described as 'cocksure'. The two most notorious types of fight were the Welsh Main, a knock-out competition with the winners of successive battles going head to head until one bloody, torn, exhausted cock was left – just about – standing, and the Battle Royal, in which any number of birds would be put in a pit, without any regard for the usual matching of weights, in a vicious free-for-all. The final battered survivor was declared the 'winner', but many such victorious cockerels died on the spot.

The most famous eighteenth-century 'cocker' was the 12th Earl of Derby. He is known today as a keen breeder of racehorses – the Derby was named after him and the Oaks after his racing residence in Surrey. But to contemporary eyes the Earl was even more keen on birds than on horses and bred an astonishing three thousand fighters a year. His womenfolk banned his cock-keepers from his deathbed so as to keep his mind on matters spiritual; but Derby got his private chaplain to arrange for some of his top birds to be trimmed and spurred ready to be lifted up through his bedroom window in a basket so he could see one final fight. He himself died shortly afterwards.

Cockfighting is, without doubt, a bloody business. But the depth of cockfighting's presence in British culture means it does still continue here today, despite being illegal for some 150 years. I discovered this for myself when interviewing an aristocratic countryman. He suddenly moved on from his eel-spearing stories to his cockfighting ones. He went to fights in the north-west, which he said was the stronghold of contemporary cockfighting.

The 'sport' of fighting cocks is an example of how humans can be cruel to chickens, yet such practices can become embedded in our culture. But it was not acceptable to the evangelical reformers who came to dominate public opinion in nineteenth-century Britain. After vigorous campaigning, cockfighting was banned in Britain in 1849. RSPCA inspectors still look out for the clipped feathers and injuries you see on fighting cocks, and prosecutions take place. Game cock breeders tend to be cagey about what they do, and where they operate: they are frightened of their birds being stolen and used for this underground activity. But even though cock-fighting continues, the practice is regarded with abhorrence when once it was seen as normal. Attitudes can change. What is 'normal' one day can come to be seen as wrong. And it can be stopped.

The Good Egg

The trend towards the frozen, fast and processed affects egg-layers as much as broiler birds. Battery eggs are everywhere in the food industry, mirroring the usefulness of eggs in the chemistry of home cooking. Many of the people who buy whole free-range eggs also unwittingly buy plenty of battery ones because they don't realize that they are in such products as mayonnaise. The website of the Battery Hen Welfare Trust, a group that organizes the rehousing of spent laying hens, makes the point that you may get a double dose of battery chicken hell in an apparently innocuous takeaway. 'Desperate for a Friday night special chicken and egg fried rice?' it asks. 'Well that's really bad news . . . it's highly likely that the chicken will be spent battery hen and the egg will be what she produced before the chop. Same goes for Indian I'm afraid.'

The consumer shift towards higher-welfare eggs when

bought fresh in the shell shows that, once we are aware of a problem, we do change our buying habits. The move has gone further than the shops. Pizza Express has gone free-range. McDonald's has turned all its eggs in Britain over to this higher-welfare system. If the company was to do the same all over the world, that really would be a massive step. Two and a half per cent of the eggs produced in the United States are bought by McDonald's.

It is now much more common for chefs and caterers to use free-range eggs. Many a café will advertise free-range eggs (even if they don't mention the status – free-range or otherwise – of the bacon and sausage on the same breakfast plate). The shift towards higher-welfare eggs has taken place to such an extent that a really good café or restaurant might not mention the fact at all on the menu; they simply take it as read. But don't assume this always to be the case. A farmer who delivers to London told me of a swanky hotel where the breakfast eggs come from caged birds. Since the cost of a Full English here is in line with the price of the bedrooms, one would have thought a few extra pence could have been spared for the hens.

The move by British consumers towards higher-welfare eggs went hand-in-hand with the political battle against the battery cage. This turned out to be a great victory. In 1999, there was a dramatic change in policy. Europe's agriculture ministers decided to ban battery hen cages by 2012. It was one of the single biggest steps forward there has ever been in European farm animal welfare, and it started in the polite Hampshire market town of Petersfield.

Compassion in World Farming (CIWF) was set up in

1967 when a Hampshire farmer, Peter Roberts, thought people should know what was happening to livestock farming. He gave up farming himself and worked instead as an agricultural representative: touring the country with his rep's card meant he could witness what was going on in great detail. 'I was astonished by the squalor in some of the battery houses,' he comments in a history of the animal welfare movement, *Animal Century*. 'Dead birds were left in their cages decomposing and live birds would be pecking at them. Some of the nipple drinkers would be leaking water everywhere and there would be mouldy food left around. It was then that I began to equate factory farming with a deterioration in farming standards.' In an early publicity campaign for the group, the model Celia Hammond crouched down in an up-scale battery cage. The memorable image was splashed around the newspapers. At this stage CIWF was a group of protesting outsiders; it has since grown into a highly respected pressure group now regularly called into government meetings with ministers.

There is still on outsize battery cage with two giant chickens beside the group's large HQ in Petersfield. The battle to free such birds continues: the egg industry is trying to delay the application of the historic ban, or to get rid of it altogether. When I went to visit, the investigations director was standing near the birds, puffing urgently on a cigarette and looking like a man focused on the job ahead. He is the man who organizes the sometimes highly risky filming expeditions that bust open the doors of these secretive factory systems and expose their workings to the public.

In a downstairs despatch room, volunteers were stuffing envelopes with campaigning literature. Upstairs, it was like any old office. People were walking between desks and photocopiers, talking on phones, talking to each other. On the walls were shocking pictures of farm animals. There has, however, been a bit of a shift in CIWF's literature towards pictures of happy creatures, rather than just these appalling exposés of man's inhumanity to animals. Documents such as CIWF's biannual supermarket awards report are now more likely to depict pigs and sheep and cows living a life in the open air on the green, green grass. The group wants to engage people through positive images rather than repel them by negative ones. Connecting the issues with the food we eat is a vital step towards better welfare for farm animals, says Philip Lymbery, the chief executive of CIWF. Some of what he told me was still, inevitably, couched in negative terms. 'If you are cruel to animals, look at what that does to our food, our health, our countryside,' he said. 'If you are cruel to animals you get BSE; if you are cruel to animals you get bird flu; if you are cruel to animals you get antibiotic resistance, you get low Omega 3.'

The strength of CIWF is that its style is eminently reasonable. The material can be graphic, yes, but they have avoided the aggression and hysteria of some animal rights and welfare movements whilst never losing sight of good clear principles. I am a card carrier for their Eat Less Meat campaign. The card states five good reasons to do so: health benefits; reduced pollution; protecting the planet; reducing global hunger; better welfare for the 50 billion animals raised for meat each year. Who can argue with these principles? The world would be a more compassionate and sustainable place if we followed them. So easy to say; so hard to achieve.

When you follow the nitty-gritty of a campaign like the one that resulted in the battery cage ban, it is both exhilarating to see the breakthroughs and disturbing when you understand the ongoing obstacles. It was Philip Lymbery, then campaigns officer, and his predecessor as CEO, Joyce d'Silva, who ran the campaign. A campaign starts, Philip explained, by deciding where they want to end up. In this case, it was to get a ban on battery cages. A review of the Laying Hens Directive was announced by the European Commission, the lawdrafting body of the European Union. This offered a chance for welfare to be improved – or made worse. CIWF worked out exactly who made the decisions. Here it was the Council of Ministers of Agriculture of the then fifteen member countries of the EU who were at the top of a 'power pyramid'. Next CIWF came up with a 'tactics toolkit': ways to put pressure upwards through each part of the pyramid in order to reach the decision makers. If this sounds like management-speak, it is worth mentioning that the toolkit included a giant hen called Hetty who was wheeled around to show the public the reality of battery cages. Then came the free-range egg breakfast events, endless meetings, letter writing, phone calls and all the rest of the day-to-day activities of lobbying that are carried out by members of the public, campaign volunteers and members of staff.

Since the decision makers were the European agricultural ministers, the campaign had to be Europe-wide. Still based in Petersfield, but with an increasingly European (and now worldwide) perspective, CIWF built up a coalition of like-minded groups. Often they made alliances with animal welfare organizations that had not previously focused on farm animals; traditionally there had been a bias towards wildlife and pets. Tackling agricultural issues is far more controversial. You are fighting huge economic interests and the fact that the public tends to see farm animals as dinner rather than as live creatures.

Compassion in World Farming kept the pressure on, constantly, and moved farm animals on to everyone's agenda. The campaigning team was ready to push an advantage at any opportunity and exploit any weakness. Two pieces of luck came their way, together with the actions of a maverick Italian.

The first piece of luck came, ironically, from a food scare. Joyce d'Silva thinks the salmonella-in-eggs scandal in 1988 did the campaign a big favour by constantly putting images of battery hens on the TV news. People can easily decide not to look at campaign literature; they can decide not to turn on a television programme about factory farming. But if the One O'Clock News and the Six O'Clock News and the Nine O'Clock News all have pictures of hens in cages, you are going to see them. People were repulsed by the idea that a disease could become endemic in intensive farming. More importantly, most people in Britain now knew, even in broad terms, what a battery cage was like.

The second piece of luck was timing. The European Commission, having announced a review of the Laying Hens Directive, sat on it for five years. This bought crucial time for CIWF and its allies to build up their campaigns, to spread their message and to get used to working alongside each other in a European alliance. By the time the document emerged for the consultation stage, the coordinated campaign was well underway. And by the time the agriculture ministers met to make the final decision, every single one of these politicians knew there was public disgust in their own country about battery cages. 'They weren't just being preached to by those silly old animal lovers from England. That was the real overall key,' says Joyce d'Silva.

One of the geographical fault lines in this continent-wide issue divided northern Europe, for instance Britain, Germany and the Scandinavian countries, who have tended to be more vocal in their opposition to factory farming, and the agricultural French and their neighbouring southern European countries. CIWF took a tactical decision that it was especially important to push forward in these more difficult places; they put adverts in the Paris Métro, for example.

Then an individual stepped in. Adolfo Sansolini is one of the quietly charismatic personalities in the animal welfare movement. He has spent his life campaigning for animal and human rights, seeing them as indivisibly part of one overall movement towards compassion. Philip Lymbery asked Sansolini to head the southern European arm of their campaigns from his native Italy. As well as motivating all the branches of the Italian animal campaigning group, Lega Anti Vivisezione (LAV), to join the fight, Sansolini joined Hetty the Hen on her tour around the country, carefully targeting first the towns where the MEPs with crucial agricultural responsibilities were based. The hen immediately attracted attention. There were volunteers showing people the size of the cage and emphasizing the fact that the hen could not even stretch a wing. That there were problems with her feet. That the wire floors meant the hen could get injuries and infections and lameness. That leg weakness and the cage conditions and the heavy egg laying meant the bird's bones would get broken. That the careless, mass haul to the slaughterhouse would mean more broken bones. 'They were mostly small towns close to the countryside,' Adolfo says. 'People had contact with real hens and so of course they said they would never eat a battery cage egg.'

After the tour and accompanying campaign were almost complete, and hundreds of thousands of signatures were delivered to the politicians, and the politicians had made promising, positive noises, it looked as though everything was going well. Then came bad news. Sansolini and his fellow workers learnt that the civil servants were not, after all, going to include a ban on battery cages in the Italian position on the Laying Hens Directive.

It was then that Adolfo took matters into his own hands. He sent a letter to all the relevant ministers, telling them there was something urgent to do. What's happening now, he said, will destroy everything that we have discussed up to now. All your commitment, all your attention, will be to no avail. The civil servants are simply going in the opposite direction. I know it's difficult, he said, but you have to do something. The only thing I can do now is to help you. But I will not ask without giving. So what I can give to you is my hunger, my thirst. From midnight tomorrow I will stop drinking and eating. I want a meeting with you and I want a different position.

When I met Sansolini in London more than fifteen years later, he said, 'I knew I was risking a lot. But living is about using life. Between birth and death you should live. I think that's about sharing. If you believe in something you should invest in it to make it happen. What I could invest at that moment wasn't anything else but putting my life on the table.' Sansolini is not a crazed martyr; Philip Lymbery describes him as 'a maverick rational radical'. His approach is to lobby and to inform, not to rant. He knew that a thirst strike put his health in imminent danger, but considered it a necessary act in order to pressurize the Italian government at a crucial point in the negotiations over a ban on the battery cage.

On the second day of his strike, already frighteningly weak, Sansolini got a meeting at the prime minister's office but collapsed twice on the way. The official put a glass of water in front of him, told him to drink it now and said they would do something. 'I refused to do that,' Sansolini told me, 'and I said: "If you do something before I leave, I'll be happy to drink it. But I won't drink it now."' The relevant phone call was made. Adolfo drank the glass of water. In the afternoon, he went to the Ministry of Agriculture. He said he would drink one more glass of water, as a mark of trust, and then await official confirmation of the new position before stopping the strike. 'I went back home. I felt very tired – it had been thirty-eight hours. I felt not very well and waited for a reply in bed. They rang around 8.30 to 9p.m. from the Prime Minister's office saying: "We called the others, the agreement is reached, this is the official position." I asked them to issue a press release, which they did. I started to drink and eat again.'

Two days later, in the crucial meeting of permanent representatives of the European Commission, the Italian representative stood up and said the Italian position had changed: they wanted a ban on the battery cage. The Italian position was hugely influential amongst the other southern European states. France, Portugal and Greece all now decided in favour of a ban.

After years of campaigning, and this final, dramatic turn, the story played out in 1999. Philip Lymbery remembers standing outside the meeting room in Luxembourg when the British Agriculture Minister, Nick Brown, emerged. 'It was a surreal moment of hanging on every word to hear that this apparent defeat had turned into a huge victory,' he recalls. Only one country had voted against banning the cages. Austria said no – because they didn't think the directive went far enough. And Spain abstained. The agricultural ministers' decision would release the 300 million birds kept in battery cages in Europe.

What happened as a result of this breakthrough? From 2003, UK and all other EU farmers were not allowed to introduce new cages into their houses, leading up to the 2012 total ban. Some countries had acted in advance. Switzerland, not a member of the European Union, had banned the cages altogether way back in 1991.

But it was still hard for people to tell from the boxes on the supermarket shelves exactly how the birds were kept. Tempting phrases like 'farm-fresh' and 'extra' could (and still can) be used for eggs from battery birds, but the packaging did not have to state that the birds were kept in cages. It was clear that labelling was important to facilitate consumer choice. This became a legal obligation in 2004, thanks to sustained campaigning. 'I think it's about information,' said Sansolini – though he added that some people did not want to be informed.

Overall, the number of consumers positively choosing higher-welfare eggs has grown enormously. But around 60 per cent of the whole eggs bought in the UK are still battery, as are a higher percentage of the non-shell eggs. There is inevitably a price reason. Whilst it is crucial that we break out of a cheap food culture and are prepared to pay for higher welfare, are we encouraged to do so by the supermarkets? It is interesting that critics say it doesn't cost much more to produce free-range eggs, but that the price differential in the shops is greater. The cost of welfare is at least partly down to supermarket ethics: they know consumers are willing to pay more, and it is hard for us not to conclude that welfare is an opportunity for extra profit. Conversely, supermarkets also conduct the occasional price war using welfare eggs, with financial consequences for the producers.

And what is going to happen when the cages are finally banned from Europe? Many fear that, despite reassurances to the contrary, there will be a rise of cheap battery eggs imported from other parts of the world. A major stumbling block for the animal welfare movement is international trade. In a climate moving towards more free trade, they have to persuade the World Trade Organization that excluding animal products from banned, lower-welfare systems is not protectionist. Unlike the European politicians, the WTO is not directly elected. How much harder it is to get to that 'power pyramid' of distant civil servants making the decisions that will affect the lives of billions of animals every day.

Even within the European Union, there are signs of a retreat. Perhaps this is not surprising; the start of change took a long time to come. Birds went into cages largely from the 1950s onwards. In the UK, the influential Brambell Report of 1965 recommended that the cages be banned. It took more than forty years for this to happen. Now this step forward may be delayed. At the time of writing, the Laying Hens Directive was under review again and the British egg industry was lobbying for the cage ban to be delayed for five years until 2017. Even within the directive there was an allowance for other ways of keeping hens that campaigners feel compromise welfare.

There are three other ways of keeping egg-laying birds: the enriched cage, barn-reared and free-range birds. The enriched cage gives the birds more space – though a third less than animal welfare expert John Webster recommends – and some opportunity to display 'natural behaviour' such as perching and dust bathing. But it is seen as a woeful option by welfare groups. The directive does not prohibit such cages, and the concern is that battery hen farmers will simply switch over to these in 2012. Then there are barn (or perchery) and free-range systems. Birds within a barn system have a chance to perch and scratch around, but cannot go outside. The chance to range outside is seen as an important part of a bird's life, especially in the longer life of an egg layer as opposed to a meat chicken.

'Free-range' is a term that conjures up images of flocks roving happy and free, pecking chirpily around their spacious green paradise. The reality can be distinctly different. Free-range systems must have pop-holes along the side of the shed, but there is good evidence that a sizeable number of birds hardly leave the house because of the size of the sheds and large number of birds. They may be able to display more natural behaviour, but unfortunately this can include vicious feather pecking and even cannibalism. John Webster concludes that, whilst he is delighted about the trend towards free-range egg production, the systems need further development so that they completely meet the public's expectations of high-welfare eggs. But he does now feel that things are going in the right direction. Progress is partly about resources being targeted towards farming that is centred on the birds rather than just on the economics. With the consumer boom in free-range eggs, this is now happening.

The organic egg section has the highest welfare standards, and the Soil Association certified organic layers the highest of all. Organic eggs make up 3 per cent of the shell-egg market; but supermarkets perceive there is a limit to what consumers will pay for eggs in general and tend to have a price ceiling on organic ones. As production costs rise, it may become unviable for the highest level of producers to continue. We are back to whether the public will pay for good animal welfare.

British consumers have voted with their money against eggs from battery cages. This is one major step forward. Furthermore, the campaign against battery cages has opened our eyes to the conditions of farm animals in general. There are more than 30 million laying hens kept in Britain; 860 million birds are raised a year for meat. We have moved towards higher-welfare for egg layers; improving the conditions of the broilers must be the next step forward.

Happy Chickens

There are three main obstacles to consumers making a difference to the millions of chickens we farm and eat for meat. First, there is a lack of knowledge and consequently a lack of anger. Consumers don't have a single symbol like a battery cage to rally round in opposition to intensive broiler farming. Many people do feel an instinctive aversion to the way chickens are mass-farmed for meat, but only once they discover how it is done. They don't like the idea of chickens being crammed in enormous numbers into vast windowless sheds and forced to endure artificial lighting and feed regimes which mean they can outgrow their basic body structure and suffer. They don't like the way breeder flocks are kept hungry. They don't like the way the birds are snatched from the sheds, transported and killed. But they need to know a little bit about the broiler chicken industry to understand these issues – it is not as simple as looking at a cage and feeling disgusted.

The second problem, and the most difficult to overcome, is money. You can vote with your pennies to buy better eggs; you must vote with your pounds to buy better meat. Where a cheap chicken can cost less than £3, a 'good' chicken will be £7 or more. At the upper end of the scale, a higher-welfare chicken will set you back £12–£20. It is two, three or even four times the amount people pay for a standard bird.

The third problem is convenience. Food shopping is hard work. Worrying about the origins of what you are buying adds to the burden. Having to hunt around for decently reared chickens makes the task even greater.

Poultry sales show, without doubt, that a larger number of people will now pay more for better chicken. As we do so, such birds will become more widely available. The total value of fresh chicken sales in supermarkets is £1.1 billion a year and is going up 4 per cent year-on-year. Within this, the market for organic chicken, one of the highest-welfare methods, may be £44 million – a tiny proportion in comparison to the broiler birds, but far from negligible. Furthermore, the annual growth for organic chicken sales is more than 30 per cent and now represents a whole quarter of the overall 4 per cent growth in chicken. This upward trend for higher-welfare is likely to rise as people become more and more interested in the quality of their food.

Since there is such a wide price difference between an ordinary bird and a better one, it is important to know what you are paying for. I visited three producers of 'happy' chickens to see what your money buys. These are individuals whose produce is, to some extent, available nationally through mail order. More importantly, they represent a movement that is growing, gradually, all over the country.

Richard Guy's Real Meat Company first got me thinking about chickens some twelve years ago, as I mentioned at the start of this book. The individual is important in higher-welfare farms. In Richard's case you are dealing with someone who has championed the issues of meat production for two decades.

The journey began for Richard when he discovered for himself that it was okay to farm animals for meat. It started with a pig. 'I was brought up on a farm,' he explains. 'My mother, who's an avid *Guardian* reader, thought it was terrible what people were doing to meat animals. So we decided to buy and rear our own. Our first pig was called Bormann after a major Nazi in the hope it would help dispatch it at the end. When it came to the slaughter we thought: "This is a bit tough on old Bormann, he's one of the lads." But if I couldn't face slaughtering an animal that I knew had had a very good life, then I shouldn't eat meat.' The day of the pig's dispatch arrived. Richard continues: 'I put Bormann in the back of a Mini Estate and drove through commuter traffic with this pig looking out of the back window. Walked into the slaughterhouse. No problem. He didn't react to the blood and start screaming as vegetarians might have you believe. I was about to give my prepared speech, when he was stunned and gone. There was nothing. No screeching, no yowling, no nothing.'

Richard Guy and his wife Gilly Metherell, a fellow farmer, decided to offer consumers an alternative to mass-produced meat. Good British beer had been saved by the Real Ale movement; could the same be done for farm animals? Their business model was to amass a number of Real Meat farmers who would supply a collection of Real Meat butchers, with strict rules about welfare and quality throughout. Twenty years down the line, ten shops bear the company's name and another fifteen sell the meat under the Real Meat Company label. They also have a substantial mail order business.

Chickens are on the front line of Richard's real meat battle, standard-bearers of his mantra that eating meat is a privilege, not a right. He and Gilly believe anyone involved in this privilege should be concerned for the animals at every stage. Their birds are kept for twelve weeks or so. They are fed by people going into the sheds rather than via automated feeders, so that they are tended as livestock rather than left to grow, or die, like lumps of matter. Richard's farmers have never given their birds antibiotics for growth promotion. They are kept in small groups in mobile houses and killed by hand at a small abattoir to ensure that the nightmare scenario of being scalded and plucked alive never, ever occurs. At the table, the result is slower-grown birds that have a maturity of flavour and a far better texture than the standardized pap of the mass-produced. They cost £15–17 each.

What about the price issue? Richard insists his customers are not 'all Range Rovers and dropping Flossie off at prep school'. They are, he says, 'people who have made a choice'. He points out that you can slightly adjust your eating habits to eat less-but-better meat and enjoy it without significant extra cost. Instead of feeding a child three ordinary sausages and two spoonsful of beans, for example, you can put two Real Meat sausages and three spoonfuls of beans on the plate.

Richard and Gilly's point of view is now much more common than it was twenty years ago. The advance has come about because the Real Meat Company and others have not shied away from a battle of words and pictures. Images of intensive farming are shown on the website. Under the More about Our Chickens section is a picture of a standard, crowded broiler house and a grisly shot of exactly what happens to the bones of a chicken with a leg disorder caused by the bird growing too fast for its skeleton.

Some of the other images on the site – of the animals you are going to eat – may not seem so controversial, but they are. At the time when the Real Meat Company was set up, it was unusual to have pictures of animals on company literature at all: the aim of meat sellers was to disassociate meat from the live creature – and in many cases it still is. Scan the shelves of supermarket meat aisles and see how many creatures trot up to you. All of this has stopped people thinking about where their meat comes from. Richard Guy thinks it is the mental and physical distance from farming that has enabled animal welfare to be compromised so badly, and allowed farmers to turn to dubious methods. 'When our parents and grandparents were young it would not be unusual to have a relative who was on a farm,' he said. 'It wouldn't be unusual to ramble across them. Traditional knowledge about farms stood farmers in good stead way beyond what they might deserve.' As regards images, Richard is a critic of specious marketing – for example, battery operations showing uncaged hens on their packaging and delivery vans (there seems to be less of a problem about showing egg-laying birds because people are not going to eat them – a classic example of the hypocrisy that surrounds farm animals).

By contrast, the Real Meat Company has always engaged with the arguments and offered total transparency. It invites journalists and any other member of the public to come and witness any part of their operation – even the slaughtering. Richard agrees that, whilst nobody wishes to dwell on it, an inability to handle 'the death thing' is an important part of people's disassociation and the resulting problems in meat production.

Does all this put anyone off eating meat altogether? I asked Richard his views on vegetarianism. When I first talked to him, in the 1990s, he gave this opinion: 'I'm not sure whether there's a moral question to eating meat,' he said. 'I don't think so. We seem to be equipped with the right teeth and stomach to eat it. What I won't tolerate is animals being made to suffer [for us] to eat meat. My chat to vegetarians is that when half the country's vegetarian and the other half is eating real meat, then we should shake hands and walk to the other side of the battlefield and do each other to death. But until then, we're fighting the same way.' Twelve years later, and with the real meat argument gaining ground, he put his opinion more strongly. He sent me his position in an email: 'I believe that, as human beings are clearly equipped to eat meat, provided the animal has had a good life on the farm and, as far as possible, an unanticipated, anaesthetized death, it can fulfil a natural process. Conversely, vegetarianism could be accused of being cruel for it denies the creature not consumed the benefit of life. Let's convert to a human parallel (always a little dodgy). If the government decided to save money on pensions by introducing compulsory euthanasia for fifty-plus-year-olds (I am fifty-two), then the question must arise, "Was I grateful to have the fifty years, or would I rather have never lived at all?" In the time I have lived I have seen the sun rise and set, I have felt rain on my face, damp grass between my toes. I have seen birds, spiders, flowers. Even if I had only lived fifteen years (the equivalent age of an animal when killed for meat), I would not want to have missed it.'

An ethical food brand thrives or falls on its high standards. The quality of meat chicken is a complicated field: some 'happy' chickens are happier than others. To value what Richard and the Real Meat Company are doing, consumers have to see that he will not compromise. He believes that the most difficult part of the battle to improve the lives of meat chickens is not the ethical meat suppliers versus the factory farmers, but the fight against what he calls 'look-alikes'.

Consumers want better welfare, and will go for a label that indicates this. If a label appears to offer the real deal, but at a lower price than that of a competitor, it is going to be popular. The Real Meat viewpoint is that animal welfare is non-negotiable. Either you pay for the job to be done properly or you don't eat the meat. 'You can't compromise without cutting out on some of the important parts of the welfare. I think it is cruel to cheat where an animal's well-being is at stake,' says Richard.

Richard Guy and his ilk think the national standards for free-range production are too low, and certainly not what shoppers think they are getting. National standards allow farmers to stay at this basic level without trying for anything better, he believes. For this reason, people should be suspicious of such standards even though, on the surface, they should be a consumer guarantee of quality. 'Volvo are obliged to keep upping their game because of their claim that they are safer than anyone else,' he said. 'That's what we do.'

What are the possible problems with free-range? On paper, chickens labelled as free-range have access to go outside. But do they? In practice, if they are kept in large flocks – and many are – they are unlikely to do so much. The openings may be too far away, and too small. Chickens kept in a large flock do not behave as they would in a normal barnyard. Furthermore, whilst the stocking density indoors is lower than the maximum for totally indoor-kept birds – about thirteen birds per square metre, as opposed to the government's recommended maximum of seventeen for intensive systems – the rest of the production is the same as for the standard chickens. Lighting, feeding, transportation and killing arrangements are the same as for the cheapest birds.

To differentiate better free-range from, if you like, 'bog-standard' free-range, there are two further categories. 'Traditional free-range' has a lower stocking density, about twelve birds per square metre, and double the amount of outdoor area. The regulations insist on a minimum age of slaughter of eighty-one days, so encouraging slower-growing breeds. The third category is 'Total-freedom free-range'. This means that the birds are given a larger area in which to run and they must be able to get to it during all daylight hours. Which makes you wonder what happens to the other 'free-range' birds. You could argue that total freedom is what a consumer would expect of the conditions for all such creatures. Sadly, this is not the case. If you really care about what you are eating, you have to look beyond the label to discover what exactly you are getting.

All of this can make you slightly suspicious of 'happy' chicken categories. The preferable alternative is to find a brand that you trust, from people who really care about the issues and take the trouble to produce meat that conforms with genuinely high standards.

The next people I got to know on the happy chicken trail were two such individuals: Peter and Henri Greig, of Pipers Farm. They live in the green, bosomy hills of mid-Devon, where the red soil matches the colour of their Red Ruby cattle. There is still a network of small family farms in this part of Britain. Pipers Farm gathers together a number of such places, gets them to operate to high company standards and sells the meat under one brand name. There is a retail shop in Exeter and an on-line butcher's shop with information about the farmers and their methods.

Peter's path into meat has interesting origins. His father was one of the first people to produce broiler chickens in Britain using the new industrialized methods. Peter and Henri themselves farmed broilers, and could make an annual £50,000 net profit from just two acres of land. But Peter recalls the way they had to shuffle between the chickens in the packed-out houses: you couldn't pick your feet up or you might tread on the birds. He remembers one night having to clear three thousand dead chickens from a shed after a problem with the ventilation. Now he has gone in the opposite direction, with the experience of profes-sional farming and a background of retailing behind him.

Chicken, he says, lends itself well to the true artisan producer, and this is now their approach.

Pipers Farm chickens are kept in flocks of two hundred. They are fed a natural grain diet without routine medication, and are kept in well-ventilated and naturally lit barns with bedding that is changed daily and is rather like a large dust-bath which also allows the chickens to scratch for their food. The birds are kept inside rather than going out, and here is something that challenges consumer perception. Peter believes that a good barn system, especially in places with lots of rainfall like the West Country, can be a better option than bad 'free-range' – so long as the welfare standards are impeccable and the stocking density and overall numbers are low. Again, you need to look at the individual's standards rather than simply at the named method of production. A testament to the high quality of husbandry here is that Peter does not need to use coccidiostats at all, either as a feed additive or as a vaccine. 'If you resort to using that as a tool you can compromise the management of the environment, and we will not go down that road,' he says. The birds are killed individually, by hand, and processed carefully, in dry conditions, so that they can safely be hung for ten to fourteen days which, as we know, makes a big difference to the taste.

Good food is the aim. When he started out, Peter Greig cut up carcasses himself, and put the joints in a frying pan so he could test their eating qualities. By this method he ended up with cuts that, interestingly, were similar to French seam-butchery, where animals are divided along the muscles rather than through them, with more tender results. The French keep a far larger percentage of their birds as slow-growers, living for at least eleven weeks in the more traditional Label Rouge scheme, simply because they taste better. Pipers chickens take twelve to thirteen weeks to grow and cost around £20 for a hefty, 2.5 kg bird. Expensive, yes. But Greig says one of his chickens is so substantial and full of good nutrition that it can feed a family of four with three meals.

The idea that a farmer is producing food is crucial. Peter and Henri are at the cutting edge of a change in British agriculture that is reconnecting consumers and producers. On regular farm walks, customers can see how the animals are kept. Their meat goes to a group of nursery schools in Exeter, to feed four hundred children. Pipers Farm is working on a project to supply office workers with 'working persons' survival packs' that are conveniently delivered to the workplace. In their shops, on the street and on-line, the approach is to supply lunch and dinner, whereas a traditional butcher may just sell pieces of raw meat and can be a touch intimidating to the supermarket shopper. Pipers supplies recipes; the meat is attractively displayed on plates rather than being piled up in trays; and the attitude of the staff is to help shoppers choose what they want to eat rather than assuming they know the names of particular cuts of meat. For people who don't want to cook, they do ready-meals that are genuinely delicious and contain high-welfare meat.

With the help of four of their network of family farms, Pipers Farm rears 7500 birds a year. This is a fraction of what a single industrial shed produces in just six weeks, but it contributes towards allowing the small family farms of mid-Devon to survive using traditional methods of animal husbandry. Such businesses have been going to the wall over the last decade; this banding together into a bigger unit is the only route to go down if they are to survive. Pipers Farm is about the whole independent network, which is why their feed millers are included on the website, as well as profiles of some of the farmers. If you are concerned about the way small, independent operations are disappearing, to be replaced by ever-bigger, more powerful and less sympathetic corporations, you have an added incentive to buy not just happy chickens but also independent ones.

Pipers Farm, like Richard Guy's Real Meat Company, believes it is important to sell other than through the supermarkets. Richard says he has seen too many people expand to supply big chains and then run into problems. Peter likens his business to a small craft at sea running alongside the super-tankers of the supermarkets. But he knows that what he lacks in size can be compensated for by being a different sort of operation altogether. 'Price will always be a very key factor,' he says, referring to super-markets and their meat sales. 'Since my father pioneered broiler chicken farming, it has relentlessly developed to get a lower and lower unit cost. That's the way the poultry industry has gone and there's no reason why anyone in the high street should want to, or can, take a stand.' He thinks higher-welfare chickens, sold through supermarkets, will suffer the same ruthless downward pressure on price. But the squeezing of margins matters with animals. He says, 'Whereas you can process potatoes in an ever-bigger factory to make crisps, if you do that with livestock there are very big implications.' From his point of view, the big difference is between an operation motivated by the bottom line and one that has quality as its guiding light.

Peter hopes that Pipers Farm can demonstrate how smaller rural businesses can band together to survive the pressures of international cheap food. 'We've come up with a model that is commercially workable,' he says. 'It could probably be done in any part of the country and sustain the local farming community.' The crucial question is whether consumers are motivated to shop at independents. He says, 'You have to start with taking cash in the high street, and it's a fiendishly competitive place. If you can do that, it's exciting.' The Pipers Farm shop is situated in Magdalen Road in Exeter, a place with a full range of small, high-quality independents including a fishmonger, a greengrocer and a baker. They too have banded together, for example organizing community events, and the street is not only surviving but thriving. There are far more independents about than you might think once you start to look around. It is a viable and rewarding way to shop, if you choose to make this a priority. It may be for an occasional shopping trip for high-quality meat, or for more goods, more regularly. The effort is rewarded immediately – with good food.

But the battle for higher welfare must also be fought in larger systems. I wanted to see a farm that did supply a supermarket, as well as selling independently.

Sheepdrove Farm produces around two thousand chickens a week, selling a number of them through selected branches of Waitrose as well as through other shops, their own two outlets in Bristol and Maida Vale in London, by telephone through a box scheme, and by on-line sales. This mixed organic farm is set in the wide-open expanses of the Berkshire Downs. Driving here, past the horse-racing village of Lambourn and into an almost prairie-like landscape, you feel up, up and away in another world. Sheepdrove is a special place, where rare birds of prey suddenly appear, or works of art: metal sheep; a wooden chicken perched on top of a sheep on top of a pig on top of a cow, like a rural totem pole. When Peter and Juliet Kindersley bought a farmhouse here in the 1970s, the tides of agrichemical cereal fields washed up to their garden fence. As Peter made money through his publishing company, Dorling Kindersley, they bought up the land and began farming it themselves organically. When DK was sold, the couple committed more fully to the farm. They are using their resources to make progress in the organic movement, not least in the world of chickens.

I was shown round Sheepdrove by Andrew Gunther, an organic farmer working with the Kindersleys who also had his own organic broiler flock in Devon. An energetic West Countryman, Andrew has a buoyant bearing not unlike a cockerel, and talks a lot, with vigour and pride – and with disgust at the iniquities of bad chicken production. He had been thrown out of his local supermarket for collaring fellow shoppers to show them the breast-blisters and hock burns on poorly-produced birds.

Sheepdrove is a showpiece organic farm, and a questing one. The Kindersleys are constantly trying to drive up their own standards; to be, as the phrase goes, 'organic and beyond'. The chickens are kept in a system which is attracting more and more interest: agroforestry. Chickens, descended from jungle fowl, are at their happiest near trees which provide them with the same sort of protective shelter that their forebears got from the jungle canopy. Such foliage also attracts the sort of insects they like to eat. There are other eco-features at Sheepdrove. The chicken house feeders are powered by solar panels, and the pasture is sown with herbs and grasses that provide the birds with more good food and insects. The plants are also carefully chosen to build up the chickens' immunity. The Kindersleys are fans of Cindy Engel's book *Wild Health*, which explains how animals self-medicate, and she has acted as a consultant to them. Next to each chicken shed is a dust-bathing area that allows the birds to have a good old wriggle to clean their feathers, unbothered by rain. The birds were kept in groups of a thousand but this number was shortly to go down to five hundred. They live for twelve weeks. A $2\frac{1}{2}$ kg bird costs £16 at the on-line shop.

As Andrew showed me around, he explained that he farmed in an organic system principally for the high standards of animal welfare. He feels the movement as a whole helps people appreciate what they eat. 'Everybody has to understand the full story behind their food. They need to know where it's from, and what it has cost an animal to give it to you,' he says. He was vociferous when asked about bad chicken farmers. 'I think they are a disgrace,' he said. 'Not all conventional farmers do this – don't get me wrong – but there are a number that have no respect for the animals. If you were a furniture manufacturer, and halfway through producing something you beat it and abused it and put dents in it, and then you tried to sell it, nobody would buy it. But farmers do that to animals, and people still buy the meat because they can hide it.'

Good chicken farming, Andrew explained, was a matter of putting good welfare into practice through attention to detail. I saw how the young chicks at Sheepdrove are encouraged to range by putting corrugated paper on the floor leading up to the feeders; they like the noise it makes. For the same reason crackly plastic containers, the sort used by the fruit trade to store satsumas, hold the birds' water. Noises from the farm – cuckoos, tractors – were being played into the sheds with the aim of making the birds' transition to the bigger sheds out in the fields less stressful. Stress is a big issue in any farming system where as little medication as possible is used and you need healthy birds. 'At this stage of the game,' said Andrew, surveying a roomful of scurrying chicks, 'we are building this immune system for life. We've got a baby with a very low immune system and we're going to take it to a place where it needs a good strong immune system.'

After seeing the birds, we went for lunch with the boss. Roast chicken was on the menu. The browned bird came out of the Aga with a great waft of the herbs stuffed into it. The Kindersleys had just bought Neal's Yard Pharmacy; there was already some herbal and organic-meat synergy going on. Little beads of fat slid quietly over the bird's thighs. The chicken was carved in a French manner, into three large pieces per side, which were then divided into juicy chunks. It was one of the most delicious chickens I have ever eaten. Alongside the Real Meat and Pipers Farm birds, it showed just how good meat could taste when it came from animals that had been respected and well farmed. The chickens from all three farms provided a totally different experience from eating a mass-produced broiler. It would be hard to compare the two types by price because they were so dissimilar.

Juliet Kindersley takes a particular interest in Sheepdrove's chickens because she keeps a small number herself. She watches her own birds and notices their natural behaviour every day. She sees, for example, how they compensate for the wind in this high spot by taking a certain direction as they set out across the yard. Juliet's viewpoint is that of someone who loves chickens and wants them to live as naturally as possible. She wants to scale this up to supply a

growing market with a top-class bird, but without com-
promising her original standpoint. Furthermore, she is an
artist, who, for all the gentleness of her manner, also has
the determination of someone with a personal vision that
must be fulfilled, whatever anyone else says. Right from the
start she was determined that the birds should have somewhere to perch, as in nature. This was not orthodox at the
time. Even in the farm's brooder houses, before the birds go
outdoors the chicks hop on and off the perches provided.

When Juliet started chicken farming at Sheepdrove it was
in order to earn regular money, in the time-honoured
fashion of women on farms finding weekly cash for the
household budget. I was struck by how many of the people
involved with the chickens here were women: the henwives
of yore had found a twenty-first-century reincarnation. It
was particularly surprising to be shown around the small
on-farm slaughterhouse and processing plant (the chickens
have the shortest possible final journey) by a woman in her
thirties with kind brown eyes, who was in charge. It was as
if she were taking a prospective parent around a nursery.
Then there was Nancy, the skilful cook at the Sheepdrove
conference centre. She serves the meat to conference-goers,
who are often people with no interest in organics who had
come to this farm in the hills for other reasons. As if by
accident, they start to learn what the movement is all about.
There is little mention of the farming system, but at lunch
Nancy speaks briefly on what they are about to eat: a
secular, organic grace. Even the person who organizes the
catching of the chickens is a woman, who Andrew describes
as a matriarch. She has the respect of her team and doesn't
need aggression or domination to get this difficult job done.
As a result there is very little damage to the birds. On the
worst systems, Andrew says, this can be up to 15 per cent.

He is constantly measuring. Conventional systems have a great deal of science behind them – the chicken was the first animal to have its genome sequenced – but the work has focused almost entirely on intensive systems. It is crucial to conduct the research that will improve these extensive ones. This is part of Sheepdrove's mission, and the Kindersleys are involved in the work of Elm Farm Research Centre which is currently experimenting with a mixed-age flock, putting chicks in with older birds as would happen in nature.

As we sat eating a Sheepdrove chicken, Andrew made a point I will never forget. A bird, he said, is not an easy animal to farm well. Despite the fact that we have found ways of shutting tens of thousands of them in sheds and making them grow quickly, it is still difficult to raise them properly with respect to their nature. This was why chicken was for so long a seasonal treat rather than a commodity meat. When you eat a chicken, it should be special. It should be the culmination of a way of farming that treats the bird with respect; and since this is difficult to do, it should make the bird even more special.

A number of people react to the issues of intensive chicken farming by saying they will eat pheasant, or guineafowl, or another kind of meat altogether. A better way forward is to eat better chicken and to reclaim it as a quality meat. The three systems I visited produced good chickens, and they did so with an underlying sense of decency. You are not just buying delicious food when you get this sort of happy chicken; you are supporting a better way of life, for people as well as for birds.

My own bias is towards trusting and supporting the individual rather than just relying on a welfare category. This is not the only way to make improvements. At any level – even for basic broilers – there can be steps forward in the way the chickens are produced. It is up to the individual to decide what to support. I tend to buy a local chicken in a local shop or farmers' market. Once you decide that this sort of food is a priority and get hooked into the local network, it can be as simple as buying meat from a butcher rather than a supermarket. If I were to get a chicken from a shop I did not trust and where I had no knowledge of the producers, I would go for a Soil Association-certified organic bird, though sadly these are not as widely available as I would like them to be. They have the highest standards on paper as far as organic chicken production is concerned. The principles of organic farming – of good welfare, sustainability and quality – are admirable. The Soil Association has done much to push food issues to the fore for six decades.

There is a certain amount of controversy about organic chicken. At the start of 2006, I witnessed a heated debate at the Soil Association's annual conference in a seminar on the Sustainable Chicken. A chicken farmer had brought in one of the Association's organic birds which he had bought in a supermarket; it had hock burns and breast blisters, indicating poor welfare. The farmer complained that, in the interests of supplying a booming market, the organic movement was allowing too many exceptions to their standards. This is not what consumers expect, he continued, as they pay for their premium bird. People have a mental image of chickens roaming free amongst wild herbs and grasses, and this was not necessarily what they were getting.

I've been impressed by the Soil Association organic farmers I have met over the years, and the chickens I bought from them did fit into what I would picture as being free-range. But as the movement has expanded, it is bound to have included people who are farming for a premium and following the letter of the law rather than its spirit. This means that the rules are increasingly important. The Soil Association's standards are getting more rigorous in respect of the way chickens must be farmed. They insist on smaller flocks than the other two big organic certifiers. They don't want chickens to be kept in groups of more than five hundred unless there are special conditions, and will not certify any flocks of over two thousand for layers and one thousand for meat birds. Other non-Soil Association organic birds can be kept in flocks as big as twelve thousand. The birds must be kept for at least eighty-one days (eleven and a half weeks). There are rules for feed, stocking density, housing conditions and lighting that enable the birds to live in a much more natural environment. A number of organic farmers will kill their own birds or put them through a small-scale slaughterhouse. In larger systems there should be less of an issue about birds being shackled, at least as regards leg disorders, since the birds are slower-growers with fewer problems of this kind. However, I personally feel that when it comes to killing small and personal is the best option.

There is an openness about the Soil Association and, being open to scrutiny, it should make the effort to keep standards high. It has a reputation and a founding ethos to maintain. The hoo-ha at the Sustainable Chicken seminar did, however, make me return to Richard Guy's words about standards. However high they are, the individual is always important. But it is useful to have a higher-welfare label as widely available as possible, so it is very much to be hoped that the individual members are truly committed. Since it is harder to be a Soil Association producer than to be any other kind of organic farmer, it is likely that the members would care.

There are chickens reared to other welfare standards, for example the RSPCA's Freedom Food label. Around 1.7 per cent of the broilers raised in the UK are under this scheme. This may not sound like many, but it is still a sizeable number of birds per year: 14 million. The stocking density is lower than the industry norm – fifteen birds per square metre as opposed to nineteen – and they are killed at fifty days compared to thirty-nine or so. This slower growth means they suffer fewer leg disorders and less incidence of hock burn and other related problems. The RSPCA says the chickens are 70 per cent less likely to arrive dead at the slaughterhouse and less likely to be rejected once they arrive. It is progress; you may choose to spend more money to take this progress further.

In France, around 30 per cent of whole fresh chickens are higher-welfare. We lag far behind. Supermarkets are starting to sell slower-growing chickens, and labelling them as such. This is a step in the right direction. The general industry standard is represented by the Assured Chicken Production scheme. This covers nearly all the chicken producers in the UK. The organization states: 'Standards have been written to include best practice in food safety, bird health, welfare and traceability.' The UK industry has made some improvements; the issues surrounding such large-scale changes are discussed in the next chapter.

Chicken welfare expert Dr Michael Appleby, having returned to Europe from the United States to work with the World Society for the Protection of Animals, says he has seen some improvements in the US egg-layer industry but fewer in the case of broiler production. In the UK, he believes, there has been a change of attitude towards farm welfare. 'Instead of never even raising the issue of welfare, and seeing it as an insult when that happened, the chicken industry has taken it on board and that pervades the atmosphere and has a day-to-day impact,' he says. There is better air quality, litter quality and management. There has been the step back from the use of antibiotics. The use of almost constant lighting has been reduced. The two greatest hurdles, Dr Appleby feels, remain the selection for heavy growth and the associated lameness, and the problems of the broiler breeders, in particular the feed restriction. The industry says that the birds keep growing so the birds cannot be said to be starved, but it is the way in which the birds are limited in their feeding which welfare scientists find unacceptable.

These problems are especially serious because of the sheer quantities of chickens we eat. In America, where Dr Appleby was working for the Humane Society of the United States, 98 per cent of the animals killed for meat are chickens – more than 8 billion each year. 'Quite apart from the problems that afflict them all, if there is a problem affecting just a proportion, such as when they don't get their neck cut properly, or they are shackled improperly, or have leg problems, then the numbers are mind-boggling. If you get to know one or two chickens well, you know that they can be, given the right conditions, charming, delightful, flexible animals. And then you think about these numbers worldwide and it is very difficult to take on board.'

Happy Chickens

It is the producers of the happy chickens who are at the top end of a trend that is set to make the most significant difference to individual birds. How big a difference, overall, depends on how we choose to spend our money.

The Bird Explorers

In a farm in England in the 1930s, a four-year-old child crept into a hen-house. She wanted to know how such a large egg could come out of a chicken. Curious and patient, the girl waited and waited. Outside, the household was going frantic with worry. The police were called. Where was she? Four hours later the little girl emerged covered in chicken mess. Her mother listened to the story of how a hen lays an egg, understood and forgave: the child was following a passionate interest in the natural world. She went on to become the world-famous primatologist Jane Goodall.

Ethology, the study of animal behaviour, is a science with a Dr Dolittle desire to 'talk to the animals'; or rather that they should talk to us. Its practical cutting edge is working out how such knowledge can be applied to day-to-day farming. This intriguing branch of zoology is starting to have a significant impact on the lives of many millions of chickens. There are many food heroes amongst the farmers and meat sellers in this book; the welfare scientists certainly also deserve this title. Largely unknown to most consumers, they have the potential to make real progress in stopping the worst cruelties of the factory farming system. Once there is proof, written down in calm black and white, that animals are suffering, it should – sooner or later – be harder for the industry and politicians to ignore the problems. And these scientists can find positive ways forward to bring animal welfare into farming.

I heard Jane Goodall relate her hen story as part of the keynote speech of a two-day international conference on animal sentience organized by Compassion in World Farming. The philosopher Jeremy Bentham laid one of the foundation stones of the animal welfare and rights movement when he wrote, in *An Introduction to the Principles of Morals and Legislation* (1781): 'The question is not, "Can they reason?" nor, "Can they talk?" but, "Can they suffer?".' The hall was packed with people from all over the world responding to this question. At one extreme was the animal rights philosopher Tom Regan, whose rallying cry was that all creatures were 'subject of a life'. Each chicken – all the billions of birds farmed every day – are individuals. If you see an animal in that light, your moral position can no longer be based just on economics. At the other end of the food politics scale was a man from McDonald's who stepped up with the unenviable task of being his company's mouthpiece in front of this audience. He talked about the corporation's conversion – in the UK, at least – to free-range eggs. As he sat down, with the prospect of questions to come, I checked out his body language; the poor man was practically eating his lips.

In the audience was a flock of bird explorers – scientists

who were discovering what made a chicken a chicken. Whilst they had a wide range of styles, all of them were 'for the animals'. They knew their work was breaking new ground; many felt the study of animal sentience was one of the most exciting and important in the whole of biology. Marian Stamp Dawkins, a leading chicken explorer at Oxford University, emphasized how important it was to try to explore the issues from the animals' perspective rather than just make changes to make ourselves feel better. How do you discover what an animal really feels or thinks? she asked. She has developed the use of 'consumer demand' tests, for example weighted doors to see how hard a hen will push for a nesting box. Other techniques include brain scans and measuring hormonal changes and non-invasive techniques such as observational learning through CCTV cameras and video. Irene Pepperberg from the psychology department of an American university spoke of her grey parrot, Alex, who she believed had the intelligence of a four- to six-year-old human child. She had developed a computer program called 'The Beakster' to stimulate his brain. In the audience was Peter Kindersley, owner of the organic operation Sheepdrove Farm, who was wondering if such a device could work with his chickens. It was after hearing this level of interest that I decided to go and see his farm.

Some of the findings of these bird explorers were counter-intuitive. For example, studies had shown that free-range hens could have problems with aggression. This was hardly 'welfare friendly'. But was this down to a system that needed fine-tuning rather than any inherent issues with free-range flocks? This was new territory. Most agricultural research money goes into establishing large-scale farming systems such as battery cages. The growing consideration of the chickens' welfare now gave a different slant to the whole picture. A number of the scientists in the hall admitted, also, the limitations of science. Peter Sandøe from the Royal Veterinary and Agricultural University in Denmark remarked that many scientists were enormously good at looking through very small windows; a neat encapsulation of the skills and limitations of this perspective.

There were other views in the conference hall. In the first session of the first day I happened to be sitting next to a broiler industry vet, one of a number of industry representatives from the USA. It was interesting that such people felt the need to attend. The recent progress of animal welfare in the USA meant that big money had to listen. I asked the vet about heart disease in chickens. 'It's like this room,' he said, waving his hand at the assembled crowd now filtering out of the hall for a mid-morning coffee break. 'Some people here will have heart attacks.' This struck me as disingenuous. The point that animal welfare groups make is that the modern broiler bird has been specifically bred and fed and kept in conditions to make it grow as big as possible in as short a time as possible, and that this can have an appalling effect on the bird's health.

Key studies done by bird explorers demonstrate the extent of the problems of fast growth. Important amongst them were studies led by Steve Kestin of Bristol University's School of Veterinary Science and published in 1992 and 2001. One showed that around 25 per cent of the most common heavy strains of broiler chicken had moderate or severe lameness as they approached their slaughter weight. This means the bird is so disabled that it will sit down even on filthy wet litter and get corrosive burns on its leg joints and breast; that it can get the hock burns and breast blisters you see on whole cheap chicken in the supermarket.

Right on the front line of current chicken research is Dr Sue Haslam in the same department of Bristol University. She has worked on chickens since 1999, and since 2003 has gone into two hundred intensive chicken farms for a new study on leg disorders. Her painstaking work is the scientific front line in an industry worth many millions of pounds.

At each farm, Sue and her fellow bird explorers took into the sheds a plastic catching pen that was hinged at one end to let the chickens in. A computer picks out ten spots where they should place the pen in order to get a random sample of what is going on. Then one person encourages the chickens to walk, using a cane, while the other person writes down a number for the bird's mobility, in a process of 'gait-scoring'. This is what the scores mean. Zero: the bird walks as it would in a farmyard, with a normal stance and furling its toes up when it lifts its feet. One: the bird doesn't look quite normal. The stride is slightly shorter than usual and there is a slightly widened stance. Two: there is a marked impairment of walking. The bird is definitely lame. It has high, goose-like steps, a widened stance and shortened pace. Three: the bird is seriously lame and will only walk if pushed to do so. Four: the bird is staggering. Five: it is immobile.

The results of the study have now been published (see p. 37) and show that the leg health problems remain. A shocking percentage of birds are suffering at the end of their life because of fast growth and heavy weight. Critics say crowded houses and breed are part of the issue; slower growth or earlier slaughter would reduce the problem.

Dr Haslam commends the mainstream chicken broiler

industry for their part in the study and their desire to make progress. Although, she says, there are some cowboys in the broiler business – she estimated around 10 per cent at the lower end of the quality scale – most of the relevant businesses wanted improvements and cooperated with her work. 'They have a genuine desire to solve the problems,' she said. 'Ten years ago it would never have happened. If we could make sure they weren't competing with outside markets, they would do whatever they could.' Here again is a major obstacle to progress: imports. Intensive chicken farmers are between a rock and a hard place, she believes. Both are made of the same material: money.

Some see economics as no excuse. I went to see Sue's colleague, one of the most respected and also the most outspoken of the bird explorers, John Webster, emeritus Professor of Animal Husbandry at Bristol University. He had recently retired after a career devoted to making practical improvements to the lives of farm animals. As well as his work at Bristol, he served on an important advisory board to the government, the Farm Animal Welfare Council or FAWC. Whilst choosing his words with great care, and always on the solid ground of scientific proof, John Webster has never shied away from publicly criticizing the industry. He does not mince his words, not least on the plight of the broiler. Now he's getting impatient with the rate of change. He was to be especially outspoken about the relationship between science and government in this respect.

When John Webster greeted me at the door of his West

Country house. I was immediately struck by his head of bright white hair, of the sort of purity of colour that might be found in a picture of Father Christmas or St Nicholas. But far from being an ethereal storybook saint he reminded me of the type of forthright, four-square Englishmen you find in the eighteenth-century novels of Henry Fielding. Beneath the hair were a strong set of features: a determined chin, a slightly hawkish nose, a focused pair of eyes and a quick, careful and direct mouth. It is a mouth the industry has learnt to be wary of. The sort of comment he makes is that the plight of the fast-growing broiler was 'the single most severe, systematic example of man's inhumanity to another sentient animal.' Strong stuff. After reading pronouncements of this nature in his first, ground-breaking book, *A Cool Eye Towards Eden*, a food business wrote to the vice-chancellor of Bristol University advising that if this outspoken professor didn't shut up they would withdraw funding from the university and advise the government to do the same. The veterinary professor's response was to say he was happy to go public about such blackmail.

In 2005, John Webster followed up with an important second book about animal welfare, *Limping Towards Eden*. Eden is irretrievable, he writes; but what we can do is make progress towards it. When it comes to broilers, I asked him, how far have we limped? 'Nowhere,' he said. 'Or almost nowhere. There are certain companies that are doing it better than others, but at the moment there's not much incentive for that because there's no real reward for doing things better. There is overwhelming evidence that the birds are suffering the physical and emotional consequences of chronic pain for a third of their lives. Still. As yet, there is no published information to show that any success has been achieved in this regard. The industry has claimed success. But the information is not on the record.' Subsequent to our conversation the government-funded report on which Dr Sue Haslam worked was published, showing that the problem of leg disorders was indeed a continuing one.

Although improvements can be made by feeding the birds less and keeping them in better conditions, the main issue is the fact that birds have been bred to be, as John Webster put it, 'pathologically greedy' in order to put on weight fast. When I mentioned the hock burn I regularly see on cheap chicken counters in supermarkets and in low-grade butchers he replied, 'Yes. And remember these are the ones coming in whole. Think of all the ones that are coming in parts. They are very much the ones that they really can't put on the shelf as whole birds.' In a 2005 *Dispatches* programme Professor Donald Broom from the Department of Veterinary Medicine at the University of Cambridge went to the high street to make a random check of chickens on shelves. Hock burn was common. Whilst some companies may be making progress, the evidence of the unacceptable is there for us all to see. Unless, of course, it has been cut off a chicken piece. How can the public be sure that the bird they are eating has not suffered?

What is needed to raise the industry standards as a whole, Professor Webster thinks, is a properly audited welfare system that has some real worth. He would like to see the farmers annually assessing the condition of their own birds, based on such statistics as the amount of hock burn, foot burn and breast burn ('welfare outputs') rather than relying on mere figures about stocking density ('welfare inputs') that may or may not improve the lives of the birds. All this would then be checked up on by visiting, independent auditors. The importance of the initial self-assessment is to get the farmers to examine what they are doing themselves rather than passively accepting an inspector and getting a piece of paper that can be filed away for the rest of the year. If what they are doing proves to be not up to scratch, the assessor would discover what they are doing to deal with the situation. If this proves satisfactory, the farmer can stay in the system. By these means a 'virtuous circle' of improvement is created, consumers get a guarantee of genuine welfare and any chicken bearing this welfare mark would be able to set itself apart from the bog-standard.

As it happens, some progress is being made in this direction, though not through getting farmers themselves involved in the assessing. The new EU broiler directive plans to make assessments by measuring 'welfare output' such as rates of foot burn that can be measured in the processing plants. If companies want to stock at higher densities, they will only be allowed to do so if their birds do not have such quantifiable problems. But will this solve the situation? Sue Haslam thinks it will weed out the cowboys. However, there are also concerns there will be ways to get around the measurements. For example, there is a generous allowance proposed for birds arriving at the slaughterhouse 'dead on arrival', as the phrase goes – even higher than the 3 per cent maximum permitted mortality in the sheds (this equals more than 25 million birds a year). Farmers could decide not to kill lame birds, which would spoil their on-farm statistics, and instead let them travel in pain to the slaughterhouse. The chicken would pay the price for the massaging of statistics.

Having seen what the scientists at Bristol University and elsewhere were up to, I became interested in the practicalities of this front line of science. How did people get into it, and what was it like trying to make a difference in this way?

Dr Joy Mench is a chicken specialist at the University of California at the Davis campus, one of the many American academic institutions set up specifically to promote agriculture. Dr Mench learnt her trade in Britain, at the University of Sussex, and was originally going to study songbirds. When she realized this would mean standing around at 4a.m. in the middle of winter in the mud and rain, feeling like an academic version of a twitcher, she switched courses and never looked back.

By a stroke of luck, the year Joy Mench graduated, 1982, was the first year in which the American government funded ten grants to study farm animal welfare. Farm animal legislation was being enacted in Europe; the Americans too were now starting to take the whole area of welfare more seriously. She went to Cornell to look at laying hens in different housing systems, having got her PhD studying the way the two halves of a chick's brain work. She then got the first faculty position in animal welfare in the USA, at the University of Maryland, to study poultry right in the heart of the broiler-belt. 'It was a real eye-opener for me that I could use my knowledge in a very practical way to improve farm animal welfare by studying behaviour,' she said. 'And I like chickens.'

Here and in her present job in California, another big chicken-farming state, she looks at such issues as the forced moulting of egg layers. Hens, like all birds, shed their feathers once a year. At this time they do not lay eggs:

from the point of view of bald economics, they are wasting time. The standard practice in the USA, though now banned in Europe, is to stop feeding and change the light levels in the houses so that the hens moult more quickly and get back into production. Dr Mench is working with the industry to find different ways to achieve this end, for example by supplying feed that is lower in nutrient density rather than withdrawing feed altogether. Four years down the line, the new methods have been tried out successfully on a large scale.

What was it like working with a vast industry which had a clear economic bias? Joy Mench's response shows chicken farmers in a human light. 'Farmers are very conservative people in the sense that a lot of the things they do have developed over years of practical experience. They don't want to change these things because they are afraid that if they change, something bad is going to happen. The way to address this is to show them that something different will have positive effects. I don't think it even has to be an economically positive effect. I think that's really powerful. The producers I've talked to are really delighted they have lower mortality in their birds, even if that doesn't mean overall they are going to get an extra six cents per dozen on their eggs. They are concerned about animal health as well. They are afraid, I think justifiably, to change things that they think are making them successful.'

As regards broiler birds, she agrees that the rate of growth is a huge battleground, and points out that it is not all down to the breed: another factor, for example, is how much the birds are fed in order to make them grow as fast as possible. She is working on a major study on the way lighting in the broiler houses affects the birds. The industry tends to keep the lights on to get the birds to eat more and grow more quickly. She is concerned that having no darkness, or very little, means that the birds cannot sleep properly, which has welfare implications.

Since Dr Mench is a chicken expert, I thought it appropriate to ask her view on the common conception that chickens are bird-brained. She gave our lunch table a firm tap with both hands. 'Chickens are absolutely not stupid,' she said, fixing me with her steady eyes. 'I get very annoyed about these remarks. Of course everybody thinks that dogs and cats are absolutely brilliant, but in general people tend to think that [farm] animals are stupid – sheep are stupid, goats are stupid, cows are stupid – it's not just chickens. That may be based a bit on our discomfort about the way we interact and use them. There may be a bit of distancing there. But chickens have very complex behaviours. They have very distinctive individual personalities. As soon as you spend some time with them, you can easily distinguish them.' She cited an anecdotal example of how a chicken in her lab flock showed intelligence. One bird would watch her break eggs against the edge of the pen (chickens like eating eggs). The hen started to do this herself, kicking the eggs three or four times against the pen in order to crack them. In the jargon of ethology, she had done a bit of 'observational learning', one indication that birds can think.

Clearly the study of birds' cognition, and a recognition of their characters and individuality, is not being done so that the farmer can go into his shed and call all twenty-five thousand of his birds individually to dinner at their own named place mats. The bird explorers work by boosting our recognition of and respect for the chicken's natural instincts and behaviour. Chicken is not some anonymous white substance that just appears on our plate; it has been a creature. This is an important step forward in how we see farmed animals. Some may say that what the scientists are proving is common sense. But proof is a weapon for change – or should be.

One of the most interesting places I discovered in pursuit of answers to the plight of the broiler was an operation in Oxfordshire. Its difference was marked in its very name: the Food Animal Initiative. The creatures were going to be food and the consumer part of the equation. The organization is also an interface between large-scale farming and welfare science. I met one of the directors, Paul Cook, at what used to be Oxford University's experimental farm. The unit still houses the queen of chicken experts, Professor Marian Dawkins, whom I had heard talk at the CIWF conference. FAI comes up with farming systems that incorporate welfare and Marian Dawkins, five doors down the corridor, can check them out in detail. In turn, she can get postgraduate students to do three- or six-month starter experiments to check out other avenues of improving the birds' lives at a practical farming level.

'What we try to do is to go back to where the chicken originally came from,' explained Paul. 'It has come from the jungles of south-east Asia. It'll have been on a fairly consistent twelve-hour day-length. It'll have been on a relatively high humidity. Marian Dawkins spent quite a lot of time studying them there and it was apparent that they tend to feed in the morning, then probably rest during the day, then feed again at night and use their crops to store food. We can't go and re-create a Thai jungle here in

Oxford but, thinking about the origins of the chicken, we can then start relating that to how they have been farmed commercially.'

Progress had already been made. Ten years ago, farms in the UK tended to keep the birds in almost constant light in order to make them feed continuously and grow fast. Paul went on, 'You were putting a chicken that was emerging from the egg expecting to find itself in an environment similar to that of its ancestors, and it was going into something where the lights are on for perhaps twenty-three hours a day.' Reducing 'daylight' hours, as the industry has generally – but by no means entirely – done, didn't cause productivity to go down. The birds learnt in the first few weeks of life to fill their crops ready for the night, rather than eating all day long, which is not what their bodies were designed to do. This promoted better leg health.

The next step was to simulate dawn and dusk in the artificial context of a broiler house. Standard practice has been to turn the lights off abruptly. Paul said, 'If you just switch the lights off at night you can hear them calling, which to us sounded as if they were quite stressed. Whereas if you use the dimming technology, they behave very differently. As soon as the lights started to dim they went and found a place to settle down, and then the lights went out and there was silence.' This had an immediate impact on welfare, and therefore also on economics. The problem of 'flip-overs', heart failure of the best-performing male chickens, disappeared overnight. 'It became very apparent that as you improved the conditions of the bird, they actually performed better. Maybe fewer died, they were perhaps better-quality when you'd finished. They were paying you back, if you like, for any investment that was there.'

FAI has also successfully experimented with going 'back to the jungle' by putting free-range chicken houses in the middle of woodland. They discovered that the birds ranged better when there was cover from predators. It makes sense; and after being proved in a place like this it can become widespread industry practice. FAI had a product called Pine Chicken, a sylvan acronym of Poultry in Natural Environments. Tesco, core funders of FAI along with McDonald's, has put the idea into practice on all its free-range farms.

Paul Cook and one of the other directors of FAI come from the chicken industry. This is why they are trying to produce tried and tested systems rather than throwing a small piece of research into an academic debate. Cook used to be in charge of the technical management of a production line of 1.2 million birds per week. He says, 'You can make a small difference to huge numbers of chickens as opposed to a huge difference to a small number of chickens. You can save birds out of battery cages and things like that, which is excellent work. But if you can make a small change with humidity or dawn-dusk dimming, then fantastic. We've probably made quite an effect.'

I went to see the broiler houses. The organic birds were kept inside for the first third of their life, as is common in free-range systems because it gives the birds a good, safe start. Paul explained that when the young birds are not crowded and stressed they seem to go on to have fewer health problems throughout their lives. The birds that were nearly ready for the market were of a slow-growing type, kept for twice as long as standard broilers, and their legs were as strong as they should be. Some had jumped on to the feeding lines inside; at this stage in an intensive non-range system the birds would be sitting down for most of the time. These birds ranged as much as they wanted.

For all its promise and success, I could see that work by FAI and other such groups would come up against the obstacle of scale. There was work the Oxfordshire group wanted to do, particularly involving processing, that couldn't get very far while the mainstream flowed in another direction. Paul said they were interested in the hanging of chicken meat to improve their flavour. This would certainly be of interest to consumers and would help differentiate birds from higher-welfare systems by emphasizing the point that better welfare means tastier meat. He was also interested in a method of stunning the birds without putting them upside-down in shackles. Such work used to be undertaken by Silsoe Agricultural Research Station, a government-funded operation; but Silsoe has now been closed. Government research money today is directed more into biotech. FAI hopes to be able to get funding to continue these worthwhile lines of enquiry. But nearly all chicken processing is done on such a big scale that making changes is almost impossible. Would there ever be the market to push such places towards higher-quality chicken? How can such consumer demand be increased without providing a substantial amount of such meat in the first place?

There are other reasons why higher welfare standards for chickens have not progressed as quickly as they might have done. John Webster is perhaps more outspoken than he was before retirement about one such obstacle to change. He believes there is an unholy alliance between scientists and government. There is, he says, a syndrome that goes like this: scientists get a research grant, then say, broadly speaking: 'Considerable further research is needed in this area. We're reluctant to make any conclusions until you've given us another half a million.' The government can then say they are spending millions of pounds on broiler research and that they are awaiting the advice of their scientists, rather than actually doing something to stop what is already known to be a problem. The scientists, meanwhile, can continue their work without ruffling too many feathers. And so the buck shuttles between the two; and the birds continue to suffer.

'I'm getting too old. I want to see more action,' says John Webster. 'Of course we can continue to learn more about the animals that we use for whatever purpose. And so we should. But we must not let this desire for further and better particulars to be used as a delaying tactic. There are plenty of things that could be done now. This scientific caution should not be allowed to delay action in relation to things that are palpably unfair on the basis of the existing evidence.' In other words, politicians duck behind the science. But Webster points out that the same evidence can be reviewed by different governments who come to different conclusions. Sow stalls, which confine pregnant sows so severely that they can do no more than stand up or lie down (they cannot even turn round), have been banned in Europe but remain in the USA and Australia despite their governments having considered the evidence of the same welfare papers. He says, 'We have to get round this argument that science can answer everything. It can't. It can inform, but it can't answer. We have to accept that these are value judgements and get the politicians to admit that.'

So what are our values here in Britain? We have fast food. We have fast-growing birds. How about fast progress on welfare? Whilst the bird explorers will continue to make steady progress and put their points in black and white, it is absolutely crucial that we, the public, know what is happening and get impatient. Public anger at the miserable situation could translate into politicians forcing the rate of improvement in the broiler industry, for example by imposing a meaningful welfare scheme. They could tackle the main issue of leg weakness in fast-grown birds simply by making it illegal to farm such birds. John Webster believes this could be done under animal welfare legislation. 'The biggest of all problems is birds that are not fit for purpose,' he says. 'They cannot sustain fitness even throughout a life of six weeks. That is the major welfare problem above all else.' Politics is about the values of a society. If we call ourselves a civilized country that cares about animals, this has to include – should especially include – the most numerous of the animals on our plates: the broiler bird.

And once consumers are properly concerned about chicken, a far greater number of us will simply take matters into our own hands and vote with our money. The importance of consumer choice cannot be stressed enough. John Webster points out that, with laying hens, it took fifty years from the Brambell Commission calling for more space for laying hens to European legislation coming up with the goods. In the meantime, shoppers became disgusted by battery cages and changed to buying free-range eggs. This is part of the way forward for broilers, too: people should just go for birds from better systems. The more demand there is, the more the supermarkets will take notice and the more farmers will turn to these systems. Lloyd Maunder, one of the big poultry companies, has already decided to go this way.

A huge push of public pressure is essential for the future

welfare of the broiler chicken. It does not mean giving up meat; it simply means eating better meat, from more humanely reared chickens. And not just the roast chicken for the family, but also the meat in the lunchtime sandwich and the work cafeteria pie.

We do not know – and will never know entirely – exactly how animals feel, nor what they think. But these scientists have gone quite a long way towards showing the way. They have given society guidelines that should be non-negotiable. John Webster came up with the concept of the Five Freedoms for animals: freedom from hunger and thirst; from discomfort; from pain, injury and disease; from fear and distress; and freedom to express natural behaviour. In the *River Cottage Meat Book* Hugh Fearnley-Whittingstall says that in the case of broiler chickens it is more a case of the Five Miseries: 'Hunger and thirst. Discomfort. Pain, injury and disease. Abnormal behaviour. Fear and distress. Stick that on the label of a supermarket chicken and see how it sells.'

One of the most pitiful expressions I learnt in my encounters with the bird explorers was the term 'learned helplessness'. This is the state of a creature that is in a bad situation and knows it can do nothing to help itself. Learned helplessness is one of the definitions of animal suffering. Imagine learned helplessness in a lame dog, or in an infant left in a cot in a Romanian orphanage. It may not be that every single broiler bird suffers like this; but enough do to make changes imperative. Consumers are not in a state of learned helplessness. We have a part to play in halting the runaway use of fast-growing strains of meat chickens. We can do something every time we buy chicken. By choosing more welfare-friendly kinds, we hasten this change. And there is another question. I believe it is important to consider not just what kind of chicken we buy, but where we buy it.

Shopping

Here is a future for food that's far more tempting than the version on offer at the International Poultry Expo. It is January. Cold fog is obscuring one of San Francisco's trademark bridges. But produce is being harvested on California's farms in the countryside beyond: here's the proof at the farmers' market in the Ferry Plaza. There's new-season citrus fruit, as well as last year's dried mandarins which dissolve in your mouth like fairy marmalade. There are stalls piled high with the greens that can grow all year round in this mild climate. Sparkling fresh fish is displayed near to deep red beef. I buy a potato and spinach tamale with spicy tomato sauce from a Mexican food stall for my breakfast, and eat this good, fresh, delicious, healthy food standing before the bridge over the Bay, in the middle of the market, near to the statue of Gandhi, the man who said: 'The greatness of a nation and its moral progress can be judged by the way its animals are treated.' I am here to find chicken and eggs.

Farmers' markets are one of the great hopes for happy chickens, as for all real food. At their best, they offer a different way of shopping from the supermarkets. Buying directly from the producer gives you a better level of knowledge about, and trust in, what you are eating. And this is food that is not available at any price in most chain stores, for the producers who come here are too small and individual to fit into such large-scale systems. Farmers' markets, by being community events with a buzz, act as an enticing shop window for independent food production as a whole. These markets have started to create a stir in Britain, too: in 2006 we had five hundred of them. I wanted to discover what gave the best ones such spirit and substance.

The farmers' market movement began partly in California in the mid-1970s. Small farmers found they were excluded from markets increasingly governed by regulations geared towards industrialized food supply chains. But some producers did not want to churn out standardized goods designed to travel thousands of miles. An unusual pairing of old-fashioned family farmers and back-to-the-land radicals came about via the invention of a different way of selling. It would be a bit of an exaggeration to say that, at the very beginning, these individuals were fly-pitching their harvests; but there was an element of taking matters into their own hands. Such enterprises soon became legal, as local and state governments caught up and saw their function. One wonders if the same would happen today. Our supposedly free-market times are geared more towards the big than the small.

The Ferry Plaza market shows that the movement's

cutting edge is still sharp. At its entrance was a series of billboards, for once not advertising odorized toiletries or processed food. Instead, these hoardings advertised an idea: an A–Z of Sustainable Agriculture. 'F' was for free-range. It was illustrated by a huge picture of some beautiful white chickens, proudly enlarged on their lush, green sward. The words explained the meaning of such creatures, and their opposite: 'Old-fashioned animal husbandry was "free-range". Animals roamed in outside areas and were provided with appropriate shelter, bedding and food. On today's large-scale agribusiness farms, indoor confinement results in poor physical development, high disease and mortality rates, overuse of antibiotics and inhumane practices. Free-range animals produce eggs, meat and milk that are high-quality, healthy and delicious.'

In the market, the people roamed. At this early hour the shoppers were businesslike, and a variety of trolleys shuttled purposefully between stalls. Some people had improvised contraptions that were essentially wire boxes on wheels; others manoeuvred natty 'hook-and-go' operations, with eight metal hooks on a golf-trolley device for hanging bags of milk, vegetables, meat and fish. A constant stream of shoppers flowed towards one particular stall. It wasn't especially glamorous. There were two white plastic tubs on a plastic tablecloth, and a granny-like figure with spectacles and curly grey hair sitting behind it. Her two granddaughters were helping out, lifting orders from a cool-box in the van. This was Mrs Hoffman, with Sada and Teresa, and they were selling chickens. Or more correctly, they had sold out of chickens by 10.10a.m. Market rules state that you must stand by your post until the end, even if you have nothing left to sell. In super-nice California people came and went for the rest of the morning, bearing shopping lists for tonight's supper party, and even though disappointed there was much greeting and how-*are*-you, and even an utterly unironic: 'Sold out. Good stuff.'

I ate Mrs Hoffman's chickens twice at Chez Panisse, the trail-blazing restaurant in nearby Berkeley. Its founder, Alice Waters, is so committed to local food that for many years she employed a dedicated hunter-gatherer to seek out excellent producers as nearby as possible and encourage them to supply what the chefs wanted. Mrs Hoffman and her late husband were raising game for shooting when Chez Panisse came calling for chickens. The resulting white Cornish-Cross birds are fed a natural diet for eight to ten weeks and live in a free-range system. I ate the superb breast of one such chicken in a *pot-au-feu* in the restaurant's set dinner, and the cheaper part of the animal in the café upstairs was equally good in what was described on the menu as Hoffman Farm chicken *alla diavola*. This was a generous joint of the large chicken thigh and wing, cooked slowly on a griddle, weighted down by a heavy pan so the skin crisped while the flesh remained juicy. The taste of this marvellous meat slicked my lips. Chicken fat salves the body as well as the soul. Next to it was a rustic sauce containing egg, bacon and parsley, and the meat had enough black pepper on it to give a fragrant heat. It came with nettles, a currently fashionable green; the vegetable farmer makes more money from nettle tops than from salad leaves. I learnt this gem from the chef; there is continual contact between the kitchen and the growers. Staff take kitchen waste to the farm for compost when they collect the produce. The chefs only write the menus once they discover what is ready to be picked in its prime: the produce is the star.

Back at the market Mrs Hoffman was very much a farmer, keenest to talk about the land. 'If you put your bottom in the ground in California, you'd grow,' was one of her mother's sayings. These days bricks were being planted, and Mrs Hoffman was upset about all the development around her farm. To accommodate the commuter overspill from the Silicon Valley builders were moving into this cheaper area, previously the sort of place where people established community agriculture schemes or just continued doing things the old-fashioned way. Now almond trees were being cut down to make way for houses. Mrs Hoffman felt that all the development was affecting the watertable. The walnut trees on her farm were dying.

After the Chicken Woman, I met the Egg Man. David Evans, from Marin Sun Farm in the acclaimed organic area of Point Race, supplies eggs as well as meat to Chez Panisse. He had another kind of water trouble. A flash-flood of 30 inches of rain had wrecked a brand-new restaurant and butchery. Despite this depressing setback David had made it to the market and was sitting at his stall, keeping out the cold with a black knitted hat that flopped over the back of his head like the French revolutionary bonnet of the *sans culottes*. He was one of many eloquent stall-holders at the market. They are the day-in-day-out educators of people about sustainable food, not least by providing it. Most shoppers who come to Marin Farm's stall have questions – about cooking, about storage. They have come to a good source. David's knowledge derives from the soil upwards, accrued through generations of family farming. His forebears came to Marin county in 1889 from southern Switzerland, bringing their dairy skills to this new land, then getting into beef in the mid-1970s. He started rearing egg-laying hens five years ago and has Rhode Island Reds, the classic egg-producing breed, plus fourteen rare breeds to promote diversity. At this time of year, when the hours of light were fewest, they produced 40 dozen eggs a day. During the longest daylight hours, this figure rose to more like 150 dozen. He does not light artificially. He does not debeak his birds. He does not clip their wings. 'They are full chickens,' he said. 'They are left intact.' The birds are killed by hand to ensure they do not suffer.

David summed up the problems facing the chicken and the egg. 'What's gone wrong is that we want cheap food at all costs,' he said. His eggs sold for $6 a dozen, as opposed to 99 cents. He couldn't supply enough for the demand. Customers loved them. 'They can't get a better egg, so we know we're doing it right,' he said.

As well as talking about welfare, David promotes his eggs and his meat through the positive point of good nutrition. This is a subject increasingly raised by shoppers. A new revolutionary herb had hit Californian consciousness. Grass, said David, is our direct link to solar energy: we should value it and use it as much as possible. His chickens eat plenty of greenery alongside their grains and bugs. I thought again of Harold McGee, writing across the way in Oakland, and his line about the egg being the sun's energy refracted into life. David spoke, too, of another kind of energy. 'After the fossil fuels are gone we'll need to adjust to a more sustainable way of living,' he said. 'We are heading for catastrophe.' It was a note that stuck in my mind. This jolly market was a good place to buy delicious eggs and vibrant greens, but its implications went further than that. By cutting down food miles and selling organic and traditionally grown food, which does not need the fossil fuels in petrochemical fertilizers, its ecological implications spread way beyond the plate.

As we talked, one of the city's hot young chefs came up. Chefs are encouraged to frequent the market. They are given nearby parking and large carts so that they can viably buy in sufficient quantity for their restaurants. Suppliers are increasingly name-tagged on menus. Around fifty chefs take part in an annual September fundraiser, with each of them cooking a three-course meal using market goods. There is a 'shop with a chef' event and there are two teaching kitchens. As a result of all this activity, the city's culinary talent is much in evidence at the market. Chefs and home cooks get inspiration as well as produce here. Crucially, they meet and talk with producers and vice versa. The most difficult and most far-reaching part of change is to get people to talk to each other who normally never meet. At a farmers' market, the consumers, producers and chefs – all part of the same food chain – get together on mutual turf in a natural, regular and useful way.

The Ferry Plaza market was buzzing even in the bleak depths of January. In the height of summer some twenty thousand people a day come to its 120 stalls. The markets are held four days a week between April and November, including a 4p.m.–8p.m. event on Thursdays so that people can shop after work. The Tuesday and Saturday markets run all year round. And this was just one of ten farmers' market sites in the city. In San Francisco, and many other parts of America, people really can do a weekly shop in such places.

But amidst all this good news it was impossible not to notice that both Chicken Woman and Egg Man had sold out. Admittedly this was winter, when the birds were less productive – if left to nature. All the same, finding chicken producers in particular was an issue even at this flagship market. Mrs Hoffman would stop one day; land prices were now so high that it seemed unlikely that her family would continue farming. The people who ran the market were looking for someone to replace her when she eventually packed up. It was hard to find someone of a similar calibre; raising chickens intensively was so much cheaper. Furthermore, the market's organizer expressed some anxiety about producers in general. The average age of an organic farmer was fifty; the Back to Farming movement of the 1970s came from 'boomers'. 'It's a worry for us,' he said, frankly. 'Who are going to take over the farms when they are gone?' I suddenly heard a more sombre strain within the generally healthy hum of the marketplace.

This note of concern came as a surprise to me; and it stayed in my ear. I'd come to realize how important farmers' markets were in the battle to re-establish real food. As well as enjoying my local market, I'd been to others around Britain and seen how much they mattered. Their significance was summed up by Hugh Fearnley-Whittingstall when he opened a farmers' market conference run by the certification group FARMA in 2005. 'For me, farmers' markets represent the single best opportunity to both preserve and develop the food culture of this country,' he said. After praising the creativity and individuality of the markets, and the way they brought consumers together and showed off local produce, he urged the stallholders and market organizers in the room to be energetic, 'possibly even aggressive', in promoting the cause. They had to get the balance of traders right and run weekly, if at all possible, so that shoppers could escape the industrialized food machine and buy the full range of goods they needed: milk and cream as well as legs of lamb.

Bernadine Prince, a farmers' market organizer in Washington DC, expanded on the significance of the movement in her powerful address to the nascent antipodean farmers' market movement at a conference in Sydney. Her starting image was the world as an apple. How much was for farming? Three-quarters of the apple represented water and could be disregarded. Half of the remaining quarter was swamps, deserts, mountains, Arctic regions and other land that was totally unsuitable for growing. The remaining one-eighth of the world-apple faced intense competition. Six hundred farms a week were being lost in America, and just 2 per cent of Americans now lived and worked on farms. In the end, only one thirty-second of the globe represented agricultural land, and just the peel of the apple, or the topsoil, really mattered. How we use this precious resource, now under intense pressure, is immensely important. Consumers shopping at farmers' markets are gaining territory in the sustainable use of Planet Earth. As the Kentucky farmer and essayist Wendell Berry put it: 'Eating is an agricultural act.' Even though broiler birds are cramped into a physically small area, intensive chicken farming still exerts a sizeable pressure on the land because of the enormous amounts of feed required for the production of such large quantities of cheap meat.

What we eat matters – not least in the way it affects our retail system. The small markets offer a crucial alternative to Britain's supermarkets, which now control around three-quarters of our food industry and are growing. One in eight retail pounds is spent at Tesco. This giant has grown so dominant that the political Right, as well as the Left, now feels uncomfortable about the situation. A huge business with many outlets and ever an eye to economies of scale is never going to bother with all the details that go into delicious, fresh ingredients that are grown and sold to the consumer via small, local networks. Everything must fit into a big supply chain, with its resulting food miles and lack of true diversity. Supermarkets may be convenient, and they may fit into part of your shopping; but are they everything? Isn't it important to have an alternative, and to support and enjoy that, even if only occasionally for your quality food shopping?

All over Britain what Bernadine Price calls 'this delicious revolution' has started at a grass-roots level. It is growing week by week, month by month, season by season, as producers produce and consumers consume and like what they get. It is growing in Orton, a small Cumbrian village, which typifies how much these markets matter to a rural community. Sixty per cent of the producers come from within ten miles of the village and 23 per cent from within three miles. Depending on the season there are between twelve and forty stalls and eight hundred regular customers. Twelve new businesses have started in this area, recently so badly struck by foot-and-mouth. The dynamic market organizer, Jane Brook, said they wanted to keep the countryside going 'not as a theme park but as a living, working, thriving community'.

The delicious revolution is growing in London. The London Farmers' Market organization now has ten markets – and there are others in their pipeline and others that exist outside their umbrella. More than half of the shoppers come weekly, and business collectively is worth £3.5 million to the local economy.

The delicious revolution is growing in Bristol. The Corn Street market has gone from fortnightly to weekly, and on the first Sunday of the month there is an additional Slow Food market – a community event with cooking demonstrations and stalls brimming with the traditionally produced food and drink of the area. It is growing too in Winchester where I found a wide choice of five chicken stalls, all with their own merits, in what is the biggest farmers' market in the UK: an inspirational place to shop.

The delicious revolution is growing in Manchester. The head of the city's markets, Krys Zasada, paints a big picture. He wants the north-west's twenty-two thousand farms to be connected to the thirty-four farmers' markets and the 10.5 million people who live within fifty miles of the city. As well as the weekly shop, what about getting local chicken in school dinners, in the Arndale Centre, in pub chains?

The delicious revolution is growing in numerous small market towns that are getting a rural beat back into the heart of their streets through farmers' markets. In Watton, in Norfolk, the egg seller brings what his hens laid last night: big, beautiful, proper free-range eggs. One local farmer was about to go out of business; then he bought an apple crusher at a farm sale, found a local orchard with spare fruit and started making apple juice. This sort of local production and selling is not an easy way to make a living, said the organizer, Jan Godfrey of the Wayland Partnership Development Trust. Volunteers and stallholders have to make an effort to turn up on the first Saturday of the month, come what may. 'You can stand on a market on a rainy day and not sell a thing,' she admits. 'People are picky and it's easier to go to Tesco than to walk up and down a wet high street.' Other days, it hums. And it is growing. For the sellers there is camaraderie, rain, hail or shine. After the market, the lady who makes fudge has lunch with the lady who sells plants.

You could farm in the countryside and never feed the people you live alongside. For shoppers, it is a way to reconnect with their surroundings. You could live in the middle of the countryside and never taste the food of the area. The market makes this happen. The delicious revolution is happening near your home, now. It cannot come soon enough.

Farmers' markets are just one way of direct selling. I went to see a great farm shop that was thriving through selling its chickens as well as other meat, fruit and vegetables, and running an award-winning box scheme supplying four hundred local households. George Heathcote's grandfather was an early organic farmer in the 1940s at Warborne Farm in the New Forest, just outside Lymington in Hampshire. George's father moved away from this system, though he was never one to pile on the chemicals. Then BSE came. George Heathcote saw the public's trust of farmers crumble away. He converted to Soil Association organic.

George's attitude, one to be commended to farmers, was to produce what the public wanted. So he asked them. Top of the list came proper free-range chickens, alongside fruit that had been ripened on the tree or bush so it was truly sweet and juicy. The Warborne Farm flock now pecks among the fruit trees and bushes. From day two the chicks are taken out of the small sheds by hand. George and his wife Kate improvized a system of tapping on the ground to encourage the chicks to forage. All this is part of careful, integrated farming, the basis of the organic system that is designed to build up the fertility of the soil and the healthiness of the food. George feels that every aspect of the Soil Association's approach is the right way to farm. 'We are not only looking after the land for the long term – and even the short term,' he said. 'We are not only looking after the animals. We are looking after the health of the people who eat the food. More and more people are concerned about how their food is produced; what they are feeding their families and what they are eating themselves. By buying our food they are entrusting us. They are not just giving us their money, they are almost entering into a contract with us that what they are buying has been produced in good faith and with integrity. It's very important that we don't let them down.'

George had a good idea for making real chickens more widely available: through farm shops. There are now four thousand such places around Britain. Chicken farming can be done well on a smallish scale. The birds look attractive as they peck around the place and instantly make people realize that they are buying goods that are closer to the soil than at a supermarket. 'Chicken farming doesn't take a great amount of skill,' he said. 'They don't take up much space, they are a point of interest and would attract people into the shop to buy other stuff. It's the kind of thing that could really make a difference and show the gulf between the factory chicken and the farm chicken. It would give farm shops a really good image: if you want good food you go to farm shops.'

The Goods Shed, a restored Victorian railway shed right by Canterbury West station, has taken the farmers' market idea and cleverly adapted it to contemporary shopping and eating habits. Its animator is Susanna Atkins, a lively woman in her thirties. Her brother is a farmer; her parents had a pick-your-own. Susanna understands the nitty-gritty of production and how difficult it is for farmers to make a living. She spotted a dilapidated, roofless building, wanted to open a restaurant serving local food, and then saw how it could work by selling the ingredients as well as the cooked food. The Goods Shed opened in July 2002, initially with twenty farmers in a permanent market. Running alongside the stalls the whole length of the building is a restaurant supplied by the sellers that are just yards away. Food miles are written down beside each box of potatoes or pile of carrots: nine miles, six miles – that sort of distance. The veg goes alongside dishes such as pot-roast chicken with shaggy parasol mushrooms and garlic. The Goods Shed has found plenty of ways to make shopping as convenient as it is in a supermarket. They've got parking and good opening hours. You have the option to pay at the individual stalls or park your credit card by a main till and pay on plastic all at once. They put a monthly newsletter though the doors of five hundred homes within walking distance to encourage local shoppers: food miles are made by consumers, not just by produce. 'It is a re-germinating thing,' Susanna explains. 'It touches on so many issues; social, economic, environmental.'

Terry, the Goods Shed butcher, has two types of chicken, Soil Association organic birds from Jubilee Farm and free-range Kentish Rangers from the McKeevers on the north Kent coast. I'd seen the birds range for myself and learnt that they are killed by hand on site. The meat was excellent. Terry takes pride and joy in selling these birds. 'I used to make steaks and go home,' he said of his previous job. 'This is proper butchery.' His perkiness made me think of Susanna's despair about the service industry in Britain as a whole. After all, why should the checkout operator care what you buy and what they are part of? 'When things get too big, the people at bottom don't have any interest in the whole,' said Susanna. 'In the old days, if there were three people working at a butcher's you knew about the other parts. If you work for a massive chain, you don't see how your bit fits in. It makes people depressed. People like to work for small companies.'

Customers, too, were taking a pride in what they were buying. Terry complained that people trailing around supermarkets had what he called 'telly-vision': they didn't look at the bigger picture beyond the rectangle of the packet they were buying. The labels told you very little about what was really going on, and customers didn't understand that they could get better value for money at a proper butcher's. His customers really wanted to know what they were getting, and enjoyed it all the more for their knowledge.

When Susanna first came to live in Canterbury, she went into a butcher's and asked for a local chicken. Not available. No demand. The profile of local food has been raised, in part by places like the Goods Shed. The butcher now sells local chickens.

Amidst all this direct selling, we are very lucky in this country still to have a network of excellent independent butchers. There is much to be proud of in our tradition of rearing and selling meat. A good butcher is a master-craftsman (or woman) and there are still a good number of them around – a testament to our status as a meat-eating country since we have plenty of pasture. The Italians have the sun for good tomatoes; we have the grass for good meat. It may be a short detour, and it can be a touch intimidating to shop at an independent butcher at first; we've become accustomed to the sleep-walking trawl around the supermarket. But the effort soon brings rewards, especially if you go regularly.

Our power as consumers is immense. But we still have to wake up when it comes to chickens in butcher's shops, even. A Q-Guild butcher in Devon (The Guild is a group of independents with high standards) told me that whilst his customers asked lots of questions about the beef and lamb, chicken was still seen as a second-class citizen. Less interest was taken – probably because it was seen as a cheap meat. We don't pay much for goods if we don't value them; we don't value them if we don't pay much. It is, as they say, a chicken and egg situation.

So we are back to the whole issue of whether people value what they are getting. It was another Q-Guild butcher, David Lidgate of Holland Park in London, who showed me yet another 'value added' point to a real chicken: nutrition. David has long been fascinated by what animals eat and how it affects their meat, for example the fact that beneficial omega-3 fatty acids are higher in the flesh of grass-fed animals. David has noticed that parents now come into the shop and buy organic beefburgers from grass-fed animals in order to give their children the best possible diet at exam times. They equate superior nutrition with optimum mental and physical health. His good news is that better-tasting meat turns out to be better for you. 'We know that extensively reared chickens taste better. All our experience indicates that things that taste better *are* better,' says David.

Inactivity is one reason why the nutritional profile of chicken has changed so much. A 2004 study conducted at London University showed that the percentage of fat on a chicken carcass has risen from 2 per cent to 22 per cent, over the thirty-year period during which our chickens have been 'improved'. What's more, the quality of this fat has declined in nutritional value. It used to contain more omega-3 fatty acids, useful for brain function and the heart – presumably for the birds as well as for us. But the nutritional status of this useful (and delicious) fat has declined because the birds are fed cereals rather than eating the insects, seeds and plants of their traditional diet. David Lidgate, who has played rugby at club level and still coaches, made an important point about the principle of having free-range birds. 'Exercise is what we really need for our health,' he said. 'It's the same for chickens.'

Lidgate told me that meat-trade buyers had progressively gone down the wrong path by judging animals on looks. Big, flavourless beasts had been favoured over smaller, tasty ones. For beef as for chicken, in Britain we have gone for quantity not quality. This was starting to be reversed. The French have always kept taste as a priority. The famous *poulet de Bresse* tends to be displayed back-side up, he said – in contrast to the way we buy chickens, with our fixation on the over-inflated breast. 'If the back is bright then the chicken is fresh,' he explained. 'The fact the breast is not such a good shape is neither here nor there to the French. By looking at the back they know it is fresh and they understand that the chicken will taste really good. That's all they need to know.'

The chickens at Lidgate's shop come from one of the most successful fine chicken producers, Label Anglais, based in Essex. Using a system of movable houses and flocks of up to a thousand, Label Anglais has built up the business over eight years and now sells a hundred thousand birds a year, entirely through independent shops and also direct to top chefs such as Gordon Ramsay and Heston Blumenthal. The birds cost around £8–14. For Chris Frederick, who runs the family business alongside his father and brother, breed is an important factor. They use a Cornish Red crossed with a French breed to produce a very slow-growing bird with fine texture and rich flavour. Taste is the key.

I started thinking about this book in front of a supermarket chicken counter. This is where many people buy their birds, and it is crucial that the quality of these chickens improves. But it is not the only place to buy them. For meat, as for all food, to sustain an alternative way of shopping is to encourage other ways of production. Where you shop has an impact on what you will be able to buy in the first place. If independents such as farmers' markets, farm shops and good butchers thrive, they form a collective that acts as an important counterbalance to the power and produce of the supermarkets. If they thrive, we have delicious food that can be part of local networks. A number of the people selling in farmers' markets would not be able to earn a living without such means of direct selling. We need more good chicken keepers; this is where such people can get a toe-hold in a reviving local food economy. By supporting farmers' markets, you further the cause of local real chickens: well reared, delicious, sustainable – and on your doorstep.

On a trip to Hawke's Bay on the North Island of New Zealand, I went to a weekly farmers' market that gave me an insight into just how such places could be an engine for reviving local food. The organizer, Ian Thomas, is a chicken farmer who keeps laying birds. He is strict about the rules for the market: only producers can sell. When a small business asked to sell coffee to drink, he said fine, but you must roast it yourself. The business invested in a roaster and now everyone in the area, and not just on market day, benefits from freshly roasted coffee from a local firm. The whole market was inspiring, with its high-quality produce and down-to-earth atmosphere.

Some farmers' markets can be disappointing. They don't always have the verve and commitment that make them special and the attention to detail that upholds standards. But many are excellent. Ultimately, they rise or fall on quality and whether they are good enough to get us away from the supermarkets, regularly or occasionally. Good food brings immediate rewards, and going to farmers' markets can easily become part of a new pattern of shopping. This should be just the beginning.

Cooking Cultures

Chicken is everywhere. Bricks of its soft, pink flesh line supermarket aisles. On the street, you get mugged by deep-fried whiffs from countless fast food chicken outlets. Their awnings feature cheery cartoon birds with beaks gaping in delight at the treat in store: 'Eat me, I'm yours!' Discarded boxes litter the pavement with slogans like 'Chicken Tasty and Tender'. The meat of this bird is now so cheap and ubiquitous that it is virtually unavoidable: the pinged ready-meal, the noodle quick-fix, the southern-fried drumstick, the gourmet lunchtime sandwich, the family Sunday roast, the TV dinner (eyes on the screen, fingers on the bones), the cheap take-out, the buffet-table spread, the salad for one, the supper dish shared with friends, the latest in restaurant 'peasant' food – *pollo cacciatore, pot au feu:* all chicken. If you are having guests round and want to feed them meat, then as likely as not it will be chicken. The main course at a wedding reception: chicken or salmon. Supermarket aisles for baby food, for pet food, for ready-meals. Chicken tonight, chicken tomorrow, chicken next week, chicken this month, next month; chicken spring to winter. Chicken, chicken, chicken, chicken. What's for supper? Nothing special – just chicken.

'Twas not ever thus. I first became especially interested in chicken for a more cherished gastronomic reason: every culture has evolved its classic recipe. There is *coq au vin* in France and drunken chicken in China, with the bird lightly poached in rice wine, southern fried chicken in the USA, and the Japanese chicken-and-egg dish called 'mother and child'. There is even a chicken dessert in Turkey, with little strands of chicken breast pulverized into a milk pudding. All these dishes developed into classic feast-day food because in times past it was a very big deal to kill these birds. They laid the eggs, the cock's crow woke the household, the bones were used for tools and divinations. They gave us omens and omelettes, and the meat was consequently regarded as a treat.

A folk memory endures of the specialness of these chicken dishes. Brits go soft-centred at the thought of a Sunday roast bird. On my trip to San Francisco I asked each taxi driver I encountered where he came from. All were recent immigrants setting out on the American dream. I'd enquire about a favourite chicken dish. The whole atmosphere in the cab would change. Often we'd sit for some time at my destination with the meter off and he'd want to keep talking about a Bulgarian stew or Ukrainian feast: it was the food of his mother and his motherland.

To put the pride back into chicken, we need to reclaim its culinary heritage. This is why on my travels I began to find my way into cooks' kitchens to gather in a favourite chicken recipe and discover not just how a dish was made but something of what lay behind it. I would sometimes go with them to buy the chicken; then I would sit in the kitchen and watch the knives that cut and the spoons that stirred, and see and taste the seasonings and other ingredients that went into the dish. I would sit at the table and note how it was set, and observe the customs and quirks of that place and that time. And then we would eat.

This essentially greedy quest can, I hope, be elevated by a quote: 'Poultry is for the cook what canvas is for a painter.' These were the words of the eighteenth-century gastronome and author Jean Anthelme Brillat-Savarin. Trained as a lawyer, he left France to escape the Revolution and spent two years in New York playing the violin in a theatre orchestra and teaching languages. He returned to France and rose in the legal profession to become a judge on the Court of Appeals. During this time his fascination with science was reflected in his interest in food, a connection that today engages such chefs as Heston Blumenthal in what they call 'molecular gastronomy'. Brillat-Savarin's book *The Physiology of Taste*, published privately in the year of his death, 1826, provided the basis for the saying 'We are what we eat': 'Tell me what you eat and I shall tell you what you are.' By looking at the classic chicken recipes in each place I can discover something of the culture of the people, even if it is simply a sensuous connection to what they eat either daily or on special occasions. Chicken is the blank canvas on which their culinary colours were painted; it is an edible national flag.

When travelling, the best place to orientate your taste-buds is a proper market. This is where you can see what cooks are buying for their families and imagine how they will use these fresh ingredients. In Mexico City, I saw maize-fed birds with their yellowy flesh displayed on top of a barrel in a circle like the spokes of a wheel, their necks included on the body as a delicious extra morsel. Maize should make the meat more delicious. These Mexican birds were also free-range. Their legs were well developed and the breast-meat elongated rather than pneumatically plump. When you see maize-fed birds in British supermarkets it does not mean that the welfare and food quality standards are higher, however: it can just be a marketing tool to make the birds look special.

In Vietnamese markets I discovered two kinds of fowl: traditionally reared Vietnamese chickens, used for boiling and stewing; and cheaper 'American' ones, produced intensively and killed at a young age to be used for grilling and in dishes that require more tender meat. There were the black-skinned chickens I'd also seen in Singapore, which are used as a health food by women recuperating from childbirth. In health shops you could even buy little concentrated phials of their essence, like super-charged, medicinal chicken soup. Native chickens roamed the Vietnamese villages; the American ones lived in sheds. When I visited, in the early 1990s, nearly three-quarters of the 8 million rural households in Vietnam kept chickens, mostly in a small-scale way. This is now changing. With the advent of bird flu, a substantially larger number will inevitably end up being American for reasons of biosecurity. News footage has shown Vietnamese villagers killing many of their free-roaming birds.

The next place to go on such explorations is a good restaurant that is rooted in the food culture of a particular place. I found one in Mexico City called El Refugio Fonda. The kitchen was entirely staffed by women, who were cooking home-style. I stood in the tiled room and watched them shred chicken, holding the breasts in their palms and scratching off little threads of flesh. Their stoves were illuminated by silver and glass asteroid lights, and they stirred dark, sensuous sauces in big earthenware pots. On the wall were cases of rose petals and pumpkin seeds and strings of dried chillis in lacquered reds, blacks and browns like the colours of old master paintings.

The owner, Daniella, described the exotic traditional dish called *mole* that was prepared around the country. It could have seventeen or more ingredients, including chillis, chocolate, sesame seed and peanuts. No one *mole* was ever the same as another, she said, and you could never write the recipe down. Furthermore, their flavours changed over time, improving in the *recalentardo*, the reheating. The most famous of all was *mole poblano*. Legend claims it came from the Santa Rosa convent in the city of Puebla de Los Angeles, when the nuns made it to honour a visiting bishop. The word *mole* came from a Nahuatl word, the language of the Aztecs, meaning a concoction or sauce made from chillis. The food writer Elisabeth Lambert Ortiz believes its origins are even older, and certainly pre-Columbian. One theory takes it back beyond the Aztecs to the Mayas: the dish could be nine thousand years old. Normally a *mole* is made with a turkey, a native bird of the pre-Columbian era, though now a couple of free-range chickens can be used instead. Chickens arrived in South America with the Europeans, who often took birds on board ship for meat and eggs.

The best *mole poblano* I found on this trip was in a little rural restaurant in Xico, in the hills above Mexico's Caribbean coast and Veracruz. Its owner, Tia Nena, was seventy-five and had been born in this house that her carpenter father had built, and where her mother had fed Zapata's revolutionaries in the early twentieth century. Tia Nena – her name a diminutive of Aunty Magdalena – had cooked here for so many family and friends that eventually she offered the same dishes to paying guests and called it a restaurant. But really this was the best kind of food: home cooking.

Tia Nena's stirring spoon was as long as her arm, the end as deep as her two hands cupped together, and the saucepan was as wide as her shoulders. A *mole* takes so long to make that it leads you towards a fiesta. She'd already cooked the chickens and was now making the sauce. Into the pan went three kinds of dried chilli that had been toasted and soaked: the red-brown *ancho*, the brown-black *mulatto* and the long, tarry *pasilla*. Their colours would produce the mysterious darkness of the sauce. Then tomatoes; an onion; five fat cloves of garlic; two chopped-up bananas – an unusual addition that was part of the Caribbean character of the place – along with peanuts, almonds, hazelnuts, prunes, raisins and pumpkin seeds. Then a small tablet of intense chocolate – essential for mellowing and melding the concoction – plus sugar and salt to season; finally black pepper, anise and cinnamon to spice. These ingredients were mixed together and fried in lard – the cooking medium is an important part of the authentic taste of a nation's cuisine. As they bubbled away, some breadcrumbs were added to thicken the sauce. It was now a black liquid-paste, strong and rich.

The meat was warmed through in the sauce for lunch that day. First we ate a clear chicken soup containing little balls of tortilla paste, pressed in at the middle with a thumb, and cooked in the broth. Then the *mole*. I was, finally, converted to the dish. Truth to tell, previously I had not been a fan. The ones I had eaten before had been strange and complex: interesting but not enjoyable. This was different – perhaps because I'd absorbed the character of the dish along the way in the kitchen. Tia Nena's *mole* was less sweet than others, and thicker. The chillis hummed happily together. It was subtle, rich, dark and good. The *mole* united us as we shared its blend of flavours and revelled in its sense of occasion.

What is it to travel through food? Is it as simple as sitting at a table and tasting your surroundings as you pause for breath in a touristic whirl-through? The day after I arrived in Mexico, crowds gathered around the news-stands. The presidential candidate Colosio had been assassinated in the street. His body now lay on every street corner, his blood splattered in newsprint. I sat at a breakfast café where the waiters poured coffee and hot milk from great heights into my cup. One placed before me the morning-carbs of hotcakes. It was only when I was still for long enough to eat that I saw the pain concentrated in the eyes of the people at the tables around me as they absorbed the tragedy in their morning papers.

Travelling through food is to taste the produce that is gathered in from the countryside; to understand the physical nature of the land and its harvests. It was the Caribbean coast bananas that I saw and then tasted in Tia Nena's *mole* – one of the factors that made it unique. With a little bit of exploring and curiosity you fall into new habits of taste and understand them better. I began to crave the flavour and aroma of the tortillas that would arrive at every meal in a little basket, freshly cooked and kept hot in a wrap of linen that gave out a faint, woody-scented sweat when you opened it. I discovered that chillis had different flavours, and started to notice their fruitiness as well as their heat.

Back in Britain, I read Mexican novels and poems and non-fiction and cookbooks. I looked at Frida Kahlo's extraordinary late cosmic paintings and her sexy, anatomical fruit, some of which I'd devoured at the market in Coyocán near her house. I hunted out the dried chillis imported by a Mexican specialist, the Cool Chile Company, and frequented the company's *taqueria* in Notting Hill Gate, eating their chicken *tinga* with smoked *chipotles*. The authentically bright flavours of Mexico remind me of the open-eyed and loose-limbed ways of my mid-twenties. And when all these thoughts and memories and new and old experiences and tastes come and go through my mind and my mouth, they are always grounded in the earthed traditions of their native place: Mexico.

In the course of an average day, I might have a French pastry or a British bacon butty and a cup of Indian tea for breakfast; an Italian focaccia sandwich for lunch; a cup of Taiwanese oolong and a piece of (local) Lewes cake at teatime; a plate of Japanese noodles for dinner, along with French, Chilean or New Zealand wine; then maybe a nip of Scotch whisky, a tot of West Indian rum. There is a vast range of chicken dishes on the menu available to the cosmopolitan palate. I might use the breasts of a chicken to make a French sauté with tarragon and cream; spice up the wings and legs with an American BBQ sauce; and later make Scotch broth with pearl barley and the bones. Does it matter if you have not eaten these dishes in their place, amongst their people? You can enjoy them in their own right, just as you can read Russian literature, or dance Latin American salsa, or look at Dutch seventeenth-century paintings. But to experience an ingredient, a dish or a way of eating in its own culture, whether in the place itself or amongst its people – wherever they happen to be – or reading about them in a recipe book that genuinely explores a cooking culture: this is to gain a whole new level of knowledge and a respect for what it is and who they are.

Finding quality examples of a cuisine can be difficult. London's cultural mix often seems more of a fruit-cake than a melting pot, with rich fragments that are separate if held together in the same place. This aspect of cities varies considerably. Sydney, for example, celebrates its racial mix more through food; its ethnic restaurants are far more than cheap take-outs. Before visiting the country, I read about them in a book with the Aussie un-PC title of *Wog-food*. Urban Australians are proud of the mix of cultures in their cities, and the second generation had often taken their parents' cooking and turned it into a classy and thriving business. New York and San Francisco too offer the world on a plate. In San Francisco, for instance, I went to a restaurant serving authentic Shanghai cooking. Yet in London I went to a number of restaurants with high expectations and came away feeling frustrated because the cooking was so bastardized. This was particularly true in chains. You'd never get a hint of the rich variety and vibrancy of Mexican food from the high-street chicken enchilada in a commercial Tex-Mex joint, where the food has been both Americanized and then exported over here. Independents can also be disappointing – though generally less often. You might expect this in the high-street sweet-and-sour chicken and the chicken chow mein. But I also went to a Georgian restaurant with a writer and former foreign correspondent from this region, once part of the crumbling Soviet Union. As we waited, she regaled me with great tales of the ebullient toasts and hospitality of Georgia's celebrated food culture. This was a part of the world where a number of plants, not least the grapevine, had been domesticated; what they eat has interesting and evolved origins. Sadly, the main course (chicken) was a sorry anticlimax.

The eating out scene is changing, especially as people travel and have greater expectations of the genuine. Vietnamese restaurants, for example, are spreading westwards from east London, carrying authentic tastes to a wider circle. But the best food, I have concluded, is often in homes.

Indeed the biggest privilege anywhere, for all the glamour of restaurants, is to eat home food. In Vietnam, I was invited back to the house of my interpreter in Saigon to eat the chicken we had looked at in the market that day. The meal started with a porridgy soup of burst rice grains mixed with chicken stock, garnished with spring onions finely sliced lengthways and plenty of coriander leaves. It was filling, nourishing and the sort of dish that is a staple in eastern Asia but rare in Europe because it is everyday food rather than restaurant event-food. Then we ate little pieces of the chicken's flesh, dipped in salt and pepper mixed with lemon juice. Next came rice noodles and Vietnamese herbs with tofu and mushrooms; followed by a salad of lotus shoots, pork belly, prawns and dry-fried peanuts, dressed in nuoc mam (fish sauce), chilli and lemon juice. Finally, a slippery agar-agar jelly of coffee and coconut milk cooled the inside of my throat.

Sitting at the table, my hostess told me about the way food is used for ritual. In the house were statues of kitchen gods. Cups of tea stood in front of them, refilled daily. On special days the family burnt paper clothes, houses and money to send them to the spirits, and put flowers and special small, sweet 'ancestor-worship' bananas before them. There was so much care and honour in the way that food was used: it had a significance beyond the material. As we relaxed and talked over shared food, my interpreter told me of her life. After the Vietnam War, when the communist North took over the entire country. Her father had been sent to a re-education camp for four years because he had fought in the South Vietnamese army. Her husband's family had tried to escape from Vietnam in an overcrowded boat: it had capsized and nearly everyone had drowned – only her husband and his brother survived. I had travelled through the country reading guidebooks that gave a perspective of the war largely from the Westerner's point of view: forever *Apocalypse Now*. Eating with this Vietnamese woman in her home was an insight into lives within a backdrop of history.

Nobody gets quite as much out of a dish as the cook – not even the eaters, who come to it complete without seeing the raw ingredients build up into their final form. The cook gets the nearest to the whole experience, with touch, smell, sight, sound and taste engaged through all the stages of preparation and on to eating it. The cook has the most fun, if also the work. Beyond this is a more fundamental point. Experienced cooks know their ingredients inside out: they know how the small amount of fat in a chicken translates into the richness of a sauce; how the long, strong bones of a free-range bird make a fine stock; how proper thighs have smooth nuggets of tasty muscle. Much is being lost now that many people cook less, or not at all. Can anyone really know or care about the quality of an ingredient such as a chicken if it does not pass directly through their hands at least occasionally? What's more, these chicken dishes are – or have been – part of folk-craft, repeated time after time, all over the world, in every country and with slight variations in each household according to whose hand stirred the pot and who had collected and measured the ingredients. These small domestic acts are part of the grain of culture that collectively give it a living strength.

How to counter the forces of processed foods? You could start by cooking chicken. There are plenty of recipes. As Brillat-Savarin said, this meat is a blank canvas that displays every part of the culinary craft: '. . . it is served to us boiled, roasted, fried, hot or cold, whole or cut up, with or without sauce, boned, skinned, stuffed, and always with equal success'.

Besides recipes, one of the most useful kitchen tricks I've ever learnt is how to joint a whole bird. Buying a free-range or organic bird and cutting it up yourself is far cheaper than buying one ready-jointed. This time spent in preparation – it takes no more than a few minutes after a bit of practice – is also repaid by the knowledge you gain from handling ingredients. You can get four quarters: leg-and-thigh, times two; breast-and-wing, times two. You can divide these further to get eight pieces: two breasts; two wing-with-breast; two thighs; two drumsticks. The following is a basic guide to what becomes clear when you use your own hands and observations. Use a heavy kitchen knife, kept sharp: good kit makes short work of kitchen tasks.

Put the bird breast side up on a chopping board with the opening towards you. Pull the legs away from the body so they are splayed out. Cut through the stretched out skin until you reach the body. Then you may choose – or not –

to make a slight detour. Turn the bird over and use your fingertips to find the little nuggets of flesh where the leg articulates with the back. Because of their position, you could refer to these as love-handles; they are more generally called the oysters. Round and delicious, an oyster is the true chicken nugget. You may not bother, and leave them attached to the back; but the French call this bit '*sot l'y laisse*': a fool leaves them. The wise will therefore use the tip of the knife to scoop round the oysters. Return the chicken to its back and yank the leg so the thigh-bone pops out of its ball socket. Cut the leg-and-thigh (with or without oyster) away from the body. Repeat for the other side. You can leave this as a quarter or cut it into drumsticks and thighs by making a diagonal cut at the joint.

As for the breasts, you need to decide if you want them on or off the bone. Ideally, it is best to cook meat and fish on the bone because fewer fibres will have been cut to let the juices out and so the meat dries out less. To do this, use a knife or kitchen scissors (a sturdy pair of dedicated poultry shears is ideal) to cut the breast and wing off the backbone by tilting the bird up on its end, parson's nose uppermost, and cut down both sides to remove the backbone. Put the meat breast-side down on the board and use your knife or poultry shears to cut it into halves. You can get two portions out of each breast quarter. To do this, use your knife to feel where the wing joint is, about a third of the way into the breast meat. Cut down firmly and you will find it divides at this point. It is not as clear-cut as the division between the thigh and drumstick, but it doesn't have to be perfect.

All this may sound complicated – but it is far easier when you follow the logic of a chicken on a chopping board rather than read the instructions on a page. After jointing a bird a few times you will become proud of the increasing neatness of your sections – even, privately, a little smug at your *bonne femme* ways.

Another great advantage of jointing your own chicken is that you can make stock with the bones. A simmering stockpot is one of the symbols of home cooking. You can cut off the wing tips and put them to good use, along with other bones and the neck and gizzard that come in the centre of a butcher's bird. In go chopped onions, carrots and celery: the holy trinity of aromatics that is at the base of so much French food. A bay leaf or two; some parsley stalks. Herbs grown in pots are the secret of making many a cheap meal special. A scatter of peppercorns. The scruffy end of some leeks. Boil it all up, skim it when it first comes to the boil if you want clarity, let it simmer away for as long as you want, then strain it through a sieve. That's it. There are endless refinements – stock uses up leftovers but it can equally well be an event. To make it more special you can get a pile of wings from a butcher for a pittance, and places that sell lots of portions often have carcasses for free. I make a consommé with shin of beef, a whole chicken, six hours of simmering and the final trick of whisking egg whites into the mix to clarify it to sparkling purity. Flavoured with a little tarragon, the result is sensational. It is interesting to offer a starter that is so purely about flavour. Quite apart from the taste and the household economy, a good soup gives your home a warmth at its centre.

I wondered how the appliance of science could help make better roast chicken, though I will admit straightaway to being more interested in eating than in experiments: I only go so far – well, almost nowhere – with goggles and thermometers. But food science also takes cooks in aprons further into ingredients, giving you a greater understanding of the materials and processes at your fingertips. For a start, it is a route into the natural history of what you are eating. The reason why some chicken flesh is dark is that it contains an oxygen-carrying protein, myoglobin, ready to give the muscles energy for movement. This is why the energetic tuna is dark red and drifting slackers like plaice are white. More practically, food science is a good way to learn how to cook. You understand why you are browning the meat – for flavour and colour, not to 'seal in the juices', as is so often said – and this gives a firmer footing in the kitchen. The American professor and food scientist Robert L. Wolke recommends, in his useful and engaging book *What Einstein Told His Cook*, defrosting flat pieces of frozen meat on an unheated frying pan or any other thick metal surface because metal is a good heat conductor and gets the room's temperature more quickly into the ice-hard food. I've used this method for chicken breasts, since I sometimes take them off the bird before roasting the rest, and found that the defrosting time is halved. But if you are defrosting a whole bird you should do it in a fridge, or the bird will reach a temperature at which bugs can multiply before it thaws all the way through.

Wolke also explains the science of thickening gravy with flour. What you are trying to do, essentially, is make oil and water mix. Different flavour molecules are fat- or water-soluble, and in a rich sauce you want them both. Flour mixed with water becomes gloopy (think wallpaper paste) and so you want to coat the flour grains with fat in order to stop this happening. At the start of a white sauce, or of flour-thickened gravy, you want to mix equal quantities of fat and flour and cook this mixture, known to cooks as a *roux*, for a while to get rid of the taste of raw flour. Once this has been done, add your liquid (a slosh of wine; water from the boiling veg) in the proportion of, roughly, eight to twelve parts liquid to one part fat, one part flour, though the amount of liquid is down to personal taste. I prefer cornflour as a thickener, or to use none at all and to keep the liquid simmering away until it has reduced to an amalgamated *jus*.

When it comes to cooking meat, there's a school of scientific cooks who go for lower temperatures. The science is this. If you cook at a high temperature you denature the proteins and the meat fibres squeeze out the moisture. Cooking at a lower temperature, ideally not going above 60–70°C in the centre of the meat, makes a real difference to the succulence of the final dish. By this method, you cook the bird at a low temperature until the inside is ready – test it with a meat thermometer – and then brown it quickly at the end on a high heat. As with all meat, it is best to leave the bird to rest outside the oven (but still in a warm place) for ten minutes or so at the end of cooking and before carving so that the heat and juices can redistribute themselves.

It is a different and ultra-precise way of cooking that will suit some cooks, but it requires precision and specialist kit. My major concern, in the case of chicken, is food poisoning. Hervé This, the French guru of the modern molecular gastronomists, admits that low-temperature cooking can be perilous even if the results are wonderful. When I asked a top British bacteria specialist about the method he was concerned that slow-cooking a chicken must carry a risk as some of the bugs could adapt to the slowly rising temperature. His advice was to make sure the temperature got up to the high sixties.

Myself, I'm sticking with the higher temperature partly because I love crispy brown skin. Roasting a whole chicken this way presents the challenge that the breast meat cooks more quickly than the rest of the bird. To get over this potential problem you can slash the thighs and legs to get them to roast at the same speed or turn the bird over twice during cooking. Start it on one side, leg-side up, then put it on the other leg for another third of the cooking time, and then put it breast-upwards for the final third. You can also ease some butter under the skin, perhaps flavoured with some chopped herbs or crushed spices, or lay some rashers of streaky bacon over the breast so that they baste the flesh in the oven.

The best way to learn how to cook is to use your senses to the full in observing and tasting what is going on. Molecular gastronomists are attractively attentive to flavour. Heston Blumenthal, Britain's leading scientific cook, suggests putting different herbs in the centre of the bird and seeing if you can taste them in the meat. Cooking the same dish many times is the best way to improve your technique and to become aware of the qualities of your ingredients, which will vary slightly. I often make chicken broth and enjoy experimenting with different flavourings, perhaps throwing in a chipotle chilli or a different kind of peppercorn or seasoning with some Asian fish sauce. Browning the chicken bones and wings before making the stock adds more colour and flavour.

It is often the interplay and contrasts of different flavours that make food interesting, which is why I am especially fond of a book by Sybil Kapoor, *Taste*. The recipes have a background of science that underpins a fascination with flavours and the way they work together. Her sweet-and-sour chicken recipe contains sour, salt, sweet and umami (a particular savoury quality prominent in such dishes as reduced chicken stock). In her recipe for chicken satay, she shows how a little saltiness increases the sweetness in a food, as does just the right amount of sour. As for that essence of chicken, stock, she shows how it can be transformed into umami nirvana by using two whole birds (with the breasts cut off for another dish), first roasted for thirty minutes and then joined by half a bottle of white wine to create a broth that is finally simmered for five hours. It makes two litres of concentrated flavour that can be kept in small quantities in the freezer for the ultimate in stock cubes. This is a glorious stock to make: vinous, toasty, herby – it smells like dinner. And it's not hard. The Portuguese have a saying, '*e canja*' ('it's chicken soup'), that is their equivalent of our phrase 'it's a piece of cake'.

A good recipe such as this instructs; it also allows you to notice for yourself what is happening, and to add or subtract according to your own observations and resources. Chicken is indeed, as Brillat-Savarin said, a blank canvas on which flavours are painted in vivid or subtle colours. I think of just some of the chicken dishes I love: tarragon chicken; a Mexican soup with chillis and lime, *sopa di lima*; a sticky BBQ chicken from my childhood; garlic butter bursting from chicken Kiev; chicken piri-piri; Jamaican jerk chicken.

Using this meat as an exploration has taken me further into cooking cultures and further into food, and this in turn takes you further into life. Cooking exercises your senses, as well as your common sense. It makes you more aware of the physical world around you. It sustains, nourishes and delights your body and your mind. It gives you life; and it makes you more alive.

Slow Chickens

It takes an appropriately long time to digest the concept of Slow Food. I first encountered it in 1999 in a deli in Bologna, a city so keen on eating that one of its nicknames is *Bologna la grassa* (Bologna the Fat). I had gone to see Tamburini, a famous delicatessen. Here was a landscape of food. On one side of the counter were snowy alps of cheese, on the other a wall of meaty stones: fat-streaked coppa, granite salamis, smooth mortadella. The vista displayed Italy's breadth and depth of artisanal goods. Yet all was not well. The owner, Giovanni Tamburini, was talking of a movement to save such produce from the welter of regulations that are imposed with regard to industrial food and were having a devastating effect on smaller businesses. Producers all over Europe, and indeed the world, were floundering amid similar problems. They needed to find a way to get together.

Tamburini spoke of an Ark that would keep them afloat. This, I later realized, was Slow Food.

It took me another six years actually to join Slow Food, having been a fellow traveller for several years. A 'convivium', as such a local group is called, started up in Brighton, near my home in Sussex. Slow Food is an international movement. The beautiful quarterly magazine is worth the annual membership alone, bringing you stories and pictures of particular depth and vividness from around the world. The movement's outlook is globalized in the best way; but Slow Food makes most sense when grounded in your own surroundings. From that base, you can see the pleasures and issues of food without losing sight of the food and drink on your doorstep, and the fact they are there to be enjoyed with convivial companions.

I now believe that Slow Food offers a unique human riposte to the industrialized food culture. It is one force that could help save and encourage good food. I came to see its many merits through looking at chicken.

Slow Food is a movement that is hard to define, but it is simplest to begin – and it is only a start – by seeing it as the opposite of fast food. It sparked up in 1986, when a group of food lovers banded together against plans by McDonald's, with its Chicken McNugget and Chicken McSandwich, to site an outlet by the Spanish Steps in Rome. Armed with platefuls of *penne*, and led by its charismatic founder, Carlo Petrini, the group 'defiantly and deliciously stated their case against the global standardization of the world's food', as Californian restaurateur Alice Waters put it.

Italy was no push-over for McDonald's. The organization only opened its first branch in 1985, and met with opposition such as Petrini and his pasta. The number of outlets boomed only when they bought up a competing fast food chain in 1995 and went from 33 to 142 outlets overnight. After that, they felt safe to brag: 'We are McDonald's, the most famous brand in the world, and we intend to conquer Italy,' in the words of Mario Resca, president of McDonald's Development Italy in a 1998 booklet.

This food Resistance movement in Italy came about through the strength of the native food culture. This is a land where local food is still relatively easy to find; where one neighbourhood *enoteca* (wine bar) I frequented in Tuscany had a choice of twelve regional wines, all open for a glass and served with local cheeses and cured meats such as *lardo*, a regional dish of meltingly tender and sweet strips of pig fat cured with herbs and wine. It is a country of dozens of types of pasta, not just *penne*. Slow Food, like Italian food culture in general, is antithetical to all that McDonald's represents. It is not so much the fastness of the food that they object to. Pasta is hardly a time-taker, and pizza can be the best of all quick meals. This is more about diversity, for a start. 'To eat a different kind of food in every street in the world in the best answer to fast food,' writes Carlo Petrini in his manifesto for the movement, *Slow Food: The Case for Taste*. It is McDonald's lack of connection to local culture, the homogenization of an international brand, that was the problem, as well as the lack of taste and the environmental concerns about industrial production.

But Slow Food is far more than just a negative opposition to Ronald McDonald and his tasteless ways. It has much that is positive to promote. The movement began in Bra in north-west Italy, a down-to-earth town with a history of workers' collectives. Nearby are the vineyards and wineries that make the famous Barolo but, equally importantly, people here make wine in the courtyards of urban apartment buildings. A group got together to promote and celebrate the wine and food of the region. The origins of the movement are firmly rooted in what the French call *terroir*, a term associated with wine that also applies to food. It means the physical nature of the land and the culture of the people and products connected to it, and a deeper understanding of what you are enjoying.

The Left-leaning nature of Slow Food's founders may, on the face of it, seem an odd quality in a group that embraces the Pleasure Principle. '[The] leftist intelligentsia . . . looked down on us as a bunch of good-timers interested only in stuffing ourselves. While from the other side, the food and wine specialists . . . distrusted us left-wing gastronomes as incompetent intruders with an ideological agenda,' writes Petrini. Yet these people were interested in food in some depth, ecological gastronomes who believed in responsibility as well as pleasure, who embraced both new technology and the evolved crafts of growing and cooking. The very oddness of the movement showed that its time would come: it filled the huge space beyond traditional party politics.

Slowly does it. The group began with a very local, rooted start, and grew gradually and in each place differently as it spread around the globe. People set up convivia with their own way to be Slow. A glance through just one issue of the British Slow Food's *Snail Mail* publication (the symbol of Slow Food is a snail) shows people making bread with wild yeast cultures; a meal in Dorset with a talk by one of the few remaining fishermen who work off the shingle expanse of Chesil Beach; a meal in honour of the food writer Jane

Grigson; a discussion on farming issues and the environment at York University; the story of strawberry growing in Somerset, including a blind tasting of nine varieties; a Slow Soup evening in Aberdeenshire organized by a woman so in love with soup that she has 124 sorts in her repertoire; and so on, from starters to cheese with a convivial backdrop of merrymaking.

At an international level, the movement does serious work in trying to save endangered foods. They catalogue such foods in their Presidia, or Ark of Taste, and give Slow Food Awards to people who keep such produce going. There is now a Slow Food University of Gastronomic Sciences in Italy with a syllabus that includes sensory analysis and the history of agriculture.

Is this, however, still a movement that will be ultimately small-scale and elite? It was when I went to Tuscany, to see the Valdarno chickens that are in the Ark of Taste, that I saw how it could play a part in the real food movement.

I was staying with friends in Anghiari, a hill town above Arezzo in eastern Tuscany. The flat overlooked medieval streets that were too narrow for cars. Life walked past at a slow enough pace to see it unfold: the old ladies watering their plants, the workers and the tourists and the dogs and the arguments and the love affairs that all passed by below our window overlooking the belltower or campanile. It was a slice of *campanilismo*, the Italian term for a passion for local life. This formed the backdrop for my encounter with the Slow chickens and their keepers.

A short train journey took me to the farm. Francesca Romano Farina and Nicola Volonnino did not look like chicken farmers. Nicola was wearing a cheap-and-cheerful Pop Art jumper. Her lively brown eyes were full of laughter and she smoked when she wasn't passing around a basket of sweets or talking. Francesca was a member of a university archaeology team before she took to the chicken life.

The setting of Nicola's farm was quintessential Tuscany, amidst the lush green corduroy of the vineyard-hills east of Florence, with sunlight on the oaks and chestnuts. This part of Italy, before it became Chiantishire, had a system known as mezzadrine farming, by which smallholders eked out a living as tenants. It was not a rich form of farming. Nicola's house, at least three hundred years old, would have had cows living in one end of the building instead of just Nicola, her builder husband and twelve-year-old daughter Veronica.

In the mezzadrine system, half the produce or its value went to the owner, half to the worker. Chickens were an exception. This meant that small flocks were kept by many households, tended by farmers' wives. The money made from the eggs and meat paid for shoes for the children, medicine and other household needs. The bird was also known as *il pollo delle buccole* because the proceeds also procured gold earrings. It was a status symbol to have a pair of these earrings, which were often decorated with semi-precious stones – perhaps in the shape of a flower. In the 1970s many were converted into rings; Nicola wore one from her family and her daughter the other. Town women had different earrings, she said; her particular kind was a badge of rural identity.

The mezzadrine system ceased and land ownership passed to the tenants. Many chose to leave for the cities; but most of those who went kept a small corner of countryside to come back to at weekends and holidays, where they could touch base with the land. Large-scale farming has never been able to take off in this area because the hilly terrain does not suit agribusiness. Some people have continued to keep a cow or two, grow some vegetables and have some chickens pecking around, looked after by neighbours as well as themselves.

The chickens that once laid the golden earrings now cluck around outside Nicola's house. She and Francesca produce about two thousand birds per year between them, sold for 11–12 euros each at some of the best restaurants in the area and at farmers' markets. All these customers know that Slow Food means quality. 'Their thoughts are for quality more than price, and I hope this sort of mentality will be the future,' said Nicola.

Because of the regional nature of agriculture a local breed had emerged, the Valdarno chicken. There they were, pecking around a spacious 7½-acre enclosure, their beautiful, clean white plumage with a smudge of gold on the shoulder, proud red wattles and polenta-yellow legs. There was a shed for shelter, though the chickens also roosted in the oak, olive and hazelnut trees on this smallholding, where wild grapevines curled in and around the branches. The ground was rich with grass and herbs, and the chickens were also fed on a mixture of grains that looked like a natural snack from a health food shop; a sort of bird muesli.

There was still a seasonality to the meat. In the spring and autumn the birds are ready to eat in four months; in the summer it takes longer because the heat makes the chickens feed less. 'We do not push them,' said Francesca. Hygiene was very important, and when the chickens go off to slaughter the land is left for a month while it is cleaned, not by dousing the place in chemicals, but with good old-fashioned rain and sun. This was a natural way of farming. 'Chickens are like people. They need good food, sun,' said Nicola. 'To fuck when they want,' she added, mischievously.

These were not just any old Valdarno chickens. Nicola and Francesca had worked with breeding experts from universities in the region to try to clean up the genetic stock that had become muddied during the many years when the chickens ran around with whomsoever they fancied. The university vets were used to working with battery chickens, and their visits to the Slow Food birds taught them and their students another way. This enterprise, small and individual as it may seem, was reaching into the wider world.

This small collective of Slow chicken farmers – four in all – had amassed an impressive depth of understanding. Francesca had interviewed two hundred chicken keepers, mostly women over the age of sixty, to discover the regional traditions of chicken farming. Some customs were no longer appropriate – such as getting male chickens drunk on a piece of wine-soaked bread in order to cut off their testicles to make them into capons. But there was still much to learn. 'The idea is not just to save the breed but to know the culture of it too,' she said. For her, as for many Italians, the countryside is a link with family roots. Growing up in Rome, she used to spend holidays, including three months in the summer, with her grandparents, who taught her country ways, such as picking tomatoes with her grandfather and eating them like fruit. 'They gave me the taste of simple, good things,' she says. Her great-aunt would keep the hatching chicks below her bed, since this was the warmest place in the house. Francesca and Nicola have an incubator, but Nicola's neighbour was still using the old-fashioned method of putting the eggs under a turkey hen, who could manage twenty at a time.

The three of us talked of hatching and found ourselves doing a nesting dance, like a wholesome version of a Jamaican batty wiggle. As I laughed about this image later I wondered: could part of the chicken's future be anything at all to do with women doing chicken impersonations? Well, undoubtedly not directly. But there was a joy and an empathy in the way Nicola and Francesca farmed that was good news for the birds. This felt like a new and viable version of the hen-wives of yore. I remembered the organic farmer at Sheepdrove, Andrew Gunther, making the feminist point that the problems of chicken production began when it was taken out of the hands of farmers' wives and into male-dominated industrial production.

When I asked them about industrial chickens, they both pulled a face. 'If people could see these places, they would stop eating it,' Nicola said, simply. She had visited one such place and seen a dead chicken standing there, wedged in by others, unable to drop to the ground.

The Valdarno chicken was taken on board the Slow Food Ark of Taste, and Nicola and Francesca began to hold events at which they cooked regional recipes and promoted the idea of regional chicken. They attend Slow Food's famous October Salone del Gusto in Turin, visited by people from all over the world. These events are an interface between Slow Food and the rest of the globe, and also between Italians and their own produce. Nicola described how parents would say their children would never touch a traditional sauce, but when they were given one with mashed up livers and hearts on crostini they found it delicious. The previous year they had met a Chinese chicken producer who killed millions of chickens to supply

McDonald's. 'When he heard what we did, he looked at us as if we were Jesus.'

I went out to look again over the chicken-dotted valley below the house. The hills beyond folded into each other. I could hear the women talk, interspersed with gleeful ciggie-cackle as they shared jokes. The grey-green of the olive leaves, like graceful flames, was lit by early evening sunlight. From the white chickens rose the soft sound of crowing, of flapping wings, and all around was running, curiosity, pecking, gathering, and a moving pattern of red combs as the birds explored their own space. The handsome fowl were as high-slung and stylish as Ducati motorbikes. Both the farm and the birds had a particular beauty. Thanks to these new-wave Slow chicken farmers, and others like them, they would continue to exist. It was biodiversity in action.

Slow Food started from Italian roots but its strength is that, with diversity at its very heart, it can adapt to local conditions. One of the strongest convivia in Britain is in north-west England. When I discovered that they were having a meal in Manchester based on the traditional English chicken dish called Hindle Wakes, it seemed the perfect opportunity to see what Slow Food meant here.

The event was Manco-Italian, set in a good restaurant called Palmiro run by a Venetian chef in south Manchester. One of the convivium's organizers, Michele Barlow, spoke to me briefly about chickens on the phone beforehand. She put the issues very simply, as everyone does. 'Tell people to get an egg and rear a chicken from it,' she said. 'Take the bird to Tesco and see whether you can make a profit.

Conversely, imagine what happens to a chicken in order for a profit to be made. It makes people think. It is surprising how people who ought to know better don't want to pay £10 or more for a chicken.'

The guest of honour was William Black, author of a gastro-travel book about traditional British food, *The Land that Thyme Forgot*. It was, we agreed, hard to find traditional food, but it was definitely out there. Good food in Britain, traditional or otherwise, is like island-hopping. You need to know where you are going or you end up with the pretentious or the dismal. William was particularly impressed by the north-west, with its black puddings and other regional foods still widely available in markets. He fell for Hindle Wakes through its name. It was originally 'hen de la wake', a celebration dish from the wakes weeks when people would stay awake carousing to celebrate a local saint's day. I rather liked this edible, licentious foodie take on a religious festival, not dissimilar to the spirit of Christmas feasting, or Easter with its chocolate eggs. The dish was traditionally made by taking a capon or a boiling fowl, stuffing it with prunes, breadcrumbs and lemon rind, simmering it for four hours and then roasting to finish it off. Like a Mexican *mole*, it sounded delicious if slightly strange; certainly a dish fit for feasting.

The room was full of warmly bubbling conversation, and I joined one of the shared tables that made the event all the more convivial. I spoke with a couple hoping to keep bees on their allotment and a woman who found beautiful pieces of wood and made them into chopping boards. She knew of trees still growing that, in due course, would end up in kitchens. The way she talked of the quality and usefulness of her boards fitted Slow Food's motto: 'A firm defence of quiet material pleasure is the only way to oppose the universal folly of Fast Life . . .'

The conversation turned to chickens. The man opposite me was not eating the meat. In a former life as an accountant, he had audited an intensive broiler business. After the first visit, he never put the meat in his mouth again.

The main course arrived. There was a piece of breast and part of a thigh on an exceptionally long bone, and it had a proper chicken smell, rich and deep, such as you might get in an evolved broth. The meat had a completely different texture and taste from most chicken. You knew it was meat – not the anonymity of modern chicken. The rich stuffing on the side was almost Christmas pudding-like in its mixture of prunes and spices and nuts. There was a little dot of very intense lemon cream. Sweet, salty, black, yellow: the dish had contrasts and strong flavours, yet held its complexity together.

William spoke to us between courses. He was against *faux* nostalgia, but after his travels really believed that British food was far more than sandwiches and Stilton. He spoke with passion about his support for Slow Food and hoped the movement could take up and promote regional dishes like Hindle Wakes. That evening convinced me it was possible. The tastes in the dish – its strong contrasts, its mixture of fruit and spice – were part of the British taste heritage. This was not an evening of food culture set in aspic; it was a living, enjoyable exploration of a native dish worth reviving.

To follow the Slow Food event one step further, I went to see the supplier of the chicken. 'Age equals taste and texture,' said Richard Charles of Ellel Poultry near the

Trough of Bowland in Lancashire. The birds that he and his wife Susie raise are a slow-growing French breed, Sasso, that take fourteen weeks – two and a half times the lifespan of an industrial broiler – to grow to around 2 kg. They range in and out of four sheds in the couple's 'backyard' – the former walled garden of Susie's family home, which itself had been in and out of the family since the sixteenth century.

A river of retrievers flowed around me as soon as I stepped inside the door. I stood beside the couple as they prepared orders for the day; their customer base includes some of the best restaurants in Britain, such as the Water-side Inn and Locanda Locatelli. Susie and Richard started the business when they inherited the house and needed something to do. Richard had previously spent twenty years in the fine food business and had plenty of contacts. The farming is not the difficult part; the marketing is clearly what requires the skills. 'People buy from people,' he remarked. It clearly meant that people had to behave well towards each other. Richard won't deal with people he doesn't like working with: 'I just say, "Toodle-poo!"' he said breezily.

The first chickens they acquired, as a trial, were one-month-old broilers that had started out in an intensive operation. In just a couple of hours these chickens, pre-viously kept indoors, took to the outdoor life and were strolling around and pecking away. Nature is clearly more important than nurture. Then problems started. The chick-ens 'went off their legs' – the expression farmers use for broilers that can no longer stand because their growth rate exceeds their skeletons. Richard and Susie needed to find slower-growing breeds, produced to commercial specifica-tions, and that eventually meant, for them, going to France.

I went out with Susie to look at the birds. The sheds stood in a large area of bushes and grass where the chickens could peck away freely, secure from foxes in this old walled garden with its wrought-iron gates. The ginger Sassos had chosen mostly to stay inside – it was very cold that day – but they could easily have gone out. Whenever they have to be confined, for example when part of a shedful has to be collected up for slaughter, Susie told me the chickens emerge like schoolchildren let out at breaktime. There was also a generous scattering of the famous *poulet de Bresse*. These small, fine, beautiful birds sport white plumage, a bright red crest and blue legs – tricolor chickens worthy of the French flag. 'The cocks are real French males,' said Susie. 'They strut around thinking they are absolutely wonderful.' The birds did look pretty pleased with themselves. They had every reason to be.

It was, in short, a very tidy little operation. Demand outstripped supply; but the couple had reached a stage in their life when they didn't want to expand. I asked Stefano Bagnoli, the chef-owner of Palmiro, what he thought of the meat. Impressed. He had found it difficult to buy good birds, and having been to the farm to pick up the order for the Hindle Wakes evening, he wondered why. 'It's not rocket science,' he commented. 'It's more puzzling why more people aren't doing it.'

Slow Food events help raise awareness and build a market for such produce; and if this happens there should be more producers. Nobody is pretending that Slow Food alone can save the chicken or feed the world. But if genuinely good poultry farming thrives, it could play a useful part in the rural economy. British farming is going through a seismic shift as subsidies shift towards agri-environmental schemes rather than farmers being paid per animal. This affects cattle and sheep farmers; chickens are not subsidized. The Good Chicken could be a decent little earner for many a farm, providing – and this is a big caveat – the infrastructure is there to kill and sell the birds in a decent way. If only we were better at cooperatives, as farmers are in other countries.

More generally, Slow Food's diverse approach is one that combines the enjoyable with the sustainable. As society becomes increasingly concerned about food, and about meat in particular, it is good to have an organization that manages to be engaged in the underlying politics in such a human way, without chewing the joy out of what is on the plate.

In the meantime, I discovered that whilst there may be a dearth of good chicken farmers, there was certainly no shortage of another breed of chicken keepers.

Pet Poultry

The number of amateur chicken keepers in Britain became apparent when the spectre of bird flu appeared. Cock-a-doodle-a-*choo*! People started counting. The government took scientific advice and decided that people with fifty chickens or more should be compelled to join the new poultry register. But for the first time there was a reason to look at the trend as a whole. Judging from the bags of food sold – a different market from the bulk deliveries for professionals – a quarter of a million small-flock keepers is seen as an underestimate, and three hundred thousand is a more likely figure.

Fear of bird flu slightly checked the boom in hobby chickens. Some people got rid of their small flock altogether. The phone was soon ringing at a Sussex chicken sanctuary, Hen Heaven of Henfield. Its owner, Linda Turvey, was disapproving of lightweights ready to ditch their chicks. 'There'll be one black, one brown, one red, one speckled,' she said after one call. She was referring to the way such keepers like a flock as pretty and variegated as a flowerbed. 'I'll only take them if they include the hut. Then they won't be tempted to get any more.'

Most owners stood by their birds. They may not have filled in the numerous pages of the chicken census, but they kept a watchful eye on all the information spewing forth. For a start, the fear it engendered was scary. Parents who had bought hens faced questions at the school gate; neighbours started looking over the fence at the not-so-innocent birds. It had the potential to get nasty, even without the flu arriving. 'There's nothing I'm scared of like scared people,' said the American poet Robert Frost. In the meantime, the disease was a marketing opportunity for people selling biosecurity products such as protective breathing apparatus. Such goods were widely advertised in the poultry press.

A more positive result of the scare was that it showed how amateurs, collectively, add up. It is not just a matter of a few people keeping a couple of pretty fowl in a back garden; they are part of a movement that now numbers hundreds of thousands. The Hen Keepers' Association kept amateurs informed of the latest news about bird flu and lobbying the government to introduce a vaccine that would safeguard the interests of the free-ranging flock.

The last time there had been such a boom in small-time chicken keepers was during the Second World War. After 1940, when the government relaxed its rules on backyard runs, local councils began to encourage home food production of all sorts. You could breed for victory as well as dig for it; a chicken provided meat and eggs, (and a rabbit produced $2\frac{1}{2}$ lb of good meat). If you had fewer than twenty birds, you were allowed to keep all the eggs; above this number, you had to have a permit from the Food Office. Birds began to appear on city balconies and roof-tops, whilst suburban streets were filled with the sound of clucking and crowing. Neighbours were pacified with fresh eggs, a most welcome gift at a time when dried gunk was universal. But keeping chickens was not as simple as it might seem: livestock production does not run like clock-work, on whatever scale. One wartime owner in a Suffolk village was horrified to find that a rat had got to the fertile eggs of her hen, Dinah, just before they hatched, halting her plans for enlarging the flock. And sometimes people bought hens only to find they didn't produce eggs at all.

Today's rise in chicken keeping has particular motiva-tions, as can be seen by a new name for the birds: 'pet poultry'. A large number of birds are kept for pleasure, as a hobby, rather than primarily as food producers. Such chickens have names like Chickpea and Clarissa; many are seen solely as egg layers rather than providers of meat and new chicks. When chickens are killed for meat it raises 'issues', rather than being seen as a natural part of country life. One Surrey vicar, the Reverend Trevor Kemp, had to face the facts of death when he and his family brought a flock into their vicarage garden. 'Culling chickens is not a process that I enjoy, but I think that it's an ability that all poultry keepers should have,' he said in a profile in the magazine *Practical Poultry*. 'In our case, it certainly threw up some interesting discussions about life and death, the eating of meat, and the reasons for keeping domestic poultry in the first place.' The dead birds were put in the freezer for a couple of months 'for emotions to settle', and that did the trick.

During the course of writing this book, I came across a huge and diverse flock of pet poultry keepers. There was the down-to-earth duchess, and there were the travellers who took in rescue birds from battery farms. There was a growing band of Tesco-refuseniks who would now turn up for a dinner party with a half-dozen home-laid eggs rather than a box of chocs as a gift for the host. The largest section of owners seemed to be women aged between thirty and fifty, but there were also plenty of men, some of whom could be heard competing with each other in the pub about how many eggs their hens had laid that week. Male, female; old, young; town or country; wealthy or make-do-and-mend: whoever you are it feels good and purposeful to care for chickens, as for any creature. It is fun watching the chickens bob, peck and scratch around, squinching down for their dust-baths and chorusing softly with their slightly melancholy clucks. Above all, it gives you a special feeling to go out and collect their eggs, wondering whether the heavy one is a double-yolker, sometimes feeling the warmth of the new-laid, and knowing that all is well in the hens' world if they are healthy and happy enough to produce something as good as an egg.

One of the factors behind pet poultry is the Eglu. This trendy chicken hut comes in bright colours and has a shape as sexily curvy as an iMac. It was launched in 2004 and immediately made national headlines. Within two years the company making the hut, Omlet, was preparing to launch in the USA. All in all, the Eglu marks a new phase in chicken keeping because it appeals to a new market: the urban hobby chicken keeper. Around 90 per cent of Eglu owners live in cities, towns or suburbs.

The people behind this poultry phenomenon are four graduates of the Royal College of Art's industrial design course. Although two of the team had been brought up with chickens, they started with a mental blank sheet of paper and visited every kind of poultry practice, from battery cage sheds to the DIY huts that smallholders knock together from a few bits of wood and some nails.

It immediately became apparent that cleaning was a crucial issue. The Eglu is made of plastic so that it can be hosed down in a jiffy, and the droppings tray can be pulled out and sluiced with similar ease. Convenience is Omlet's watchword, falling in with this pressing modern desire. When testing the prototype on six families, they soon saw that people wanted to get the whole kit in one fell swoop. Omlet began to deliver the henhouse complete with chickens – one ginger, one black. They sell the feed and provide a total back-up service, including a website forum which has 1500 users. Part of their design training, explains one of the Eglu's designers, Johannes Paul, is that you don't ignore what people want; rather, you find a way to make your design fit your clients. 'People may toy with an idea, but if you put it into a desirable and convenient form they will change to someone who is serious about doing it,' he says. 'They've seen a way that makes sense and that they can achieve.'

Whilst chicken keeping is a great leveller, it has to be said that you pay for the convenience of an Eglu. Hardy smallholders are somewhat mocking of this aspect. The whole kit – everything down to the egg-boxes – costs £395. But that's chicken feed to many people who are affluent enough to want to keep chickens as a hobby rather than as a necessity. Johannes has delivered to roof terraces in Hackney and to Eton. At one posh pile, the owner enquired whether her cat might be a problem. It was a mini-leopard.

I became interested in these new chicken keepers and wondered how this step into livestock related to their interest in food, farming and nature as a whole. Damian Oliver is a typical Eglu owner who speaks affectionately of keeping the family's two chickens, named Amelia and Abigail after the ducks in *The Aristocats*, in the garden of a 1930s suburban semi in Surrey. The colour of their pink Eglu was chosen by his two daughters, Evie and Mabel, aged seven and three. Talking to Damian, it became immediately apparent that the eggs, although most welcome, were not the main reason for the enterprise. He spoke first of the sheer pleasure of having the chickens around. On a summer's evening he and his wife sit in the garden talking and watching Abigail and Amelia. 'It's the same sort of draw as an open fire,' he explains. 'It's almost hypnotic. They are always busy, and you watch them. They give you a warm, smiley feeling.' The two chickens have different characters. Amelia is the stronger personality and won't let herself be caught so easily. Abigail is more biddable, which is why she helps him with the odd bit of media work in promoting the Eglu. When we spoke, they had just been doing a photo shoot for the *Guardian* to illustrate an article on jokes. Why did the chicken cross the road? Now we know: because of a request from G2.

Damian's father had been a farmer and he grew up in a Suffolk village amongst a small domestic flock. At this stage, only the most sociable chicken had a name – Mrs Henny Penny. Sometimes Damian's dad used to disappear, and then there'd be roast chicken on the table. Damian once went to help pluck a bird himself but found it strange. He didn't get into shooting or fishing either. It took a while for his own family to decide to get chickens for themselves, largely because they were living in London. It was the Eglu that got them going because the hobby suddenly suited a largish urban garden.

The Olivers' initial fears about comments from the neighbours were quelled when the eighty-year-old next door immediately said it was good to have chickens back on the street; everyone had kept them during the war. As for admin, Damian cleans the birds out thoroughly once a week, changes the water and tops up the feed bowl once every two to three days, collects the eggs and shuts them up at night. That's pretty much it. If the family wants to go away for the weekend, they put the birds in the fox-proof run and have no worries.

A background motivation for keeping chickens was the whole issue of knowing where your food comes from. In his early teens, Damian was taken on a school trip to a battery egg farm. The industry was showing off its Brave New World production to the consumers of tomorrow. The idea backfired. 'The whole class trooped into what seemed like an endless row of cooped-up chickens. It was a horrific sight,' he says. 'I can recall the noise. Chickens make this low noise. Times that by thousands and you get a loud, continuous droning noise. They had artificial daytime and were producing eggs at an unnatural rate. It was quite a shocking experience.' It is part of the purpose of the Eglu to help the family keep in touch with where food comes from. The henhouse is not, however, called the Roast-U. They buy their chickens to eat as pre-prepared free-range meat from a supermarket.

The only real drama, apart from some concern about

bird flu, has been rescuing Abigail, twice, right from the jaws of an urban fox. The first time, there was an almighty rumpus in the garden as the family was eating lunch. Damian leapt up to find the ginger hen in the fox's mouth. A few carefully aimed stones and Abigail was free, wandering around punch-drunk. The fox jumped over the fence and looked at Damian, brazen as can be, with a few feathers still in its mouth. A week later, Damian was on the phone when he heard the same sort of shrieking. He dashed outside and rescued her again. This time the hen was punctured in the chest and bleeding a little. But the next morning she was up and running around, though it was a month before she laid eggs again. There's a much greater threat to the chickens during January and February when the foxes are building their dens and breeding. From now on, says Damian, his two birds will range a little less freely at this time. 'It's only nature,' he comments. 'They are only trying to feed their young and live. I'd just rather it wasn't my chickens.' Soon afterwards the family gathered, fascinated and charmed, to watch and film five fox cubs play on the lawn in front of the chickens in their fox-proof Eglu-run.

Another big impetus behind the pet poultry movement is the Battery Hen Welfare Trust. A human version of *Chicken Run*, its thirteen regional rescue coordinating centres scoop up large loads of ex-battery egg layers and give them homes with volunteers. The bird 'girls', as they are known, soon pick up hennish ways, giving the lie to the idea that such creatures are bred to be adapted to their conditions. Nearly 11,500 hens were rescued in 2005. Not many, perhaps, compared to the tens of millions that are produced annually for the national flock. But it's still a handsome number, and the movement as a whole has caught the public's imagination, attracting new types to chicken keeping and thereby engaging more people in the issues of farmed animals.

You can see why battery rescue feels worthwhile. Even the most extreme reality TV programme cannot produce the sort of transformation you can get with a rescue hen. There is poignancy and a sense of triumph in seeing an animal come back to its nature. One series of photos on the website shows a particularly terrible case. 'This is Yoko,' the caption reads, 'who arrived with two broken legs, a broken toe and a chronic chest infection; she was also skeletal.' This pitiful picture – the creature looks half-dead – is then replaced by a better image, taken three weeks later, when Yoko can sit up and support herself. Five weeks on, she manages to stand up. It's heart-wrenching stuff.

Since the motivations of the pet poultry movement are different from those of traditional chicken keepers, it is hardly surprising that some old-timers see the newcomers as a tad sentimental. Many older keepers tend to be more matter-of-fact about their birds. 'They keep birds for a purpose,' explained Chris Graham, editor of *Practical Poultry*. 'They are either working or showing birds. If they don't meet the standards, the bird goes. So they can't quite grasp why anyone would want to keep and nurse back to health a tired battery hen.'

But many aspects of poultry keeping remain the same whoever you are. Chris spoke of some of the problems that have to be dealt with: feather-pecking; blood-sucking red mites; cocks harming the hens as they mate; the need for good ventilation in the hen-house; recognizing disease before it was too late. Chickens tend to look fine, he said, unless you know the signs, and then everything can go wrong very quickly. 'If you get to the point where the bird is away in the corner huddled and hunched up, the chances are it is getting on for too late to do anything about it,' he warned. 'You have to be responsible. The birds depend on you for their welfare and health and happiness. If you don't do it properly, they suffer.'

There are risks attached to pet affection. Chickens are more than a garden accessory; they bring you face to face with hard facts, and sometimes it doesn't help to be sentimental. The next step from keeping chickens is to get a cockerel and hatch out some eggs. Only half the chicks will be egg-laying females. Do you dispatch the boys straightaway, or kill them later for meat? Or pass them on to some bloke from the small ads? There was even a macabre rumour going around that people are unwittingly selling their unwanted birds into the underground world of cockfighting.

Yes, there's an element of nostalgia in chicken keeping. People had them as children, or remember their grandparents having them. It has an old-fashioned, cottage-garden type of image. This certainly explains the likes of the granary-look, staddle-stone mini-chicken 'barns' you see advertised (yours for £475) in the poultry press. But the emergence of the Eglu shows that chicken keeping is not fixed in sepia. And it is never going to be a light decision to keep chickens. Even if some people may go into it with a slightly soft-focus view, that is soon sharpened up by day-to-day reality.

The world of special breeds that first boomed in the Victorian era still exists today. The Domestic Poultry Trust in Honeybourne, Worcestershire, is an extraordinary place to visit. I'd recommend it to anyone with an ounce of curiosity and a love of variety. There are some 120 kinds of chickens here, housed in sections based on origins. You wander the globe, from Chinese chickens in pagoda-style huts to the Egyptian Faverolles that can roost quite high and are good at escaping the fox. There are Orloff chickens with big eyebrows, and birds with gigantic earlobes or with beautiful markings or a comic way of running. I stood in this remarkable place and listened to the planet of fowls calling out, and wondered if they all spoke the same language. Could the Japanese bantams be understood by the American turkeys? I met an artist here who was drawing the birds. We agreed they could be hard to pin down: whenever I raised my camera lens, or she her pen, they would dart off, instincts alert to the predator.

The chicks hatched here are sold to amateur keepers. Some amateurs belong to breed clubs that meet and show regularly, both at their own specialist shows, generally in the winter when the birds are in full feather, and at county shows during the summer. Showing does encourage people to focus on the rarer breeds, which is important. Some types of endangered chickens are down to their last hundred-odd, and dedicated groups of enthusiasts are crucial keepers of the genetic flame. It is important to maintain biodiversity, in chickens as in every other part of life.

I went to see the secretary of one such dwindling breed, Toddy Hamilton Gould of the Scots Dumpy Society. All around her place in Oxfordshire were unusual breeds: frilly geese, Wiltshire Horn sheep, dogs, cats, horses. I could see her husband tending a vintage car in his garage. The Dumpy's main characteristic is its very short legs, and Toddy's hens and cockerels scuttled about their enclosure like hats on wheels. Or, as she put it rather more elegantly, sailed along like boats. Like a number of chicken breeds, with their firm stance and erect hearing they also reminded me of the animal welfare professor John Webster – although their dignity is somewhat undermined by the fact that in long grass they appear to have no legs at all. Not all the birds inherit the short-legged gene, however, and Toddy gives these ones away because she is trying to preserve the true characteristics of the breed. She shows the birds but also enjoys their food production, collecting the eggs and serving them to her b&b guests and her family and friends, and sometimes fattening up cockerels to eat. They taste like chicken did thirty years ago, she said, 'Slightly gamey, with a much darker meat and really tasty.'

The Dumpy only lays an egg a day for four to five months, when the daylight hours lengthen, and even then there can be gaps when individual birds get broody. It's hardly in tune with modern mass-production, and you can see how the breed became rare, with only about five or six hundred in existence today. But numbers have gone up considerably in the last thirty years thanks to the society. There is a Rare Poultry Society concerned with all such breeds, but twelve years ago the Dumpies were strong enough to have their own group with a biannual newsletter and an annual meeting at the National Poultry Show in Stoneleigh, Warwickshire. Avian flu has highlighted the vulnerability of such birds. 'People have suddenly realized there are rare breeds of poultry as well as pigs, cattle, sheep and everything else,' says Toddy. 'If there's an outbreak of avian flu and the government insists on a culling regime, they will die out very quickly.'

Showing birds is one way in which rare breeds are kept going, but it is done for looks more than for productivity. Judy Hancox at Butts Farm near South Cerney in Gloucestershire has been a keen breeder since she was given her first birds at the age of eight. She enjoys all the paraphernalia of showing: washing and drying the birds, putting oil on their faces and legs to make them shine. She says there's even one show-man who is a hairdresser and puts his birds under the salon's dryers for a final fluff. You need to find the perfect bird at the perfect stage, she says. Appearance matters. When people come to the farm to buy birds they may talk initially of egg numbers, but in the end most of them fall for looks.

Some of the most extravagant-looking birds are the ones which lay the fewest eggs precisely because so much energy goes into the externals. The reliance on looks makes one fear for the future of the rarer chicken breeds. They will remain the domain of interested amateurs unless useful traits, such as good egg production, are also selected for. One of the strange truths about rare breeds is that their future depends on how much they are used. Their future depends, at least partly, on us eating them and their eggs. If this aspect interests you, the Rare Breeds Survival Trust website has a list of accredited butchers.

The issue of eating rare breeds is – with one notable exception – squarely addressed at Butts Farm. You can wander round admiring all the animals and then you can buy their meat from a farm shop. But not that of the rare chickens. A veteran breeder said to Judy, 'Why try to reinvent the wheel? People have spent millions of pounds crossing to get the perfect table bird. Make the most of it.' The twenty-odd chickens she produces for the shop every week are a hybrid breed developed specially for meat. She feeds them on chick crumbs, then growers' pellets and, by the time they are twelve weeks, on pure wheat. The birds are killed at six months – a lot older than the six-week broilers. The quality of the birds can be judged by the fact that some go off to London restaurants to such meat-savvy chefs as John Torode and Fergus Henderson. Sure, there are some Indian Game running around the place, the type that was crossed to produce more breast on meat birds, but by the time these pure-breeds are ready for the pot, at about a year old, Judy thinks they are only good for boiling.

The closeness of farm and shop is important to the whole enterprise; this is about showing where meat comes from. Judy does educational work with the Countryside Foundation, showing children the animal origins of food and other products such as wool. She has noticed a real change in attitude as people get more involved and feel less uncomfortable about the facts of meat eating. A primary school-teacher once asked Judy's daughter Rosie, 'How can you eat your own animals?' The child turned the question around, replying, 'How can you eat animals that are not your own? I know how they have been reared.'

Judy is a country person, with a down-to-earth, knowledgeable attitude to her birds. She has affection rather than sentimentality for the chickens. I asked many of the chicken owners about their animals' intelligence. Toddy Hamilton Gould asserted, 'Chickens aren't stupid. They definitely have characters, and some have much stronger characters than others.' Another person, who spends most of his working life thinking about chickens, said straightaway, 'They aren't very deep-thinking creatures. They are wily and perhaps a little bit crafty at times, but I don't think there's anything desperately dramatic going on between the ears.' Some breeders just replied that of course chickens were stupid. Judy's answer showed respect. 'In lots of ways they are much more intelligent than we are,' she said. 'It's just they are not very good at knowing what we want. You have cats and dogs and horses that seem to have a greater understanding of what we want. Chickens don't have that. But they're not stupid.'

One of the most unusual places I visited on the chicken trail was a school farm. When Warriner School was built on a greenfield site, Oxfordshire County Council bought 70 acres and devoted 40 of them to agriculture. Some of the land has ancient ridge-and-furrow fields, showing the lines of historic cultivation. Another field was used within living memory as large allotments, where villagers would grow strips of corn to take to a local mill. Not many of the pupils have direct experience of farming these days – under 3 per cent. But the farm gives everyone at the school, and young people beyond, a proper chance to learn about how food is produced.

John Hirons is the teacher in charge. When he took over funding had been cut dramatically, yet persistence and hard work have kept the place going. Now this hands-on approach is back in favour. All the eleven-year-olds visit the farm in their first year at the school, and then it plays an intermittent role for the rest of their time – for example in the science curriculum, or when domestic science students run out of eggs. A small group focuses on the farm in a GCSE on environmental and land-based studies. Thirty pupils were taking this subject when I visited, but numbers were likely to double because an additional teacher had been appointed. Other schools visit the farm; it is an unusual resource these days, and one that is increasingly valued.

'We're into measuring everything these days,' said John when I asked about the advantages of having a school farm. 'I don't think you can measure some of the benefits, but you can see and feel them when you're here.' At lunchtime there are thirty or forty children around doing chores or just visiting. For some of them, the place is a haven. 'They can create a bond with animals that they may not have with their peers,' says John. 'It gives them an opportunity to care when they might come from a very uncaring background. Then there's simply the opportunity to see animals behaving naturally. They get used to that, and it's then much easier to talk about spotting abnormal behaviour. It's training them in observation and in using their eyes to see rather than to look.'

When John arrived, the farm had a battery cage system. That went. Now they keep a number of breeds, including the rare-breed Old English pheasant fowl, which are good layers – about 320 eggs a year – and hatch well, too. All the breeds produce fertile eggs that go off to be incubated and hatched at other schools, and the progeny then come back to Warriner. There are a number of different types of chicken hut in the yard, including an Eglu, so the students can learn how they work. They are also encouraged to keep chickens themselves, buying farm birds for a modest price.

The chickens, along with the pigs, tiny Dexter cattle and goats, help the pupils learn about the RSPCA's 'Five Freedoms': that animals should have food, water and shelter, be free from illness and injury and be allowed to behave normally. What do they learn from the chickens in particular? Take just the eggs. 'They understand that most of the eggs you buy in a supermarket would be no good at all in an incubator, that you need a cockerel,' says John. 'So there's a bit of sex education going on there. They often hadn't thought about what they eat as the raw materials that, given the right conditions, will turn into feathers and eyes and brains and so on. They look at eggs in a quite different way when they think about that. Adults as well as children take things for granted. We are so far removed from our food.'

A farm that produces meat, eggs and milk makes this link in many ways. Visiting primary school pupils, from Year Six, will weigh newborn lambs and then older lambs, and then take a lamb out of the freezer to weigh that too. At one level it is a maths exercise, demonstrating growth rates and so forth; but it also shows where their chops come from. Education doesn't get much more real than this.

Because of the farm, the children see chicken as chickens. John's dissections of dead cockerels show all the bits inside a bird. The pupils are fascinated by the fact that chickens have earlobes and therefore ears. He pulls the tendons to make the claws move. Even the squeamish who have gone off to the other side of the classroom come back to watch that. 'You need,' John repeated, 'to get them to see rather than look.'

The bird flu scare meant there was some disquiet in the school about the chickens. John kept calm and sorted out the real risk from the hype. He made it clear that if the birds went, it wouldn't be just for a season. The birds would be gone for years and years and years. Chickens are the one type of animal on the farm that pupils take home and look after for themselves; these are the next generation of chicken keepers, who understand through personal experience what makes a chicken a chicken and an egg an egg.

The chicken keepers matter, and this is why: knowledge is the best anchor against the storm-swells of scares and the background machinations of industry with its ever-hardening bottom line. The more people keep chickens, the safer they are – and not just from the fox.

Home to Roost

Lewes, the county town of East Sussex where I live, is draped over hills. Because a number of its streets curve downwards you can see the countryside beyond, framed between the buildings in tall, vertical slices that combine town and field. Did a vast digestive system still connect these green surroundings with the stomachs that resided within the houses?

Local food is not especially easy to track down. The independent shops do have a certain amount, and now flag it up. The highest concentration by far is in the monthly farmers' market, where there are two local poultry sellers. As well as free-range meat chickens the Hanburys also offer boiling fowl from their old egg layers, which make the mother of all chicken soups. It is unusual to see such hens on sale; most farmers have to pay to get rid of birds like these. This was an example of how such markets offer

271

different produce. The Hanburys' free-range chickens have long, strong legs; their free-range eggs have perky yolks. One detail caught my eye on the information board at the side of the other stall. At Ersham Farm the birds were barn-reared. Was 'free-range' the be-all and end-all? I had come to be slightly suspicious of categories for their own sake. I decided to take a look for myself.

Driving deeper and deeper into the Sussex countryside, I was drawn into some kind of enchantment. It was a beautiful day with an autumnal glow. Pheasants wobbled out of hedges. The scene was lit with the liquid clarity of October sun. Yet this was not some impossible rural idyll; I was about to meet one of the people who make this beautiful English countryside a real, working place.

Ersham Farm is a bucolic remnant amongst the industrial sprawl and housing estates on the edge of Hailsham. Here Michael Vine rears, kills and sells five to six hundred chickens a fortnight. The youngest live for eight weeks and the oldest for up to eighteen weeks or so. Some reach $6\frac{1}{2}$ lb, a mighty weight for a bird to reach without 'going off its legs'. This is possible because they are fed a relatively low-protein feed and therefore grow at an unhurried rate. The birds are kept in what is called a deep litter system. Groups of five hundred are kept in barns with natural light and ventilation. Wood chips from local joineries cover the ground and are replenished daily to give the birds a dry, clean place to scratch and peck around.

The birds were kept in a terrace of sheds, each holding a batch at a different age. Michael pulled back the first door. Before me scuttled the newly arrived day-old chicks. They were like animated eggs, still yellow from the egg. It was hard to believe that the creatures were so young – they seemed bigger and more active than mere infants. Michael explained that they come wet out of the shell and then fluff up, adding to their tiny volume. Standing before this farmed clutch, I instinctively went 'aahh' and felt myself puffing up like a broody hen. The chicks were kept within an eight-foot circle inside the shed, with feeding bowls and a heat lamp. They rushed around like clockwork toys, running into each other, stopping and then starting again. I couldn't believe that there were five hundred in this small space until Michael pointed at the five boxes, each of which had contained a hundred birds. The day-old chicks now come by van. They used to arrive by train until British Rail stopped transporting animals. It is now only just possible for a small farm, like all places reliant on the big hatcheries, to get supplies in such relatively tiny quantities. Not for the first time, I felt the fragility of local food. We may think its future lies in consumer demand for a quality product; but what if it really depends on the logistics and economics of freight?

I asked Michael about the drugs required to rear the birds. As well as the routine vaccines given by the hatcheries, Michael gives the chicks a one-off dose of a coccidio-stat in the water right at the start, rather than routinely giving them drugged feed, so that they build up their own immunity. We moved into a shed of four-week-olds. They still had yellow heads but had grown enormously, though less than conventional broilers.

In the six-week olds' shed, I found myself looking at the birds in a different way. These white-feathered creatures were now large enough to imagine in a roasting tin. It was a serious thought that these animals existed for me to eat. But I didn't feel disturbed by their welfare. They seemed well looked after, not least because the operation was being carried out on a scale that made it possible for Michael to be aware of every single one, every day. The welfare of the birds really was important. In one chicken shed was a turkey from another barn that had been picked on by its fellows. Birds go for shimmering, reflective things. They move in on even a bead of blood. Michael had taken the turkey out of its barn to be amongst the chickens. It now looked entirely at ease, if egregious. It was, he said, like a turkey 'hospital'. I bought one of the turkeys for the family Christmas lunch, and felt happy to put it in the centre of a festive table.

I went back to Ersham Farm. It was a Monday, the day the birds are killed. I had a cold and it was raining. The February sky was dark. I sat for a couple of minutes in the car, psyching myself up for the experience. I half wondered whether I would throw up. The queasiness of the subject; the need to depart from the pleasures of food and get my pen dirty; my physical state: all combined with the difficult idea of seeing animals die. But this was a place that I sensed I could trust. If I couldn't face up to the facts of death here, then it was all over.

The killing shed was clean and workmanlike. Michael was in the back and greeted me with a wave. It couldn't have been easy having a curious stranger coming into your life, but he had nothing to hide. There was one man doing the killing, and he has worked for decades at this family farm, since he was twelve. Like many of the butchers I've met, he was a cheerful chap. Would this be the case in a big processing plant where the workforce are economic units, just like the chickens?

The birds were in crates at one side of the shed. They

didn't seem distressed, but just sat there quietly. Watching the slaughterman work, you could see it was a craft. He didn't rush. It was a calm, ordered job. He took each bird by hand, individually, and put it head-down into a metal cone. Then he put an electric charger to its head. This stuns the bird. Then he cut its throat. The blood ran. It was the reddest red that I'd ever seen. A pan below collected the blood. Each bird twitched for a short while, but was definitely dead. It was a job the slaughterman did once a week and he was good at it; and he did not have to do it all the time. Buying this chicken was also buying into a system that did not push people to their limit and beyond.

When the carousel of cones had been finished, the birds were plucked. I watched the chickens I ate, softened from the scalding tank, go into a churning metal contraption that was full of rubber fingers beating the birds softly so their feathers came out without bruising the flesh. While all this was going on Michael was at the back, cleaning the plucked birds off by hand and putting an elastic band around the legs to show off the breasts. The birds would next go into a refrigerated room. Even though the chickens had been wet-plucked, they could still be hung for several days and then be gutted. The place was dry and clean; and the chickens would not be sitting wrapped in sweaty plastic on a shelf. It was safe to hang the birds like this and contributed to making them taste so good. You could produce a high-welfare bird and yet lose out in terms of taste without this sort of attention to the last part of the process. I've eaten Michael's chicken most often roasted. Its flavour comes through in the crispy skin, the running juices, the slightly caramelised, tacky goodness of the gravy, as well as in the meat. Good chickens; good food.

When I think back to seeing the birds die, most of it is in black and white in comparison to the blood. However much we think of chicken as innocent white meat, colourless as a blank page, this is an illusion. I found it profoundly important to see this blood. In an unhysterical way, it made me take the whole business more seriously and more realistically. That is a good thing. If you are going to eat meat, or 'eat animals' as the food writer Hugh Fearnley-Whittingstall puts it, then it is best to do so well and know some of the detail of the way the bird is produced.

Michael said people often asked him, 'Are they happy chickens?' 'I like to think they are,' he said. 'How do you judge happiness?' Good question, and like all good questions, hard to answer precisely. You could start with what makes an unhappy chicken. Michael did not criticize the broiler farming industry, but I had my own views. An unhappy chicken is one that is grown to the point at which the bird can hardly stand. One that is shoved in a lorry for a long journey when it can get too hot or too cold. One that is shackled upside-down with painful legs on a long killing-line. In contrast, there were many positives at this small chicken farm on the edge of Hailsham.

I had begun to see that scale was, for me, one of the issues surrounding meat. Of course you can get small producers who keep animals badly, but few such places survive now unless they offer a quality product. Part of the point of local food, and of a farmers' market, is being able to meet the person responsible, and feeling that, where chickens are concerned, he or she respects the birds. You could never do this on a large scale. If bird flu means chickens have to go indoors, this could be done to an adequate welfare standard. But it could not be done by the million, and it could not be done without the skilled attention to detail that is given at Ersham Farm.

I found other Sussex chickens, but it wasn't easy. The county used to be famous for its fowl, but now special local birds were thin on the ground. Many chefs and shops commented that they couldn't get enough meat of this kind. I ate some sensationally good chicken that probably wasn't strictly legal; the farmer didn't want to get involved with regulations and sold to friends. The bird I ate had pecked its way around for nearly four months and was a good size, which meant it had had time to develop more flavour. This farmer had begun keeping broilers when, like me, he had stood in front of the poultry counter in a supermarket and was disturbed by an odd fact. 'They were all the same,' he said. 'Every one was the same – right down to the ounce. And they are *not* all the same: chickens are all so individual.'

One of the most encouraging places I visited was a small farm shop at Furners Green, a short drive north of Lewes. Fourteen years ago, Sharon Barnard and Trevor Gregory had featured in a piece in the local paper about young farming couples who could not afford to get their own place. Twelve years later, they finally managed to get the Old Dairy. This is the sort of place that could give skilled, local farming a future. And it is the answer for a number of shoppers. You can visit the farm and then buy its produce just metres away. The Portakabin shop sells freshly picked vegetables, ready-prepared foods and meat from a mix of livestock, including local breeds. It was homely, friendly, unvarnished, real and honest. Sharon's mother, Linda, made this straightforward comment about meat eating: 'Either you decide you are going to be a vegetarian or you are going to eat meat and take responsibility for it.' The Old Dairy wasn't going to feed the world, or the county; but the people who came here would be happy eaters, and they would come back. In contrast the vast pig farm down the road, with thirty thousand animals, had shut down.

It is easy for industrialists to scoff at the small-scale. But a large number of such operations mount up to a significant movement. While British farming is in a state of some turmoil, one way forward is locally produced quality food. William Kendall is one farmer who fervently believes this is the future. He is a man with a foot in two kinds of agriculture. He helps run a large conventional farm in Bedfordshire with his cousin, who happens to be the president of the National Farmers' Union. And for the last three years he has been setting up his own small organic family farm, Maple Farm in Kelsale, Suffolk, selling directly to local shoppers. The Suffolk project is the polar opposite of the monoculture of agribusiness. Instead of churning out a commodity William is learning many different skills, from milling the farm's wheat to selling eggs at farmers' markets, through a box scheme and at their own farm shop. The family's three hundred hens forage in woodland and on pasture to the extent that a sizeable amount of their food comes from this source rather than from grain feed. Beyond this, William has a great deal of experience in marketing food through building up two successful businesses as the chief executive of Green & Black's chocolate and of the New Covent Garden Soup Company. This sort of outlook and experience should bring to fruition a modern version of a family farm. Can it work?

Take a few statistics. A tonne of potatoes produced organically and sold locally gets William £1200, compared to the £100 he might get selling chemically produced potatoes into a commodity market. He employs around nine people on the farm, often women or retired men who want this sort of work and fit into a place like this when they wouldn't slot behind a desk. His eggs are sold for around 30p each. Expensive? Yes. But he cannot produce enough, such is the demand. But instead of upping production and putting the birds under pressure, he is keeping them as part of a patchwork of goods that add up to make the whole enterprise viable. 'We need to get food on to another agenda – that it's not just another commodity,' he says. 'The cheap chicken you buy may fill your stomach, but does it lift your spirits? Does it help you live a long and healthy life, or does it keep you going until your next trip to the doctor?'

The Real Choice, a report by Caroline Cranbrook published in 2006 by the Council for the Protection of Rural England, showed how, over eight years, the network of good local food producers thriving in this part of east Suffolk has brought many benefits to the area including fewer food miles, fresh produce, characterful high streets rather than clone towns, and more wildlife in a living countryside – benefits that are appreciated by a wide range of consumers and not just the wealthy. 'High standards of sustainable production, good animal welfare, and viable rural communities are key elements in our national quality of life whether we live in the rural communities portrayed in this report or in densely populated areas,' writes Barry Gardiner MP, Minister for Biodiversity, Landscape and Rural Affairs, in the report's introduction. Is this lip service or will politicians really get into the nitty-gritty – the planning consents, the processing infrastructure, the regional distribution centres, the small slaughterhouses – that will make a difference?

There is a demand for this type of chicken, this type of food; there are farmers who need to make a living from the countryside. What, then, can pull them together and make the good, local chicken more available? I went to see Topsy Jewell at the Netherfield Centre for Sustainable Food and Farming, an organization that promotes local food. On the wall of this working farm in mid-Sussex was a board showing the bookings for their course, including one on producing poultry for the table, tutored by Michael Vine.

Topsy said there really had been a resurgence of people producing naturally reared and grown produce. Lots of small producers in the area were successfully doing their own direct marketing. There was word-of-mouth advertising through children's schools and neighbours, and a new development in the form of the village markets which were starting up. As a founder of the organization Common Cause, Topsy had got the Lewes farmers' market going ten years ago. I listened to her talk of the early days – getting up at the crack of dawn to put up stalls that took your fingers off, and the ups and downs of raising money and negotiating practical and legal obstacles – and got a sense of the pioneer spirit behind this local food movement. Now the farmers' market is heaving every month and there's a waiting list for stalls. The issue of whether it could be held more frequently was a tricky one: it wouldn't be right to take too much custom away from the local shops in Lewes. There will be a way forward, eventually, that will have to be negotiated carefully within the town; it will have to enlarge the overall market for local food rather than pitting small producers against each other.

There is a genuine grass-roots movement in favour of local food, but at the same time an urgent need to hook it into a slightly larger system. 'The local food network has been completely destroyed by supermarkets,' said Topsy. 'A lot of what we're doing is re-creating that network. We're putting producers back in touch with the butchers, for example. It's a bit of a slow *ad hoc* process, but it is building. I'd like to see a much stronger network re-created. It's only putting back what was there fifty years ago. In a way that's a big frustration, because it was there and now it has gone.'

Topsy mentioned that farm shops and markets couldn't get enough chickens. What were needed were the infrastructure of killing and processing plants, refrigerated vans and pick-up points that could help smaller farms to be part of a local food supply. This infrastructure will only get going when there is volume. But then again there will only be volume once the infrastructure is in place.

One way forward for increasing the volume of local and regional food is procurement. This term covers the food that goes into hospitals and local authority operations, not least school dinners. Organizations such as Sustain, the alliance for local food, are doing ground-breaking work on getting such places to source locally. The NHS in London gets through 1.3m chicken legs a year. That's a lot of chickens. If Sussex, and any other county or city, found ways for restaurants to use the chickens' breasts (since this seems to be what customers want), and for schools and hospitals to get the nourishing thighs, and perhaps some pubs to have the wings as bar snacks, then a whole local bird would be starting to look really profitable. All this would take a great deal of coordination and organization at a regional and local level. It would need some government help as well as the drive of local and regionally minded entrepreneurs. This kind of initiative isn't about heavy-handed intervention; more about enabling alternative systems to exist. Can local government help local production?

We think of front lines as being in distant places. But they are also at our front door and connected to our own lives and shopping habits. Whilst scale is important, the individual is too. Buying a local chicken is a big personal step forward because it puts us shoppers back in touch with where food comes from and engages us in the arguments at all levels of food production. Local food may seem like a small movement, but its importance is greater than the single purchase.

Local food can be found anywhere, albeit in increasingly smaller quantities: it is in itself a global movement. I learnt of a Sustainable Livelihoods Programme being organized by OXFAM with EU funding in Colombia. The aim is to reconnect poor rural farmers with the cities so that they can sell fresh goods to urban consumers. Alongside this has been a successful campaign by the city authority to keep regional distribution centres going in the capital, Bogota. This means that local markets can continue to operate even as multinationals pant at the gates trying to set up ever larger, more streamlined systems of food distribution that would push such small producers out of the marketplace altogether. There are 4 million small-scale farmers in Colombia who could benefit from being able to sell their goods in this way, and half a million consumers who would then have better access to fresh local produce.

A (literally) graphic depiction of the global food system can be found in the award-winning *Atlas of Food* (2003) by Erik Millstone and Tim Lang. Its forty-two spreads vividly illustrate the international reach of such issues as animal feed, pesticides, food miles, trade disputes, animal transportation, food ownership – just about every issue that touches on the chicken, as well as the rest of what we eat and drink. Erik Millstone is Professor of Science Policy at the University of Sussex, and I seized the opportunity to hear his global take on local chicken.

He immediately snapped any precious ivory fork in two: if you live on a council estate with no transport other than a bus then local, fresh organic produce is inaccessible both physically and in terms of cost. 'I get very bored and irritated when some of my more wealthy friends sit around boasting about the lengths they go to to have local, fresh organic produce when actually it's an exercise in conspicuous consumption – showing off their wealth and leisure. It's not a solution to the problem for the whole of society,' he said. In the case of the chicken: 'I don't want food dipped in disinfectant so it can survive a pointless and unnecessary eight-thousand-mile journey just so some fat cat in Bangkok can buy some more cocaine and pornography, but I don't see why honest, decent Thai farmers should be prevented from sharing in the benefits of globalization. The fact that a chicken is produced in Thailand doesn't mean that somehow the chicken is treated less favourably than in Buxted in Sussex. I don't want high-end exotic foods coated in pesticides coming in from Kenya, but I think farmers in developing countries should have as good access to our markets as industrial farmers have to theirs.

That isn't a matter of localization against globalization. Its about globalizing equity and localizing equity.'

   Local, clearly, is not the whole solution to the chicken story; but it is part of the solution, and it may well be one of the options most directly available to readers of this book. Erik's comments were none the less a good splash of cold water on my thinking. However much your own choices matter – and they do – you should never forget the bigger picture. By 2050, the fifty poorest countries in the world may have free access to global trade in all products other than arms. Whilst it is hard to argue against poorer countries being given access to bigger markets and raising their gross domestic product, can this happen in a way that takes into account animal welfare, fair trade and sustainability? Will local markets be destroyed by more ruthless global ones? Will locally produced (and eaten) free-range chickens be replaced by ones produced by US-owned broiler multi-nationals partly to be exported? Even if you are not flying fresh birds to far-off markets but deep-freezing them by the tonne to travel by boat, you are still considerably upping the carbon count compared to what happens in fresh local production. Wouldn't it be better to develop or sustain regional markets, as OXFAM is seeking to do, rather than further globalizing the meat trade? These questions are big and complex. But clearly the battle for good food is a global one: a chicken is a chicken wherever it is raised. Dr Michael Appleby, of the World Society for the Protection of Animals, is just one of those who wants to see less movement of animals and animal products around the world. 'We need more self-sufficient countries in food rather than racking up the commercial arms race and therefore the pressure on how we treat animals,' he says.

At a national level, there's no use being 'ivory fork' about progress. Change can come from many directions, not least with more supermarket shoppers choosing to buy free-range birds. Supermarkets are moving towards a greater number of slower-growing, free-range and organic birds. Changes are starting to happen, very gradually, at the quality end of ready-cooked food. One development is that Leon, an interesting healthy fast food chain in London, has gone for free-range chicken meat, using the cheap thighs left over from super-market breasts to make delicious nuggets that sell for a reasonable price. Dividing a bird so that it makes a good profit need not just happen at an international industrial level, with dark meat heading east and white meat heading west. This move by Leon raises the bar for similar 'posh' chains. People have long been aware of free-range and other higher-welfare chicken in fresh produce; now we want to know more about the origins of the cooked meat, too. Prêt à Manger was at one time sourcing chickens from Brazil. Now it has moved its supply base to the UK, buying barn-reared chickens kept at a density of eleven birds per square metre. Responding to a customer enquiry, a company spokesman said Prêt was frequently considering a move to a free-range option. The stumbling block was the cost and resulting higher retail prices, and whether customers were yet ready to take that increase. 'As free-range farms increase in number so does availability and quality. However prices still look at least 25 per cent higher than current,' he wrote. If a competitor in the quality food sector can manage to go free-range, the company will feel pressure to do the same. All these changes are steps forward. We are building towards a critical mass of opposi-tion to the crudest form of factory farming. Change is coming. One of the largest chicken-producing companies in the UK, Lloyd Maunder in the West Country, now rears around 60 per cent of its birds (some half a million a week) using more extensive methods: free-range, organic and Freedom Food, using its own slow-growing bird, the Devonshire. They say there is no question that farmers prefer working with such systems and that consumer demand for such meat is accelerating.

More broadly, it was encouraging to hear Erik Millstone's view that progress was – slowly – being made in some areas of food politics; he combines his cynicism about the food system with optimism. 'For me it's a question of power,' he said. 'Enormous amounts of power are held in the hands of the food industry and public policy makers. They make many decisions about how our food is produced and what is or is not acceptable. And the public is ignorant of this because decisions are taken behind closed doors. But things are changing because of the BSE crisis.' From that point, he has observed a wave of reform rolling through the institutions in charge of the food we eat. In his own area of expertise, additives, he is finally being allowed into government committee meetings on toxicity and carcinogenity. Once public bodies are more accessible to the public, it is harder to keep convenient industry practices going at the expense of consumers and farm animals. This fundamental principle is making headway, as can be seen by the fact that GM crops have so far been halted in Europe because a climate of openness meant that the information was put on the label (though not in the case of animal feed). Millstone calls the change 'sleepwalking into the sunlight', since he thinks governments were not entirely clear about the enormous implications of such access to information. Knowledge is power.

When I asked the Bristol University professor John Webster about attitudes towards animal welfare he said there were two extremes: mulish indifference and impossibilism. Most of us operate somewhere between the two. I came to see, in the course of writing this book, that the issues of chicken production were multi-layered and that there was no one single solution. Buying a sustainable chicken covers much on a personal level – and this is an option increasingly available to us. Improvements beyond this matter too. Steps can be made in the right direction from many different angles. Shopping, feed, drugs and killing are all part of the equation. It matters whether we cook the chicken, and if not, where it is sourced by the business that cooks it for us. It matters whether the birds' feed comes from deforested parts of Brazil. It matters that we enjoy and respect what we are eating rather than shoveling cheap protein into our bodies. As far as consumers are concerned, some will find a small-scale local chicken preferable to one that is part of the industrialized chicken industry. Others will change to a slower-growing breed from a supermarket. It may start with the food you feed your children, and go on to include what you will or won't buy for yourself in a restaurant or takeaway or work canteen.

But there is a bottom line. The production of cheap meat at a terrible cost to the chicken's welfare is wrong. The reality of fast-growing breeds that are pushed to the point where a quarter of the birds suffer lameness as they reach slaughter age stands as an everyday symbol of man's inhumanity to animals. Killing lines that don't always work must be improved or replaced by more humane methods of killing. Stocking densities that exacerbate welfare problems should be made less intensive: this should be a priority, not just a luxury. We are responsible for these birds' existence; we must give them a decent life. Solutions are at our disposal. They are available now.

Changing the practices of such a large and powerful industry is not going to happen overnight. The issues of international trade and rapidly expanding food supply chains are hard to grapple with if you are a consumer standing in front of a meat counter with opaque labelling. But these are our governments; these are our meals. Just as with the struggle against global warming, the message is not one of despair but of a move towards healthy, sustainable, engaged solutions that make life better for us straightaway. As individuals and citizen-consumers around the world, we can make choices that will help shift the economic and political balance sooner rather than later. We can make a difference.

What gives you hope? I asked Joyce d'Silva of Compassion in World Farming. 'The human heart,' she said. Heart, head and stomach can combine on the plight of the chicken that gives us meat and eggs. Together, they will take us all forward.

Acknowledgements

Nearly everyone I spoke to for this book wanted to shed light on what can be a contentious and murky subject. My thanks to them for their judgement and generosity. I got much inspiration from Compassion in World Farming's conference on animal sentience and the global yet grounded views on food politics at the Soil Association's conference in London in 2006. The Food Ethics Council continues to offer a thoughtful and thought-provoking perspective and I've long been glad of the existence of the Food Commission. Thanks to Richard and Mary Young for time at Kite's Nest Farm and to Farmed Animal Net, CIWF and the Soil Association for regular news updates on animal welfare and other issues. Sue Clifford and Angela King at Common Ground are guiding lights and *England in Particular* sits near by desk and armchair.

From my initial chicken travels, I'd like to thank Gus

Grand for Singapore chickens, Liddy Manson and Jeb Boasberg their kind hospitality for San Francisco chickens, John Lowry and his aunt for Mexican chickens, Hugh Thomson for Tia Nena's chickens, Daniel Fearn for Hungarian chickens, Alice Thomson and Edward Heathcoat-Amory for Moroccan chickens, Rupert Denyer for his flat in Anghiari for Slow Italian chickens, Michele Barlow for Slow Food's North-West chickens, Lizzie Fairie and Henrietta Pinney for getting me to New Zealand chickens, and Clare Moberly for Colombian markets. Great thanks to John and Ann Dezikes for *The Chicken Book* and for sharing a memorable meal at Chez Panisse.

For feeding me with chickenalia and other help, thanks to Emily and Ben Faccini, Gail Vines, Frances Price, Debbie Oates, Sue Reddish, John May's blog The Generalist, especially an interview with Jeff Nuttall, Mark Mansbridge, Toby Champion, Chandos Ellotson and Steve Harris at the estimable Sportsman near Whitstable for thoughts on cooking chicken, and all those working on chickens at Keo, including Nick Fisher for Fred Wiseman.

For bringing this subject to book form, my thanks to Richard Atkinson, Nick Davies and Nicola Doherty. Many thanks to my agent Georgina Capel and to Hugh Fearnley-Whittingstall for his powerful foreword. Helen Mander and Roger Ellis read through drafts and to them and to Sophie Orloff and Julia Ellis I offer cluckerty clucks of appreciation for their encouragement and belief.

Bibliography

Appleby, Michael, Mench, Joy and Hughes, Barry, *Poultry Behaviour and Welfare*. CABI Publishing, 2004.

Bateman, Michael. *Good Enough to Eat*. Sinclair-Stevenson, 1991.

Blumenthal, Heston. *Family Food*. Michael Joseph, 2002.

Blythman, Joanna. *Bad Food Britain*. Fourth Estate, 2006.

Blythman, Joanna. *Shopped*. Fourth Estate, 2004.

Blythman, Joanna. *The Food We Eat*. Michael Joseph, 1996.

Brillat-Savarin, Jean Anthelme. *The Physiology of Taste*. Counterpoint, 1999.

Clifford, Sue and King, Angela. *England in Particular*. Hodder & Stoughton, 2006.

Coe, Sue. *Dead Meat*. Four Walls, Eight Windows, 1996.

Cook, Christopher. *Diet for a Dead Planet*. The New Press, 2004.

Davidson, Alan. *The Oxford Companion to Food*. Oxford University Press, 1999.

Davis, Karen. *Prisoned Chickens, Poisoned Eggs*. Book Publishing Company, 1996.

Dixon, Jane. *The Changing Chicken*. UNSW Press, 2002.

Engel, Cidy. *Wild Health*. Weidenfeld & Nicolson, 2002.

Fearnley-Whittingstall, Hugh. *The River Cottage Meat Book*. Hodder & Stoughton, 2004.

Fiddes, Nick. *Meat*. Routledge, 1992.

Gordon, John Steele. *The Chicken Story*. American Heritage, 1996.

Grandin, Temple and Johnson, Catherine. *Animals in Translation*. Bloomsbury, 2005.

Green-Armytage, Simon. *Extraordinary Chickens*. Harry N. Abrams, 2000.

Grimes, William. *My Fine Feathered Friend*. North Point Press, 2002.

Gurdon, Martin. *Hen and the Art of Chicken Maintenance*. New Holland Publishers, 2003.

Halweil, Brian. *Eat Here*. Worldwatch, 2004.

Hams, Fred. *Old Poultry Breeds*. Shire, 1999.

Harrison, Ruth. *Animal Machines*. Vincent Stuart, 1964.

Honoré, Carl. *In Praise of Slow*. Orion, 2004.

Humphrys, John. *The Great Food Gamble*. Hodder & Stoughton, 2001.

Kapoor, Sybil. *Taste*. Mitchell Beazley, 2003.

Kennedy, Diana. *The Cuisines of Mexico*. Harper & Row, 1972

Lambert Ortiz, Elisabeth. *The Book of Latin American Cooking*. Penguin, 1985.

Lang, Tim and Heasman, Michael. *Food Wars*. Earthscan, 2004.

Lawrence, Felicity. *Not on the Label*. Penguin, 2004.

Lind, L.R. (ed.). *Aldrovandi on Chickens*. University of Oklahoma Press, 1963.

Mason, Jim and Singer, Peter. *Animal Factories*. Crown, 1980.

Masson, Jeffrey. *The Pig Who Sang to the Moon*. Vintage, 2005.

McGee, Harold. *The Curious Cook*. HarperCollins, 1992.

McGee, Harold. *On Food & Cooking*. Hodder & Stoughton, 2004.

Millstone, Erik and Lang, Tim. *The Atlas of Food*. Earthscan, 2003.

Newall, Venetia. *An Egg at Easter*. Routledge & Kegan Paul, 1971.

Pearce, John. *The Colonel*. Doubleday, 1982.

Petrini, Carlo. *Slow Food*. Columbia University Press, 2001.

Pollan, Michael. *An Animal's Place*. New York Times Magazine, 2002.

Pollan, Michael. *The Omnivore's Dilemma*. Bloomsbury, 2006.

Pringle, Peter. *Food Inc*. Simon & Schuster, 2003.

Bibliography

Sams, Craig. *The Little Book of Food*. Alistair Sawday Publishing, 2000.

Schlosser, Eric. *Fast Food Nation*. Penguin, 2002.

Sidney, Russell. *The History of Californian Farmers' Markets*

Singer, Peter and Mason, Jim. *Eating*. Arrow Books, 2006

Smith, P. and Daniel, C. *The Chicken Book*. North Point Press, 1982.

Striffler, Steve. *Chicken*. Yale University Press, 2005.

Stull, Donald and Broadway, Michael. *Slaughterhouse Blues*. Thomson Wadsworth, 2004.

Symons, Michael. *The Pudding That Took a Thousand Cooks*. Viking, 1998

Tansey, Geoff and D'Silva, Joyce (eds). *The Meat Business*. Earthscan, 1999.

Thear, Katie. *Free-Range Poultry*. Whittet Books, 2002.

This, Hervé. *Molecular Gastronomy*. Colombia University Press, 2006.

Tudge, Colin. *So Shall We Reap*. Allen Lane, 2003.

Verhoe, Esther and Rijs, Aad. *The Complete Encyclopedia of Chickens*. Rebo International, 2003.

Visser, Margaret. *Much Depends on Dinner*. Penguin Books, 1989.

Webster, John. *Animal Welfare: A Cool Eye Towards Eden*. Blackwell, 1994.

Webster, John. *Animal Welfare: Limping Towards Eden*. Blackwell, 2005.

Weeks, C.A. and Butterworth, A. (eds), *Measuring and Auditing Broiler Welfare*. CABI Publishing, 2004

Winstson, Mark. *Travels in the Genetically Modified Zone*. Harvard University Press, 2002.

Wolke, Robert. *What Einstein Told His Cook*. W.W. Norton & Company, 2002.

Chicken Contacts

Battery Hen Welfare Trust www.thehenhouse.co.uk
Big Barn 01234 871005 www.bigbarn.co.uk
Bordeaux Quay Cookery School 0117 904 6679 www.quartiervert.co.uk
British Egg Information Centre 0207 808 9790 www.britegg.co.uk
Butts Farmshop 01285 862 224 www.thebuttsfarmshop.com
Compassion in World Farming 01483 521970 www.ciwf.org.uk
Domestic Fowl Trust 01368 833083 www.domesticfowltrust.co.uk
Earsham Farm 01323 841272
Eglu/Omlet 0845 450 2056 www.omlet.co.uk
Ellel Free-Range Poultry O1524 751200 www.ellelfreerangepoultry.
  co.uk
FARMA (National Farmers' Retail & Markets Association) 0845 45 88
  420 www.farma.org.uk
Farm Animal Welfare Network www.fawn.me.co.uk
Farmed Animal Net www.farmedanimal.net
Farms for Schools 01706 218614 www.farmsforschools.org.uk
Federation of City Farms and Community Gardens 0117 923 1800
  www.farmgarden.org.uk

Food Animal Initiative (FAI) 01865 790880 www.faifarms.co.uk
The Food Commission 020 7837 1141 www.foodcomm.org.uk
Food Ethics Council 0845 345 8574 www.foodethicscouncil.org
Friends of the Earth 020 7490 1555 www.foe.co.uk
The Goods Shed 01227 459153
Graig Farm Organics www.graigfarm.co.uk 01597 851655
Greenpeace 020 7865 8100 www.greenpeace.org.uk
Guild of Q-Butchers 01738 450443 www.guildofqbutchers.com
Hen Heaven of Henfield 07754 550193 www.henheaven.org
Hen Keepers Association www.henkeepersassociation.co.uk
Humane Society of the United States www.hsus.org
Humane Slaughter Association 01582 831919 www.hsa.org.uk
Kelly Turkeys 1245 223581 www.kelly-turkeys.com
Label Anglais 01279 792460 www.labelanglais.co.uk
Lidgates 020 77278243
Lloyd Maunder 01884 820534 www.lloydmaunder.co.uk
London Farmers' Markets 0207 833 0338 www.lfm.org.uk
Maple Farm 01728 652000 www.maplefarmkelsale.co.uk
Marin Sun Farm www.marinsunfarm.com
McKeever Kentish Ranger Table Poultry 01227 751227
Netherfield Centre 01424 775615 www.thenetherfieldcentre.co.uk
PETA 020 7357 9229 www.peta.org
Pipers Farm 01392 881380 www.pipersfarm.com
Poultry Club of Great Britain 01476 550067 www.poultryclub.org
Practical Poultry 01959 541444 www.practicalpoultry.com
Providence Farm Organic Meats 01409 2544421 www.providence-farm.co.uk
The Poultry Site www.thepoultrysite.com
Rare Breeds Survival Trust 02476 696551 www.rare-breeds.com
Real Meat Company 0845 7626017 www.realmeat.co.uk
River Cottage 01297 630300 www.rivercottage.net
RSPCA Freedom Food 0870 33 35 999 www.rspca.org.uk
Scots Dumpy Society 01869 346554 www.scotsdumpy.org.uk
Sheepdrove Organic Farm 01488 674747 www.sheepdrove.com
Sierra Club www.sierraclub.org
Slow Food (00 39) 0172 419611 www.slowfood.com
Slow Food UK 01584 879599 www.slowfood.org.uk
Soil Association 0117 9142412 www.soilasociation.org

Chicken Contacts

South of England Rare Breeds Centre 01233 861493
www.rarebreeds.org.uk
Sustain: The Alliance for Better Food and Farming 020 7837 1228
www.sustainweb.org
TFX (Campaign Against Trans Fats in Food) www.tfx.org.uk
United Poultry Concern www.upc-online.org
Warborne Organic Farm 0590 688 488 www.warborne.co.uk
Warmwell www.warmwell.com
World Society for the Protection of Animals 020 7587 5000
www.wspa.org.uk

Index

abattoirs *see* slaughter houses
Aberdeenshire 242
agri-environmental schemes 251–52
agribusiness 106
agriculture, change in 167
agroforestry 170
Aldrovandi, Ulisse 15
Alexander the Great 14
Anderson, Pamela 87
Anglo-Saxons 14
Animal Century 146
animal welfare: public opinion on 109,
    178, 197
Animal Welfare and Meat Science 69
animal welfare movement 150, 154, 155
animals:
    attitudes to 109,149, 178, 197
    five freedoms for 198, 268–69
    looks and 216
    self-medication 171
antibiotics 30, 51–54, 178:
    growth rates and 51
    resistant bacteria 51, 52
'antimicrobials' 78

Appleby, Dr Michael 177–78
Araucana 18, 130
Archibold, John 30–31
argon 73
arsenic 61
ascites 38
Asda 110, 111
Asia 8, 12, 16, 117, 130
Assured Chicken Production scheme
    177
Atkins, Susanna 213, 214
Atlanta 100, 103
Atlas of Food 283
Australia 22, 196, 227
Austria 153
avoparcin 52
Aztecs 223

bacterial chondronecrosis (BCN) 37
BAE Systems 105
Bagnoli, Stefano 251
bananas 224, 225
Barlow, Michele 247–48
barn-reared hens 154, 155

Barnard, Sharon 277–78
barnyard chickens 164
battery cages 25, 29–29, 42–45, 154:
    banning of 145, 148, 154
    campaign against 156
Battery Hen Welfare Trust 144, 260
battery-cage birds: rescue of 136, 260–61
beaks 42, 43, 136
Belgium 48, 59
Bell, Lord Justice 41, 71
Bentham, Jeremy 181
Berkshire 169
Berry, Wendell 208
Berwick-on-Tweed 16
bird flu 8, 95, 103–4, 117–19, 140, 222,
    253–54, 264–65, 269, 276
Birmingham 17, 108
Black, William 248, 249
bleed tunnel 72
blood 66
Blumenthal, Heston 217, 221, 235
Body, Sir Richard 54
body temperature 69
Bogota 282
Bologna 238
bones 36, 150, 232
Bordeaux Quai 96
botulism 60
Bra 240–41
Brambell Report 154, 197
Brazil 30, 59, 68, 99, 105, 109, 116, 285:
    rainforest cut down 116
breast burn 187
breasts:
    blisters 37, 170
    large 36, 37, 85, 103, 109, 216
breeding 15, 17, 19–20, 26, 41, 44
breeding flocks 25 *see also under* broiler
        industry
breeds 17–18, 263–65
Brighton 239
Brillat-Savarin, Jean Anthelme 221, 230,
    236
Bristol 96, 210
Bristol University 40, 49, 71, 183, 185,
    287
broiler industry:
    basis flawed 33
    breeder flocks 41–42, 107, 117
    campaigns against 86
    conditions 30, 41, 44, 96–97, 109

    description of 32–35
    feed 114
    growth speed 29, 34, 111, 178, 183,
        184, 190, 287
    intensity 37, 38–40
    mortality rate 37, 54
    numbers in shed 37
    opposition to 157, 285
    origins 29–30
    problems 36–40
    slaughter 34, 36, 64–80
    slaughter age 36, 137, 164
    specialization 25
    stocking density 39–40
    US model 30
    ventilation 30
Brook, Jane 209
Broom, Professor Donald 187
Brown, Nick 152–53
BSE (bovine spongiform encephalopathy)
    6, 95, 147, 211, 286
Burger King 85, 88
burns 39
butchers, independent 214–15
Butler, Samuel 125
Butts Farm 265–66
buying habits, changing 145

California 25, 100, 189, 201
campaigns 86–88, 92
campylobacter 48–50, 72
Canada 42, 92
Canterbury 212, 213
caponizing 14
carbon dioxide 73
Cargill 116
Carrington, Lord 21
cat food 107
catching machines 68
catching teams 68
celebrities: campaigns and 87–88
Centre for Science in the Public Interest
    91
chalazae 128
change: obstacles to 44–45
Chanticleer 14–15
Charles II, King 140
Charles, Richard and Susie 249–52
Chaucer, Geoffrey: *Nun's Priest's Tale*
    14–15
Chez Panisse 203

Index

chicken:
  beef protein and 95
  as blank canvas 236
  buses 102
  cheapness of 4, 33, 34, 40, 96, 104,
    114, 287
  consumers 198–99
  consumption of 7, 67, 178, 265
  curry 99
  dark meat 106, 233
  fat 216, 229
  flying 131
  frozen 82–83
  GM 113
  higher-welfare 158
  imports 58, 78, 105–6, 108
  international dimension 105–19
  jointing 230–31
  labelling 94, 153, 177
  local 280, 282, 284
  money made from 109–10
  nuggets 82, 93, 95
  organic 75, 97, 114, 158, 175–76
  price 104, 158, 163
  processed 92, 93–95, 195
  roasting 98
  slow-cooking 234–35
  status of 66
  as treat 21
  white meat 106
  see also following entries and broiler
    industry
Chicken Book, The 17, 139
Chicken Cottage 86

chicken farming, industrial:
  companies' concentration 29, 107
  growth speed 29, 34
Chicken Run, The 94–95, 260
chicken sheds, intensive 10
chicken-keeping: hobby/backyard 17, 135
chickens:
  appearance 17–19, 265
  characters 123
  cloned 113
  diseases 25, 109
  ears and earlobes 19, 269
  egg eating 191
  feeding 136
  gender 33-34
  genome sequenced 174

  happy 163, 276
  history of 13–17
  inactivity 216
  intelligence 191, 266–67
  keeping, non-commercial 124, 253–70
  numbers 7, 164, 178
  organic 59, 194
  origins 12–14, 192
  respect for 124
  self-medication 123
  shelter 137
  sleeping 191
  slower growing 177
  study of 188–99
  transgender 133
  transport of 9, 24, 35, 77
  trees and 131, 194
  waste from 62–63
  water and 95
  see also preceding entries and broiler
    industry; free-range chickens;
    hens
ChickMaster 101
chicks 134, 135, 137
children:
  cooking by 82
  fast food and 85
  obesity 98–99
Chile 18
chilli 224
China 13, 35, 100, 106, 117, 246, 263
cholesterol 89, 90, 127
Chunky Chic 29
Clarke, Margi 72
claws 43–44, 69
Co-op 110, 111, 114
coccidiosis 54–58, 166
coccidiostats 57, 273
Cochins 16
cockerels 42, 137–43:
  aphrodisiacs 140
  folk traditions 138–39
  mythology 138
cockfighting 13, 15, 140–41, 142, 262
Colombia 282
Colorado 64
combs 19, 137, 140
Common Cause 280
Compassion in World Farming 32, 44,
    110–11, 145–46, 181, 288
consumer choice 197, 215, 285

convenience 81, 88–89, 104, 158
Cook, Paul 192, 194
cooking 82, 99, 219–37:
   lack of knowledge of 97, 98
cooks 221, 223–25, 229, 234, 235
Cool Chili Company 226
Cool Eye Towards Eden, A 40, 186
Coqrock 88
Cornish Red bird 217
Cornish-Cross birds 203
coronary heart disease 89
Council for the Protection of Rural
   England 279
Countryside Foundation 266
Coutts, Martin 86
Craig, Alison 60
Cranbrook, Caroline 279
cruelty 41, 44, 86–87, 181
Currie, Edwina 47

Daniel, Charles 17, 139–40
Danish Nutrition Council 90
Davis, Karen 38
Dawkins, Marian Stamp 182, 192
Deans Foods 108
death checker 72
deep dermatitis 39
Delaware 26
Denby Poultry 94
Denmark 39, 91–92
Derby, 12th Earl 142
dermatitis 39
developing countries 107
Devonshire 286
Dew, Aloma 62
diabetes 98
dioxin 48
direct selling 211, 214 *see also* farm
      shops; farmers' markets
Dispatches 187
Diss 100
dog food 107
Domestic Poultry Trust 263
drugs 25, 30, 51–60, 95, 109, 273
d'Silva, Joyce 148, 149, 150, 288
dust-baths 136

E. coli 6
ear-lobes 19, 269
Eat Less Meat campaign 147
Edmondson, Drew 60–61

eggs:
   air sac 130, 131
   battery 144
   cheapness 44
   cholesterol 127
   colour 130
   companies' concentration 108
   cookery and 126
   cuticle 130
   embryo 131–32
   fat 127
   formation of 126–28
   free-range 42, 145, 155
   freshness 130, 131
   hatching 132, 134
   higher-welfare 144, 145, 153, 154
   imports 23, 47–48, 50, 56, 106, 154
   just laid 130
   laying 131, 134, 135
   light and 24
   myth and 125–26
   numbers eaten 56
   numbers produced 22
   nutrition 126
   organic 155–56
   processed 106
   production 16, 22
   shell 129, 130
   as treat 21–22
   whites 128, 129
   yolks 24, 126–27, 128, 132
   see also battery cages
Eglu 256–58, 259, 268
Egypt 14, 22, 125, 263
Ellel Poultry 249–52
Elm Farm Research Centre 174
Engel, Cindy 171
enriched cages 154, 155
environmental health officers (EHOs) 94
Ersham Farm 272–77
ethology 180
EU (European Union) 47, 52, 58, 60, 61,
      75, 105, 152, 154, 282:
   broiler directive 188
   Council of Ministers of Agriculture 148
   see also following entry
European Commission 39, 114, 152
   Laying Hens Directive 148, 149, 151,
      154
European Food Safety Authority (EFSA)
      47, 78

Index

Evans, David 204–7
Eye 62
eyes 123

Faccenda Group 108
'factory farms' 7–8
'faecal soup' 72
faeces 11, 39, 54, 55
Farina, Francesca Romano 242–47
Farm Animal Welfare Council (FAWC)
    39, 40, 74, 110, 185
FARMA 207
farmers' markets 200–11, 217–18, 271–72
farmers' wives 21
farming: industrial 7, 8, 26
farms shops 211, 277, 281
fast food 81, 82, 83–93, 95
Fast Food Nation 85
Faverolles 263
Fearnley-Whittingstall, Hugh 198, 207, 276
feed 30, 44, 55, 187, 190, 193:
    additives in 101
    antibiotics in 30, 51–54
    arsenic in 60, 61
    deforestation and 116
    GM 113, 114, 115
    protein-high 36
    restriction of 41, 178, 187, 190
Ferry Plaza 200–7
fertilizer 60, 73, 106, 206
Fibrowatt 62
Fiddes, Nick 65, 66
First World War 22
fish 106
Flint, Caroline 92
Flip-Over Syndrome 38
flock husbandry 5
Food Animal Initiative 192–95
'Food for Freedom' 27
food industry: dodges of 91
food labelling 90, 92 *see also under*
    chicken
food miles 106
food poisoning 46–50
Food Standards Agency 49, 50, 59, 89, 95
foot burn 39, 187, 188
foot-and-mouth disease 6
force-feeding 14, 29
France 19, 22, 29, 150, 152, 166–67, 177,
    216, 250
Frederick, Chris 217

free trade 114, 154
free-range chickens:
    aggression 182
    bird flu and 118
    'bog-standard' 164
    bones 36
    feed 114
    problems with 164
    reality of 155
    standards too low 163
    total-freedom 164–65
    traditional 164
Freedom Food 286
Friends of the Earth 113
Frizzles 18
Fruita 64
Furners Green 277
Future of Food, The 115

Game Cock 140
Garcia: Deborah Koon 115
Gardiner, Barry 279
gassing 73–74, 87
genetic engineering 112–15
genetics 17, 19
Georgia 227–28
Germany 17, 22, 53, 59, 92, 138, 150
gizzards 136
globalization 79, 106, 283, 284, 288
GM food 113, 115, 286
Godfrey, Jan 210–11
Goodall, Jane 180, 181
Goods Shed 212–14
Gould, Toddy Hamilton 263–65, 266
Graham, Chris 261
Graig Farms 75
Grampian 108, 114
grass 205
gravy 233–34
Greeks 14, 152
Green Revolution 7
Green-Armytage, Stephen 18
Greenpeace 41, 116
Gregory, NG 69
Gregory, Trevor 277–78
Greig, Peter and Henri 165–69
Grievink, J.-W. 108
Grigson, Jane 241–42
Grimsby 106
Guardian 258
Guelph University 42

Guillain-Barré Syndrome 48
Gunther, Andrew 170, 173, 246
Gurdon, Martin 133
Guy, Richard 8–9, 159–63, 176
Gwynn, Nell 140

Hammond, Celia 146
Hams, Fred 29, 130
Hanburys 271, 272
Hancox, Judy 265, 266, 267
hanging 77, 195, 275
Harper Adams Agricultural College 77
Harrison, Ruth 44
Harvard University 112
Haslam, Sue 184–85, 187, 188
Haughton, Barney 96–97
'head furnishings' 18–19
heart disease 37–38, 89, 98, 127, 183, 193
Heathcote, George 211–12
'Hen Fever' 16–17
Hen Haven 253
Hen Keepers' Association 254
*Hen and the Art of Chicken
        Maintenance* 133
Henderson, Fergus 266
Henfield 253
hens:
    barn-reared 154
    broody 132–33
    cocks and 135
    as mothers 133
    pecking order 137
    specialization 25
    see also battery cages
Hetty the Hen 148
Hillside Animal Sanctuary 86
Hindle Wakes 247, 248
Hirons, John 267–70
hock blisters 39
hock burn 37, 184, 187
Hoffman, Mrs 202–3, 204, 207
hollandaise 128
home cooking 82
Hoover, Herbert 26
hospitals 281
Hoyte, Arthur 91
Humane Methods of Slaughter Act, 1958
        74
Humane Slaughter Association 68, 71, 73
Humane Society of the United States 74,
        178

Humphrey, Tom 49–50
Hurd, Professor Louis 24

incubation 13, 23–24, 134, 135
India 125
Indian Game cocks 15, 266
infection 37, 47, 48–50, 51
Institute for Agriculture and Trade
        Policy 61
International Poultry Expo 100–5, 119
Ireland 57
Italy 150–51, 215, 239–40, 242–47

Jacobson, Michael F. 91
Jewell, Topsy 280
joints: problems 37
Jubilee Farm 213
Julius Caesar 14
jungle fowl 12–13, 129, 135, 192
junk food 92, 97

Kahlo, Frida 226
Kaoor, Sybil 236
Kelly, Paul 78
Kemp, Reverend Trevor 255–56
Kendall, William 278–79
Kennard, Bob 75
Kentucky 62, 83
Kentucky Fried Chicken 83, 84, 85, 86,
        91
Kentucky Fried Cruelty 86, 87
Kestin, Steve 183
Kindersley, Peter and Juliet 170, 172–73,
        182
Kraaier, Bergse 138

Label Anglais 216–17
Laffoon, Ruby 83
Lancashire 250
Lancet 89
Land that Thyme Forgot, The 248
Lang, Tim 283–84
lasalocid 55–56, 57
Lawrence, Felicity 94
layers: slaughter 43, 67, 77
'leaking liver' 38
'learned helplessness' 198
leg problems 37, 40, 44, 109, 178, 183,
        187, 197
Lega Anti Vivisezione 150
Leghorns 25

Index

Leon 285
Lewer, S.H. 16–17
Lewes farmers' market 271–72, 280–81
Lidgate, David 215, 216
light 23, 36, 43, 134, 178, 190–91, 193
Limping Towards Eden 186
Lincolnshire 62
Lion Quality Eggs 114
litter 30, 37, 39, 41, 53, 60, 62, 272
Live Fast, Die Young 32–35
'Livestock Revolution' 7–8
Lloyd Maunder 285–86
Locatelli, Locanda 250
local food 75, 271, 278, 279, 280, 281,
    282–83
London 16, 141, 209, 227, 285
London Farmers' Market 209
London Underground 88
London University 216
Lorenz, Karl 43
Luxembourg 47
Leg Health and Welfare in Commercial
    Broiler Production 37
Lymbery, Philip 147, 148, 150, 151, 152

McCartney, Sir Paul 87
McDonalds:
    deforestation and 116
    development of 84–85
    eggs 145, 181
    FAI 194
    libel trial 41–42, 71
    McNuggets 85, 116
    opponents of 238–39
    trans fat and 91–92
McGee, Harold 126, 127, 129, 205
McKeevers 213
McNuggets 85, 116
mail-order 160
maize 30
Malta 22
Manchester 210, 247
manure 60
Maple Farm 278
Marans 130
Marks & Spencer 110, 111
Maryland University 189
mating 19
Maunder, Lloyd 197
Mayas 223
mayonnaise 128

Meat 79–80
meat:
    cheapness of 6
    cooking 234–35
    eating 7, 65–66, 117, 198
    eating less 160
    live creatures, disassociation from
        161
    price 81–82, 104
    production quantity 7
    quantity eaten 117
    trade's deceit 94–95
    unease about 6
    unfit 94
    see also chicken
Meat: A Natural Symbol 65
Meat Hygiene Service 75
mechanically recovered meat 95
Mench, Dr Joy 189–91
merat: eating less 160
meringue 128
Metherell, Gilly 159, 160, 161
Mexico 223, 225
Mexico City 221–22
mezzadrine farming 243
Millman, S.T. 42fn.
Millstone, Erik 283–84, 286
mole 223–25
Morocco 22
Morrison's 59
moulting 44, 189–90
Moy Park 59, 108
mutagenicity 59
myoglobin 233

narasin/nicarbazin 57
National Farmers' Union 278
National Institute of Poultry Farming 22
National Poultry Show 264
Neal's Yard Pharmacy 172
Nebraska University 62
Nena, Tia 223–25
Netherfield Centre for Sustainable Food
        and Farming 280
Netherlands 90, 94, 95
New English Journal of Medicine 90
New York Times 91
New Zealand 217
Newman, Martin 87
NHS 281
nicarbazin 57, 59–60

nitrofuran 58–59
nitrogen 73
Noble Foods 108
Normans 14
Northamptonshire 108
Northern Ireland 95, 108
Norway 22
Novak, David 87
Nunan, Coílín 56

Oakham chicken 110
Old Dairy 277–78
Old English pheasant fowl 268
Oliver, Damian 258
Oliver, Jamie 82
Olsen, Lloyd 64–65
omega-3 fatty acids 215–16
Omlet 256
On Food and Cooking 126
Organic Farmers and Growers 114
organic farming 176 *see also under* chicken; chickens
Orloff chickens 263
Ortiz, Elisabeth Lambert 223
OXFAM 282, 284
Oxford University experimental farm 192

Palmiro 251
Panorama 94
Paul, Johannes 257, 258
Pearce, John Ed 83
pedigree birds 41
People for the Ethical Treatment of Animals (PETA) 86, 88
Pepperberg, Irene 182
Perdue, Frank 28
Persia 13
Pertelote 15
Petersfield 145, 146, 148
Petrini, Carlo 239, 241
Pine Chicken 194
Pizza Express 145
Pizza Hut 85
Playing Chicken: Avoiding Arsenic in Your Meat 61
Pliny the Elder 14
plucking 35, 72, 77–79, 275
plumage 18
Poland 47
Polish 18

pollution 60–62, 63
Portugal 22, 59, 152
poulet de Bresse 29, 251
Poultry in Natural Environments 194
Practical Poultry 261
Pret à Manger 285
Price, Bernadine 208, 209
processed food 89–93, 98
processing plants 35, 40, 67, 70
Puebla de Los Angeles 223

Quartier Vert 96, 97

Raj, Dr Mohan 71, 73, 74
Ramsay, Gordon 217
Rare Breeds Survival Trust 265
Rare Poultry Society 264
ready-meals 93–94, 98
Real Choice, The 279
Real Meat Company 8, 159–63
Refugio Fonda 222–23
Regan, Tom 181
Reiter's Syndrome 48
Renaissance 15
Renderer 107
Resca, Mario 240
Rhode Island Reds 25, 205
River Cottage Meat Book 198
Roberts, Peter 146
'roosters' 140
Royal College of Art 257
RSPCA (Royal Society for the Prevention of Cruelty to Animals) 142, 268
Russia 106

*Safe*Food 57, 58
Sainsbury's 110, 111
salmonella 6, 46–48, 50, 51, 72, 149
Salt Lake City 84
Salt Lake City University 65
San Francisco 200, 206, 220, 227
Sanders, Harland D. 83–84, 91
Sandøe, Peter 183
Sansolini, Adolfo 150, 153
Sasso 250
scalding tank 72
Schlosser, Eric 85
school dinners 82, 281
school farm 267–70
School Food Trust 92

Index

Scientific Committee on Animal Health and Animal Welfare (SCAHAW) 39
scientists:
  animal studies 180–99
  government and 195–96
Scotland 16, 62
Scots Dumpy Society 263–65
Second World War 23, 27, 28, 254–55
Shankar, Ravi 87
Sharpton, Reverend Al 87
Sheepdrove Farm 169–74, 246
shopping 200–18
shows 17, 263
Sierra Club 61
Silkies 18, 133
Silsoe Agricultural Research Station 195
Silver Supreme 29
Simpson, Alan 115
Singapore 222
slaughter 34, 36, 43, 64–80, 287:
  conditions of 76
  methods of 70–72, 274–75
  numbers 67
  see also following entry
slaughter houses:
  closing down of 76–77
  numbers of 75, 76
Slovakia 47
Slow Food 238–52
Slow Food University of Gastronomic Sciences 242
Smith, Page 17, 139–40
Soil Association 55, 56, 57, 59, 114, 155, 175, 177, 211, 212
Somerfield 110, 111
Somerset 242
sores 39
soufflés 128
soup 232, 242
soya 30, 113–14, 115
Spain 47, 48, 153
spurs 42, 140
Staphylococcus aureus 53
Steele, Cecile 26
Stobart, Tom 131
Stonegate 114
Stoneleigh 263
stress 172
Striffler, Steve 27

Stubbs, George 16, 17
stunning 35, 70, 195
subsidies 251, 252
Sudden Death Syndrome 38
suffering 40, 41–42, 181, 184
Suffolk 62, 278
Sun Valley 108, 116
Sunday Mirror 86
Sunday Times 108
supermarkets 3–6, 9, 10, 37, 58:
  alternatives to 168, 208
  changing attitudes 111–12
  cheap chicken 4
  chicken, attitudes to 110, 111–12
  eggs 77, 156
  GM feed and 114, 115
  higher welfare and 153–54
  local food and 281
  power of 108–9
Surrey 16
Sussex 16, 277
Sussex University 283
Sustain 281
Sustainable Livelihoods Programme 282–83
Swann, Sir Michael 52
Sweden 22, 40, 47
Switzerland 153

Taco Bell 85
Tamburini, Giovanni 238, 239
Taste 236
Terry 213–14
Tesco 59, 110, 111, 194, 208–9
TFX (Campaign against Trans Fat in Food) 92
Thailand 59, 68, 105, 108, 109, 283
'thinning' 49
This, Hervé 234
Thomas, Ian 218
tibial dyschondroplasia 36
Tickell, Oliver 92
time 97
Too Hard to Crack 55
Too Hard to Swallow 56, 59
Torode, John 266
trans fat 89–93
Tudge, Colin 52
Turin 246
Turkey 22, 274
Turkey Twizzlers 82

turkeys 73
Turner, Fred 84
Turvey, Linda 253–54
Tuscany 242–47
2 Sisters 108
Tyson Foods 85, 107, 117–18
Tyson, John 27–28

Uganda 66
Uhelmann, Sarah 74
Ukraine 107
umami nirvana 236
Union of Concerned Scientists 53
United Egg Producers 104
United Poultry Concern 38
United States of America:
  animal welfare progress 183
  antibiotics 51, 53
  chicken:
    broiler production 26–27, 38
    companies' concentration 107–8
    consumption 26, 178
    farming in 23–28
    rendering 107
    slaughter 74, 102
    transporting 27, 102
  farms lost in 208
  fast food 83–88
  fat deaths 89
  food labelling 90–91
  meat exports 107
  meat imports from 107
  pollution 60–62
urbanization 117

vaccines 25, 47, 58, 273
Valdarno chickens 242–47
vancomycin 52–53
Varro 14
vegetarians 67, 162
verts 75–76
Victoria, Queen 16
Vietnam 222, 228–29
Vine, Michael 272–76, 280
vitamin D 24
Volonnino, Nicola 242–47

Wageningen University 90

Waitrose 16, 59, 110, 111, 114
Wald, George 112
Walker, Alice 87
Wallace Collection 129
Warriner School 267–70
washing 78–79
'water belly' 38
Waters, Alice 203, 239
Waterside Inn 250
wattles 19, 137, 140
Wayland Development Trust 210
Webster, John 40, 155, 185–88, 195–96,
    197, 198, 264, 287
weight 37
welfare 111, 119, 147, 148, 171, 189, 193,
    197, 287:
  cost of 154
  public opinion on 109, 178, 197
  see also following entries
Welfare of Animals during Slaughter or
    Killing Regulations 73, 75
welfare campaigners 68
welfare regulations 105
welfare scientists 73, 181
welfare system, audited 187–88
Welsh Main 141
Welsummers 130
Wild Health 171
Willett, Walter 89
Willow Farm brand 111
wings 106, 150, 205
Wiseman, Fred 79–80
Wolke, Robert L. 233
women: domestic work 82
World Health Organization 90
World Society for the Protection of
    Animals 178, 284
World Trade Organization 154
Worldwatch 117

Xico 223

York University 242
Young, Richard 55, 58
Yum! Brands 85, 87

Zasda, Krys 210